Beyond the Victim

Beyond the Victim

The Politics and Ethics of Empowering
Cairo's Street Children

KAMAL FAHMI

The American University in Cairo Press
Cairo   New York

Material in this book is drawn from Kamal Fahmi, "Social Work Practice and Research
as an Emancipatory Process," in *Social Work in a Corporate Era: Practices of Power*, eds.
Linda Davies and Peter Leonard, Ashgate, 2004. Reproduced by permission.

Map on page xiv by Ola Seif.

ISBN 978 977 416 063 9
Dar el Kutub No. 15645/06

1 2 3 4 5 6 7   07 08 09 10 11 12

Designed by Hugh Hughes/AUC Press Design Center
Printed in Egypt

For my parents

Practice that is about genuine empowerment can never be certain of where it is heading, but—contrary to the views of some post-modernists—it can, and indeed must, proceed in a way that takes account of universal value, moral and ethical principles, even if the way in which these are defined and operationalised will vary over time and across cultural settings.

(J. Ife 1999, 222)

Contents

Acknowledgments

This book is the outcome of many years of fieldwork and research aimed at developing an understanding of the lived experiences of some of the youngsters called and labeled 'street children.' My deepest gratitude and respect go to all those boys and girls, and young men and women who allowed me and my team of street workers and researchers into the habitat they have made of the street in an attempt to resist exclusion and chronic repression and to affirm their human agency. From these youngsters I learned a great deal about myself and about the social realities that encourage them to continue to struggle to survive in circumstances that most of us would find, at the very least, unbearable.

I am forever indebted to Linda Davies from McGill University for her enthusiastic and committed encouragement, support, and guidance during the preparation of the original manuscript.

I would like to express my sincere appreciation and gratitude to my friend and colleague Jacques Pector for the inspiring and enlightening dialogues we had and for his help in identifying appropriate documentation regarding many of the themes discussed in this book.

To the team of street workers and researchers who participated in the different phases of the participatory action research reported in this book, I am deeply grateful for their commitment, hard work, and love.

Finally, I am very lucky to have family and friends who have encouraged and supported me throughout the years that culminated in the writing of this book.

Acronyms and Abbreviations

AR	Action Research
l'ATTrueQ	*Association des Travailleurs et Travailleuses de Rue du Québec*
BCJ	*Bureau de Consultation Jeunesse*
CAPMAS	Central Agency for Public Mobilization and Statistics
CIDA	Canadian International Development Agency
EAD	Egyptian Association for Development
EASSC	Egyptian Association to Support Street Children
EC	European Community
ILO	International Labor Organization
MISA	Ministry of Insurance & Social Affairs
NCCM	National Council for Childhood and Motherhood
NGO	Non-Governmental Organization
PAR	Participatory Action Research
PIaMP	*Project d'Intervention auprès des Mineur(e)s Prostitué(e)s*
PO	Participant Observation
PR	Participative Research
SDC	Social Development Consultants
UNICEF	The United Nations Children's Fund
UNESCO	United Nations Educational, Scientific and Cultural Organization

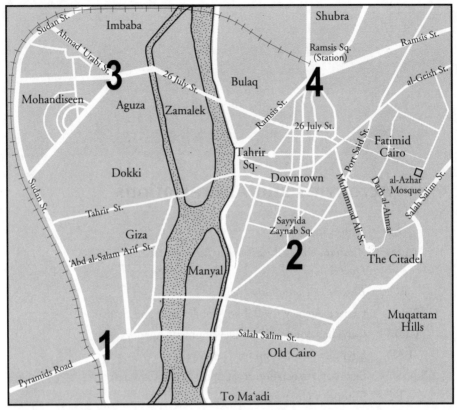

Greater Cairo: numbers indicate zones of street work

Introduction

Despite widespread concerns and numerous intervention programs aiming at its eradication, the street children phenomenon continues to escalate throughout the world. Indeed, the resilience of the phenomenon matches, if not surpasses, that of the children themselves. I believe that the failure to adequately address this complex and very diverse phenomenon is the result of conceptual confusion with respect to defining who a street child is. The dominant discourse on street children obstinately defines them as victims or deviants to be rescued and rehabilitated. As such, the capacity of many of these children for human agency is occluded by excluding them from participation in the construction of solutions to their problems. I argue that far from being mere victims and deviants, these children, in running away from alienating structures and finding relative freedom in the street, often become autonomous and are capable of actively defining their situations in their own terms. They are able to challenge the roles assigned to children, make judgments, and develop a network of niches in the heart of the metropolis in order to resist exclusion and chronic repression. I further argue that for research and action with street children to be emancipatory, it is necessary to acknowledge and respect the human agency the children display in changing their own lives and to capitalize on their voluntary participation in non-formal educational activities, as well as in collective advocacy.

My arguments are based on fieldwork undertaken with Cairene street children and youth over a period of eight consecutive years (1993–2001), which I reflectively narrate and report in this book. One major objective is to demonstrate how this fieldwork was implemented through the articulation of a participatory action research (PAR) methodology of social development practice and research that eclectically combined street ethnography, street work, and action science. In my view this combination is particularly pertinent for PAR undertakings that target excluded populations.

Over a period of more than ten years prior to beginning fieldwork in 1993, I had incorporated a PAR framework into my professional work in the youth sector, in both Montreal and Cairo. Indeed, an abiding interest in praxis, that is, making research an integral part of practice, has been a major professional concern on my part since the late 1970s, when I first started my career in social work, and in subsequent international development activities. I have experimented with methodologies drawn for the most part from the Southern (Freirean) PAR tradition (see Chapter 1), which conceives PAR as basically a grassroots practice methodology with a built-in mechanism of ongoing reflection and dialogue that serves to enlighten action, empower participants, tackle contradictions, and generate experiential knowledge.

My personal bias and conviction, as will be seen, are for a conception of PAR as an open-ended process of action and participatory research incorporated into everyday activities and work with excluded, marginalized and oppressed groups. This conception differs from other conceptions that view PAR as essentially a research methodology associated with action within a limited scope and timeframe. In my view, the 'practice-biased' conception is better positioned to effectively work on the gap separating action/practice and research/theory, which is a main, if not the major, tenet in PAR.

Another equally important purpose of this book is to contribute to the meager literature on both PAR and street children by providing a critical and reflective 'view from the field.' The major analytic focus will be on the 'natural history' of the PAR process as it unfolded in terms of the developmental stages and the contingencies that characterized it. In tracing these stages and contingencies and reflecting on them, the objective is twofold: to demonstrate the challenges that PAR undertakings face, and by the same token, to demystify the 'promises' (Finn, 1994) of PAR, which is often presented as a panacea.

Given the 'processual' nature of the reported PAR case, I have not opted for a traditional reporting format, following the sequence of introduction, methodology, findings, and conclusions. Instead, in the chapters that follow, I tell the story of a PAR process that gradually developed after two professionals decided to act upon their desire to 'do something' about Cairene street children. In the summer of 1993, I was introduced to Dr. Samia Said, a sociologist by training and president of Social Development Consultants (SDC), a private consultancy firm.[1] In discussing possibilities for collaboration, we realized that we were both interested in doing something about the street children phenomenon in Cairo. This is how the story I tell in this book began.

The story is essentially that of a process of experiential learning. The narration follows the progression of 'action' in terms of the interwoven and dynamic cyclical 'acts' of interpreting, planning, anticipating, doing, experiencing, assessing, and readjusting. It is a story of an undertaking that actively assumed the problematic and uncertain features of group life, the dilemmas of the actors' experience, and the *savoir-faire* they brought to bear in coming to terms with these dilemmas. The main endeavor narrated in the story was focused on incorporating the perspectives of participants, people's ability to influence one another, their capacity for reflectivity, and for intentional and meaningful activity. As such, the unfolding story is one of an interactive, open-ended process of participatory action research.

Finally, the narration that follows is not just about the realities of Cairene street children; it is equally—and probably more so—about the realities of undertaking research and action with their participation. Therefore, a dual focus will be maintained throughout the book: on the lived experiences of these young persons individually and collectively on the one hand, and the lived experiences shared with them by the group of practitioners on the other.

Presentation of the Chapters

Six chapters and two appendices make up the bulk of this book divided into two parts. In Part 1, I present a critical review of PAR and street work since they constituted the two major theoretical and methodological frameworks of the fieldwork program with Cairene street children. The review highlights the convergence in the values and assumptions underlying both PAR and street work, justifying their combination in programs targeting excluded street populations.

In Chapter 1, after reviewing the historical background of PAR, I examine its major assumptions and values, as well as questions of ontology, epistemology, and methodology. I then discuss the limitations of PAR and some of the critiques emanating from postmodernist/poststructuralist perspectives.

In Chapter 2, I attempt to organize available knowledge regarding a community organizing practice called 'street work' that is little known and poorly understood with a meager and often sporadic and sketchy literature. I start with an overview of the historical development of street work. I then examine the major parameters of street work practice before presenting the underpinnings of its present situation.

For both PAR and street work, I discuss two diametrically opposed conceptions at the two ends of a practice continuum stretching from radical/critical to instrumental/control. I discuss the discourses emanating from these two conceptions, and show that the polemic around them has been a consistent feature since their origin. Finally, I discuss two major tensions underlying this polemic and suggest a dialectical approach to analyzing and struggling with them.

In Part 2, I reflectively reconstruct the PAR process undertaken with the Cairene street children. In Chapter 3, I start by describing the beginning, exploratory phase of the process in which street ethnography constituted the bulk of street work aiming at elucidating some of the realities of street children and street life. I discuss these realities in Chapter 4, and present the conceptual framework that was developed in conjunction with them. This framework was used to inform the progression of the PAR process, the reconstruction of which I resume in Chapter 5. Lastly, in Chapter 6, I present the impact of this process at the individual, collective, and policy levels, and I end with a discussion of some methodological considerations and unresolved issues.

In Appendix 1, I sketch the profiles of some of the street children we came to know in order to illustrate the diversity in the trajectories that led them to the street, as well as the diversity in street life circumstances and styles. In Appendix 2, I sketch the profiles of some of the street localities in which the street workers established a meaningful presence. My purpose is to highlight the diversity in the use of public space by street people as well as the diversity in the milieus that they create.

Finally, throughout the book I set aside commentary sections to relate and reflect on some of the ethical issues emanating from practice as well as to make links with theoretical aspects. While some of the incidents related here may appear sensationalist, my purpose in relating them is twofold: I want to document some of the situations of extreme marginality and exclusion that we came to witness, and by the same token demonstrate the depth and complexity of the ethical dilemmas faced by practitioners. I remain convinced that the major challenge for PAR and street work practitioners, who work with excluded populations, is ethical in nature because of the value-laden, ambiguous, complex, and uncertain character of many of the situations in which they become involved; and for which established academic knowledge is of limited use and which, in addition, often require an immediate response. Hence, PAR and street work practitioners constantly need to construct their own experiential knowledge based on the artistry, spontaneity, and intuitive *savoir-faire* that they bring into their practice. Moreover, the strength of this kind of reflective, praxis-based practice resides in its ability to tackle ethical dilemmas with a dialectical sensitivity that helps to elucidate the issues that emanate from within the gray zones of practice, and avoid the trap of Manichean moralism.

Institutional Frameworks

In the summer of 1993, after agreeing with Dr. Said to 'do something' about the street children phenomenon, I started exploratory fieldwork in the streets of Cairo with the help of two volunteers, Samir (male) and Ranya (female), whom I identified through informal networks. In December of the same year, a UNICEF grant to SDC was used to conduct a situation analysis of the street children phenomenon.

Samir, Ranya, and Dr. Said were to be involved throughout the eight years of the PAR process described in this book. Fieldwork was conducted under the umbrella of The Egyptian Association for Development (EAD) until The Egyptian Association to Support Street Children (EASSC) was set up in 1998 as a non-profit NGO to specifically target street children and youth. Throughout the process, Dr. Said acted as technical advisor to the project, Samir and Ranya headed up the street worker/researcher team, and I was the project leader. Additional workers were recruited from 1996, and the average number of workers was maintained at five, with very little turnover.

International donor agencies, including UNICEF, CIDA, the Canadian Fund for Local Initiatives, Oxfam-GB, *Médecins sans Frontières*, the Ford Foundation, the Air France Foundation, and several European embassies in Cairo offered grants and in-kind support to EAD and EASSC. From their response to our proposals and work it was clear that they liked and appreciated our program.

In April 2001 the process was abruptly brought to an end when EASSC was dismantled by a decree issued by the local governor, under whose jurisdiction it was formally registered. In the decree the governor stated that the decision was made upon recommendation from the Ministry of Insurance and Social Affairs (MISA), which had allegedly observed sixteen administrative and financial infractions in EASSC's registries. EASSC went to court to contest the decree. The case is still being reviewed.

In December 2002 some of the EASSC street workers and the children who had started to assume street work tasks just prior to the dismantling of the association, decided that they would not wait for the court to settle the dispute between EASSC and MISA, realizing that it could take another couple of years. They studied the feasibility of establishing a new association, and in November 2003 they finalized all the tedious paperwork and formalities necessary for registering it and filed an application. The new organization resumed operation in September 2004, and many of the donors who had supported the defunct association, EASSC, resumed their support.

Part 1

Theoretical and Methodological Framework

In this part of the book I discuss the theoretical and methodological framework that informed the implementation of the PAR case which targeted street children in Cairo, Egypt, and which I narrate in the second part. In the following two chapters, I review two methodologies of social action/practice and research—participatory action research and street work—which, in combination with street ethnography and action science, were used in an eclectic manner to implement the PAR reported in this book. I refer to street ethnography and action science in Chapter 2 as essential parameters in critical street work.

In the review that follows I trace the origin of these two methodologies. I specify the context in which they emerged, and I examine their historical development. This emphasis on the historical background reflects my belief, in line with Germain and Hartman (1980, 323), that the sense of continuity in the historical content "can advance the formation of a sense of professional identity" and "can lend perspective and depth to understanding the ideological struggles within contemporary social work practice." I believe that today there is need for grounding social movements into a historical perspective that bypasses the trashing of Marxism and highlights the continuity of the thread of *resistance* to social injustices.

My objectives are twofold: firstly, to demonstrate the convergence in the values, assumptions, and *raison d'être* of the emancipatory version of PAR (Freirean/Southern) and critical street work methodologies that justifies their combination in programs targeting excluded street populations; and secondly, to add historical and analytical elements to the rather meager (especially with respect to street work) body of literature concerning these two 'marginal' methodologies. These elements along with the practice demonstration in Part 2, are intended to add further legitimacy to the marginal emancipatory versions of PAR and street work associated with critical thought.

1

Participatory Action Research

For a great number of international development practitioners, researchers, social workers, and civil society activists who are committed to social
justice and to the empowerment of oppressed and excluded social groups,
participatory action research (PAR) seems consistent with this commitment
(Finn 1994; Healy 2001; Reason 1994; Sohng 1996). Indeed, PAR is now
endorsed as an alternative methodology able to respond to the philosophical
and methodological challenges facing contemporary social exclusion and the
need for the development of effective strategies for social inclusion (Healy
2001; Reason 1994a).

Authors addressing the general topic of participative inquiry, including
PAR, usually acknowledge the fact that it refers to many diverse definitions,
concepts, practices, and typologies of research and action/practice endeavors
conducted in different disciplines and fields of study. Trying to put some
order into this diversity requires such a high degree of energy that many
researchers opt instead to devote their efforts to the practice of PAR, arguing
that it is too early to define its reality.

Indeed, there are many approaches to participative inquiry: participatory research, feminist research, collaborative research, appreciative inquiry,
action inquiry, cooperative inquiry, critical ethnography, applied anthropology, transformative research, empowerment research, research partnerships,
action research, critical action research, participatory action research, and
others. These approaches are often based on quite different premises, and
emphasize different aspects of the participatory inquiry process. Within
a given approach, one is likely to encounter different communities of
researchers who represent their work in different ways. Moreover, the degree

and quality of articulation in theory and practice differ significantly from one approach to another (Reason 1994a).

Many scholars refer to participatory research (PR), action research (AR), and participatory action research (PAR) as a general paradigm that assumes that communally generated knowledge should be dedicated to transforming unjust and oppressive social relations confronting the community. However, a close examination of the literature reveals that there is strong resistance to assimilating all action-oriented research into one category and thereby undermining the difference in the degree of their politicization. According to Reason (1994a), the lack of a unified and/or clear position regarding the relationship between the action and research dimensions in participatory research may very well be the source of the ambiguity and vagueness that characterize the various descriptions of the interactions between these two fundamental dimensions.

McTaggart (1991) observes that PAR has been used as a way to improve and inform a wide spectrum of socio-economic and cultural practices in such a variety of fields that it is has come to mean different and sometimes contradictory things to different people. McTaggart (1991, 168) also argues that the misuse of the term 'participatory action research' is not only due to a lack of understanding, "but also because there are attempts to represent research deliberately as inspired by communitarian values when it is not."

In this chapter I conduct a critical review of PAR literature. I begin with a brief historical review of the origin of AR and PAR in both Western and Third World contexts,[2] highlighting their differences. I then examine the major assumptions and values underlying the PAR tradition that emerged in the South, as well as issues related to ontology, epistemology, and methodology, before discussing its limitations. Lastly, in the commentary section, I draw upon my own experience as a PAR practitioner to reflect on these limitations.

Historical Background

In tracing the origin of action research, many authors refer to the early fieldwork of Engels and his alignment with the working classes of Manchester. They also refer to Karl Marx's (1818–83) *L'enquête ouvrière* and his use of 'structured interviews' with French factory workers as a type of AR, since it made the workers reflect on their living conditions (Marx 1979). For a more recent history, some writers consider John Dewey (1859–1952), who developed a philosophy of pragmatism (Dewey 1916, 1938), as the founder of the first generation of action researchers that emerged after the First World War. However, it is the social psychologist Kurt Lewin who is generally acknowledged as the father and inventor of the term 'action research' (Argyris and Schön 1989; Barbier 1996; Brown and Tandon 1983; Fals-Borda 1991; McTaggart 1991; Zuniga 1981).

The Lewinian Tradition

Kurt Lewin (1890–1947) was a specialist in Gestalt Psychology at the *Frankfurter Schule* when, in 1933, he fled from mounting Nazism and took refuge in the United States, where he became an American citizen and developed the concept of action research. He suggested that "causal inferences about the behavior of human beings are more likely to be valid and enactable when the human beings in question participate in building and testing them" (Argyris and Schön 1989, 613). This is possible, he argued, through the creation of "an environment in which participants give and get valid information, make free and informed choices—including the choice not to participate—and generate internal commitment to the results of their inquiry" (Argyris and Schön 1989, 613). The essence of Lewin's thought is perhaps best summarized in the well-known saying commonly attributed to him and passed on by his followers, to the effect that "there is nothing so practical as a good theory" (Brown and Tandon 1983, 281).

Lewin's originality resides mostly in his suggestion that the best way to learn about social systems is to try to change them through action (Lewin 1946). His determination to make the researcher a practitioner outside of university walls was considered unscientific, and he was severely criticized.

Lewin described AR as a process that begins when a group of people decide that there is the need for some kind of change or improvement regarding a specific problem area of shared concern. The group then decides to work together through a spiral process in which every cycle is composed of analysis, fact-finding, conceptualization, planning, implementation, and evaluation. This process not only helps in solving problems, but it also generates new critical knowledge about the situation itself. Participants play increasingly important roles in determining necessary adjustments and future directions. Group decision and commitment to improvement are crucial ideas in Lewin's approach. This implies that change comes from within the group, and that solutions are not imposed from outside. Furthermore, the deliberate overlapping of action and reflection requires flexible and responsive action plans that can be changed as people learn from their own experience. This reflects Lewin's conviction that the complexity of social situations precludes the possibility of anticipating everything that needs to be done in practice (Lewin 1946).

Since Lewin did not prescribe a rigid set of procedures for AR, contemporary action-oriented researchers still vigorously debate what really defines and constitutes this approach. The AR tradition, developed by his students and followers after his premature death in 1947, has for the most part been associated with private industry, organizational development, and more recently, with the work of scholars in the disciplines of education, agriculture, and human development (Small 1995). This Lewinian tradition of action research, articulated around the concept of group dynamics developed in the United States, is often criticized for reducing the larger implications of Lewin's insight: "Practice-oriented scholars became so client-centered that they failed to question how clients themselves defined their problems and they ignored the building and testing of propositions and theories embedded in their own practice" (Argyris 1983, 115). Whyte's (1987, 1989) research model for organizational development is often used as an example to demonstrate how an action research model based on a participatory strategy can serve to reinforce and perfect the status quo. Furthermore, critics of the Lewinian tradition argue that the overemphasis on group and interpersonal dynamics, efficiency and effectiveness of task accomplishment, common values, social integration, and incremental problem-solving approaches has not only reduced the scope of his insights about the relationship between theory and practice and the social use of science, it has also helped to perpetuate the culture of consensus social theories of affluent nations as a basic ideological assumption (Brown and Tandon 1983; Fals-Borda 1991; Finn 1994; Zuniga 1981).

According to Kemmis (1993, 2), the emancipatory insight of Lewin's AR is congruent with the fact that he was strongly influenced, prior to his departure to the United States, by Moreno, the inventor of group dynamics, sociodrama, and psychodrama, who "was interested in research as a part of social movement," and "had already developed a view of action research in which the 'action' was about activism, not just about changing practice or behavior understood in narrowly individualistic terms."

Kemmis (1993, 2) further argues that a view of this kind could not be advocated in the United States in the late 1940s and early 1950s, in light of the escalating concern about Marxism and communism that provoked "self-censorship among leftist scholars." Indeed, as we will see below, the connection between action research and social movements was to be articulated outside the United States.

Radicalization of the Lewinian Tradition

In his historical review of AR, Barbier (1996) acknowledges both the contribution of Lewin and the reduction of his ideas by his followers in the United States. However, Barbier argues that since the beginning of the 1970s there has been a gradual and sustained radicalization of AR, led by researchers in Europe and Canada. For Barbier, the term radical, when used in conjunction with AR, refers primarily to the status of the practitioner, that is, the more the practitioner becomes a researcher while remaining a field worker, the more radical the AR approach becomes. This radical view represents what Barbier and others regard as an epistemological break from traditional positivist research: action research is the science of praxis carried out by positioned and politically aware practitioners in the very context in which they are working.[3] The objective of research is viewed as the elaboration of the dialectics of the action with the participation of the concerned group, with a view to radically transforming the social reality at hand and improving the well-being of individuals and groups.

However, Barbier notes that we are still far from witnessing a universal radical AR approach. Indeed, in his view, the existing diversities make AR look chaotic, and the proliferation of writing about AR has reduced it to a sort of "sociological gadget." Yet Barbier sees this current manifestation as a step on an evolutionary process toward the consolidation of the epistemological break, favoring the emergence of existential, integral, personal, and collective AR.

Although Barbier's historical review of the AR tradition is generally colored with the 'who is more radical' syndrome, he does acknowledge a wide variety of contributions and influences from different thinkers and schools. However, this acknowledgment only briefly mentions the contribution of Third World thinkers and activists by citing the names of Freire and Fals-Borda. Barbier is not alone in undervaluing the contribution of Third World intellectuals and activists to the development of AR. Indeed, this absence is a common feature of the literature. One of the aims of this chapter is to remedy this deficiency.

Contribution of the Third World

Another school of action-oriented research emerged from work with disenfranchised groups in the Third World (Brown 1985; Fals-Borda and Rahman 1991; Finn 1994; Hall 1981, 1992; Healy 2001; Petras and Porpora 1992; Schapiro 1995; Small 1995; Sohng 1996; Zuniga 1981). This school shares many values and concerns with the Lewinian tradition: the sense of social responsibility and the option of using the intellectual resources of science to improve human well-being (Zuniga 1981, 36); the rejection of positivism as the sole philosophical conception of science (Small 1995, 944); the emphasis on the value of useful and popular knowledge and developmental change (Brown and Tandon 1983, 283); the focus on research questions that have implications for action (Small 1995, 948); and the active participation of those being studied throughout the research process (Finn 1994, 28).

However, the two schools differ ideologically with regard to how these values can be translated into practice. Whereas the Lewinian tradition is based on Consensus Social Theory, the school emerging from the Third World assumes that societal groups have conflicting interests. Moreover, whereas the Lewinian School believes that enhanced efficiency and effectiveness improve the situation of all system members, the equitable distribution of resources and the enhancement of the self-reliance of disenfranchised groups are central to the Third World school, even at the cost of economic efficiency and growth. Furthermore, the values and ideology of the Third World school (empowerment, equality, self-reliance, and commitment to the interests of local participants) often entail challenging oppressive political and social arrangements, with the result that the research group is often positioned in opposition to dominant and mainstream forces.

Following the tradition observed in English literature, the term AR will be used to refer to the Lewinian School, and the term PAR to refer to the Third World (Southern) tradition. It should be noted that only one term is usually used in the French-language literature: *recherche-action*. However, the literature acknowledges the distinction between the two main schools discussed here, usually referring to the Third World tradition as 'radical' and the Lewinian tradition as 'non-radical.'

Paulo Freire is generally considered to be the father of PAR (Finn 1994; Gaventa 1993; Hall 1981; Selener 1997). The ideas expressed in *Pedagogy of the Oppressed* (Freire 1970) and the concepts of 'liberating dialogue' and 'critical consciousness' developed in *Education for Critical Consciousness* (Freire 1973) continue to be basic tenets of the type of PAR that maintains a focus on power and its relationship to knowledge production. Freire's understanding of and commitment to praxis, as well as his attempt to develop a methodology for involving disenfranchised people as researchers seeking answers to questions raised by their daily struggle and survival, were guided by his many years of grassroots field immersion. His influence has not been limited to Latin

America. Since the early 1960s, radical intellectuals quickly spread the model of liberatory pedagogy throughout the developing world. Taking a stand on the side of the poor and powerless, these intellectuals found in Freire's concept the possibility of espousing reflection and practice so as to promote personal liberation, political mobilization, and social transformation.

Indeed, the Third World's contribution to the development of participatory research is quite significant. According to Hall (1981, 8), by the late 1950s and early 1960s, the dominant positivist research paradigm had been extended to the Third World "through elaborate mechanisms of international scholarships, cultural exchanges, and training of researchers in Europe and North America." Reactions from the Third World, beginning in Latin America, took many forms. Dependency theorists (Amin 1974, 1977; Said 1994) unraveled the mechanism of economic and cultural dependency, as well as its contribution to the maintenance of existing class distinctions and to the aggravation of the problem of poverty. At the grassroots level, young scientists from the First World working as development experts in Africa, Asia, and Latin America experienced difficulties when trying to apply their research methodologies in the Third World context. They realized that by placing the control of the production and distribution of knowledge in the hands of experts, their techniques and methods were actually reinforcing the imposition of the Western development model with all its contradictions (Park 1992, 33). These international development workers also realized that their local assistants were more effective in gathering pertinent data from the targeted groups, as they were able to resort to methods deeply rooted in cultural contexts that promoted the communal sharing of knowledge. Thus, the orientation toward more reliance on local knowledge, experience, wisdom, and skills began to surface as a valid and justified approach. In this sense, the PAR tradition emerged within the context of resistance to the imposition of the Western model of research and development on the Third World.

According to Hall (1981), while PAR was being developed in the South (Latin America, Africa, and Asia), critiques of positivist research paradigms were becoming increasingly loud and articulate in the North, leading to the emergence of action- and participatory-oriented methodologies. Solidarity and collegial networking with Southern researchers were established. However, Hall deplores the fact that the majority of writers in the North often neglect the contribution of the South when tracing the origins of participatory research. Fals-Borda (1991) goes further, arguing that the lack of clarity of the different theoretical positions with respect to PAR today could be largely remedied if due attention were paid to earlier attempts in the Third World (since the early 1960s) to construct PAR philosophy and techniques with a view to producing and remaking science and knowledge.

Review of Participatory Action Research in the Third World

Muhammad Anisur Rahman and Orlando Fals-Borda are acknowledged in the PAR literature as two influential PAR authorities from the South (Colombia) whose contribution, both to the field and to the international intellectual arena, is highly regarded (Hall 1992; Park 1992; Reason 1994a; Small 1995). In a book that they edited and to which they contributed several chapters, they review the Southern PAR school from its emergence in the early 1960s (Fals-Borda and Rahman, 1991). They firmly situate it within the long tradition of liberationist movements: "Those who adopted PAR have tried to practice with a radical commitment that has gone beyond usual institutional boundaries, reminiscent of the challenging tradition of Chartists, utopians, and other social movements of the nineteenth century" (Fals-Borda and Rahman 1991, vii). Their theoretical discussion is "written also with a view to undertake a dialogue with academic scholars and in particular those who consider themselves 'post-modern'" (1991, viii).

The authors describe their initial work (from the early 1960s until 1977) as an iconoclastic period characterized by an activist and anti-professional bent, with the organization of a political party in mind. In March 1977, at the time of the World Symposium on Action Research and Scientific Analysis in Cartagena, Colombia, this early activism and radicalism gave way to a period of self-assessment and reflection (Fals-Borda and Rahman 1991, 25). A revision was undertaken, resulting in the discovery of Gramsci and in the rejection of the then dominant interpretation of historical materialism, which viewed social transformation largely as the task of an intellectual vanguard supposedly having a more 'advanced' consciousness than that of ordinary people. It was also realized that although vanguard parties from both the left and the right might have produced structural changes in some situations, they had also instituted new forms of domination over the people (Rahman 1991, 13).

Accordingly, a new radical analysis emerged, one that maintained that "domination of masses by elites is rooted not only in the polarization of control over the means of material production but also over the means of knowledge production, including control over the social power to determine what is useful knowledge." (Rahman 1991, 14). It then became necessary to simultaneously tackle the two gaps since history had demonstrated that decreasing disparity in access to the means of material production did not ensure a similar reduction in disparity in knowledge relations. On the contrary, it triggered new processes of domination (Rahman 1991, 14).

The new challenge for PAR was producing a countervailing, liberating knowledge "upon which to construct power . . . for the poor, oppressed, and exploited groups and social classes" (Fals-Borda 1991, 3). Gramsci's proposal to convert common sense into good sense becomes the basis for the production of this new emancipating collective knowledge. Committed intellectuals and the base-groups come together as equals in a process of research and social action, whereby each group contributes its knowledge, techniques, and experiences, forming what Fals-Borda calls a subject/subject relationship. The dialectical tension produced in this joint venture results in the synthesis of a new liberating knowledge combining the intellectual's critical rationality with the common sense and cultural values of the people. Knowledge thus produced is not offered to the dominant elite for consumption. Rather, the people themselves use it to acquire more power in their struggle for a more just social structure.

Fals-Borda and Rahman are perfectly aware of the fact that since they made the statements above, PAR has been gaining recognition, and many officials and researchers have begun to claim that they are working with PAR, whereas in fact, they are co-opting it as a methodology and a jargon, without subscribing to its ideology. Despite Fals-Borda's and Rahman's worries with regard to this seemingly unavoidable appropriation and co-optation, they refuse to be PAR "watchdogs," to decide what is and what is not authentic PAR (Fals-Borda 1991, 162).

In the foregoing, I have broadly reviewed the contexts within which two different traditions of PAR—the Lewinian and the Southern—have emerged. In reality, it is common to encounter PAR undertakings that borrow from both schools, in addition to those that clearly adhere to one or the other. The remainder of this chapter discusses the Southern tradition of PAR and its influence on critical/progressive social work and development.

Values and Ideology in PAR Literature

The basic ideology of PAR is that a self-conscious people, those who are currently poor and oppressed, will progressively transform their environment by their own praxis. In this process others may play a catalytic and supportive role but will not dominate. (M. A. Rahman 1991, 13)

PAR's main assumptions and values are consistent and convergent with the tenets of critical theory and progressive forms of social work practice and research (DePoy et al. 1999; Healy 2000, 2001).[4] Commitment to genuine socio-political change, coupled with a strong belief in the capacity of participants, through collective and conscious actions, to influence the political and economic factors that shape their existence, are pillars in both critical theory and PAR. This emancipatory view is believed to be conducive to greater social justice.

Criticizing Positivist Epistemology

Whereas "the orthodox scientific worldview is the product of the Enlightenment and represents a liberating step for human society in releasing itself from the bonds of superstition and Scholasticism," it has led us "to narrow our view of our world and to monopolize knowing in the hands of an elite few . . . [and] to place the researcher firmly outside and separate from the subject of his or her research, reaching for an objective knowledge and for one separate truth . . . . There is an emerging worldview, more holistic, pluralist, and egalitarian, that is essentially participative . . . [that] sees human beings as co-creating their reality through participation: through their experience, their imagination and intuition, their thinking and their action" (Reason 1994a, 324). In these few lines, Reason succinctly summarizes the position held by PAR practitioners. Although the merits of traditional science are not denied, a growing number of scholars and practitioners strive to go beyond the limitations of positivism, which may be appropriate for natural sciences, but not for social sciences.

Since PAR practitioners work for the most part with subordinated communities, they are critical of research methodologies that serves the interests of the dominant culture by monopolizing the production of knowledge and using the latter to sustain the subordinate status of disadvantaged communities. Tandon (1982, 1989) developed a four-point critique of the monopolist research to which most PAR proponents subscribe: absolutist, purist, rationalist, and elitist. The absolutist critique emphasizes that pure knowledge cannot be generalized across contexts, thus its creation cannot be the aim of social research. The purist critique condemns the drive for objectivity and value-free research, and claims that a separation between researcher and subject (in order to uphold academic rigor) only maintains the researcher's full control. The rationalist critique asserts that the classical research paradigm overemphasizes thinking as an objective means of knowing, at the expense of feeling and acting. Finally, the elitist critique challenges the exclusive accessibility of the dominant research paradigm to elite professionals, with the result that their research only serves the economic and ideological interests of their class.

Knowledge and Power

As we have already seen, the Southern tradition emphasizes the political aspect of knowledge production. Those involved in the PAR process understand that knowledge for social change is produced in a context of unequal power relations (Gaventa 1988, 1991). The definition of ordinary people's problems and decisions affecting their lives are based on scientific/expert/ specialist knowledge. This knowledge is heavily loaded with technical terminology, jargon, and specialized language of argumentation unfamiliar to ordinary people, who are thereby excluded from the debate. Expert representations are so powerful that people often end up internalizing the dominant constructions and discounting their own experience (Sohng, 1996).

This analysis demonstrates the importance of understanding the role of knowledge as a key instrument for maintaining control and power. Therefore,

> the PAR tradition starts with concerns for power and powerlessness, and aims to confront the way the established and power-holding elements of societies world-wide are favored because they hold a monopoly on the definition and employment of knowledge. (Reason 1994a, 328)

This starting point aims at establishing an understanding of both oppressive and enabling sources of power. However, inasmuch as understanding of this kind requires an appreciation of history, PAR strives to be contextualized in the socio-political environment in which it is conducted and in the historical conditions that culminated in the situation under study (Freire 1970; Fals-Borda and Rahman 1991). PAR's goal is to go beyond official and elitist constructions of history in order to allow the multiple histories of people's cultural and daily life expressions to surface.

PAR is People-Centered

> If I perceive the reality as the dialectical relationship between subject and object, then I have to use methods for investigation which involve the people of the area being studied as researchers, they should take part in the investigation themselves and not serve as the passive objects of the study. (Freire 1982, 27)

Participatory action researchers challenge top-down approaches to knowledge production, and seek to promote egalitarian relations in the research process (Brown and Tandon 1983). They refuse to separate themselves from the research subjects and they join in as committed participants in a process of co-learning that honors and values the knowledge and experience of oppressed people. The wisdom of "organic intellectuals," whose critical awareness is grounded in personal experience, is a valued source of knowledge (Gramsci 1987, 1992). A major point of departure is thus the lived experience of individuals and communities and the belief that through that actual experience, we may "intuitively apprehend its essence; we feel, enjoy, and understand it as reality" (Fals-Borda and Rahman 1991, 4).

PAR values people's knowledge. It aims to foster their ability to conduct research and to appropriate knowledge produced by the dominant knowledge industry and to use it for their own benefit. It encourages them to explore problems from their own perspective, and, significantly, it liberates their minds for critical reflection and inquiry. In this way, PAR contributes to the development of freedom and democracy (Tandon 1989).

PAR is about Praxis

> Praxis was one of the first articulating concepts of the PAR movement. Proscribed as unscientific by positivists, it has from the beginning had the advantage of moving away from those schools where practice means technological manipulation or social engineering of humans, and instrumental control of natural and social processes. (Fals-Borda 1991, 156)

Antonio Gramsci (1891–1937), an Italian Marxist, critical theorist, and political activist, is generally acknowledged to be the major influence on the development of praxis as a political methodology for work with the oppressed (Burrell and Morgan 1979; Fals-Borda and Rahman 1991).

Gramsci's thought was focused on introducing a subjective element into orthodox Marxism by stressing the capacity of the oppressed to develop a critical consciousness that represents a concrete force for a political end. In so doing, Gramsci reconnected with the young "radical humanist" Marx before the epistemological break in the latter's thought that led him to move toward 'radical structuralism' (Burrell and Morgan 1979, 282). By merging elements of structure and consciousness, Gramsci made a strong plea for integrating the subjective and objective aspects of experience by calling for a dual focus on the structural situation and on people's subjective experience.

One major implication of this renewal with the young Marx is that transformation could no longer be perceived as the sole task of an intellectual vanguard supposedly having a more 'advanced' consciousness than that of ordinary people. Instead, the path to transformation is through praxis-based modes of inquiry in which the intellectual's critical rationality works in a dialectical tension with the common sense and cultural values of the people, which results in the synthesis of a new liberating knowledge.

Praxis-based research suggests an ongoing process of engagement, adult education, communication, action, and reflection. The objective of this process is to produce, with a group of people, knowledge and action that are directly useful to them in terms of empowerment and liberation. As such, a praxis-based approach attempts to unify theory and practice by suggesting that "one cannot 'do' theory or practice in isolation; rather, it is a reflexive process of learning by doing and doing by learning" (Ife 1999, 220).

The above account of PAR values and ideology must now be situated within the ontological, epistemological, and methodological frames of reference.

Ontology, Epistemology, and Methodology

Before presenting the way in which PAR theorists address ontological, epistemological, and methodological questions, a word of caution is necessary. These questions are usually raised in conjunction with the construction of paradigms that are basic belief sets that represent a worldview regarding the nature of reality: what can be known and how to go about finding it. While it is true that PAR does hold some beliefs regarding these issues, as will be shown below, its proponents—especially those in the Third World—refuse to think in terms of building a new paradigm. As Fals-Borda (1991, 162) puts it: "The participatory approach to producing and remaking knowledge would go so far as to accept the general epistemic change in the overall nature of its search, short of claiming that PAR is a new paradigm or is

building one on purpose." This aversion to paradigm-building reflects a
basic refusal to play the role of

> watchdogs of the new knowledge to decide what is scientific and what is
> not. It would mean playing the same game of intellectual superiority and
> technical control that we have been challenging in the academic world.
> Perhaps we should be content to follow Foucault (1980) and develop a
> more modest conceptual systematization of heretofore 'subjugated knowl-
> edges' as a more stimulating and creative task. (Fals-Borda 1991, 162)

Accordingly, the alternative to paradigm-building is an insistence on viewing PAR as a rigorous search for knowledge in the context of:

> . . . an open-process of life and work . . . a progressive evolution ended
> toward an overall, structural transformation of society and culture, a pro-
> cess that requires ever renewed commitment, an ethical stand, self-critique
> and persistence at all levels. In short, it is a philosophy of life as much as
> a method. (Fals-Borda and Rahman 1991, 29)

In the following discussion, I will examine how critical researchers treat
PAR's philosophical assumptions in general without dogmatically adhering
to a particular paradigm or insisting on constructing a new one.

Ontology

PAR's ontological position is quite different from the positivist one, which
assumes that a 'real' and 'factual' reality exists independently of the observer.
From a positivist perspective, this kind of reality can be apprehended ratio-
nally, and knowledge of the true state of affairs can be achieved through
objective inquiry. This basic ontological posture is criticized as being both
reductionist and deterministic (Hesse 1980).

According to Reason, PAR's ontological position is well expressed by
Freire:

> The concrete reality for many social scientists is a list of particular facts
> that they would like to capture . . . . For me, the concrete reality is some-
> thing more than isolated facts. In my view, thinking dialectically, the
> concrete reality consists not only of concrete facts and (physical) things,
> but also includes the ways in which the people involved with these facts

perceive them. Thus in the last analysis, for me, the concrete reality is the connection between subjectivity and objectivity, never objectivity isolated from subjectivity. (Reason 1994a, 332)

This is a relativist ontology that maintains that there is no unique, pre-existing 'real' world, independent of human mental activity and human language (Guba and Lincoln 1994). Reason (1994a, 333) notes that advocates of this ontological position draw on several philosophers (Dewy, Habermas, Maxwell, Skolimowski, and so on), for whom constructions of reality are manifested not only through the mind, but also through the reflective action of individuals and groups.

This relativist ontological position maintains that "valid human inquiry essentially requires full participation in the creation of personal and social knowing." (Reason 1994a, 332). In this light, dialogue becomes a key notion:

because it is through dialogue that the subject-object relationship of traditional science gives way to a subject-subject one, in which the academic knowledge of formally educated people works in a dialectic tension with the popular knowledge of people to produce a more profound understanding of the situation. (Reason 1994a, 328)

Epistemology

The common critique and stand against dominant positivist philosophical conceptions have made most action-oriented researchers particularly sensitive to and aware of epistemological issues and their implications for conducting research. They strongly argue, as we have seen, that logical positivism is just one theory of knowledge creation, one that is neither unique nor the best. Furthermore, action-oriented researchers make a strong plea for an alternative epistemology that is to a large degree a reversal of the positivist conception of knowledge. Firstly, it calls for clarifying and positioning the relationship between epistemology and ideology, and between knowledge and power:

If an inquiry is primarily engaged in service of a dominant class it will not need to dialogue with people; it is not interested in their reality, but rather in imposing on them a dominant reality . . . If an inquiry is engaged in the service of the development of people, it will necessarily engage with them in dialogue. (Reason 1994a, 333)

This claim stresses the importance of recognizing the value of popular knowledge, common sense, wisdom, and intuitive learning.

Secondly, the new epistemology strives to understand the complex world of lived experience from the point of view of those who live it. Major emphasis is placed on the fundamental importance of experiential knowing, developed within the framework of an existential concept of experience. Research is no longer viewed as the study of people who are regarded as passive objects of inquiry and unaffected by the research process. Instead, the research object is conceived as a situation in which human subjects are actors who play a critical role and are capable of undertaking self-reflection regarding their world and their action within it (praxis).

Thirdly, by embracing the idea that experiential knowledge arises through participation with others, action-oriented research believes that people can and should participate in the identification of their own problems, the analysis and interpretation of these problems, and the generation of relevant knowledge (Reason 1994a; Small 1995). Thus, participation gives rise to experiential knowing and helps to break up the relationship of subordination by transforming the relationship between the researcher and the researched into subject-subject rather than subject-object. In other words, knowledge is created in the interaction between investigators and respondents.

A fourth philosophical difference concerns the aim of inquiry. From a positivist perspective, the aim is to produce, through verified hypotheses established as facts or laws, a universal explanation (prediction and control) primarily based on cause-effect linkages (Guba and Lincoln 1994). Action-oriented research places more emphasis on the specific situation or context and less emphasis on universal laws because the primary concern is to create change that will benefit those who are being studied. Moreover, unlike positivist research, which is concerned with describing 'what is' and refrains from proposing what 'should be,' action-oriented researchers believe that any scientific endeavor is value-laden and that judging the morality of proposed solutions to social problems cannot and ought not be avoided.

Finally, the objective of promoting the interests of those being studied leads action-oriented researchers to place considerable emphasis on the ethical implications of the research study. Unlike positivist researchers, whose primary ethical concern is that subjects consent to be studied and are neither harmed nor deceived, action-oriented researchers believe that using the subjects for the exclusive gain of researchers is exploitative. Thus, not only do they maintain that subjects should gain from the research results and implications, but they are also concerned with how the actual process of research affects the individuals and systems studied.

Thus, concerns for epistemology and ontology appear to be secondary to the primary concern of confronting "the way in which the established and power-holding elements of societies worldwide are favored because they hold the monopoly on the definition and employment of knowledge" (Reason 1994a, 328).

Methodology

PAR is a methodology for an alternate system for knowledge production based on the people's role in setting the agendas, participating in the data gathering and analysis, and controlling the use of the outcomes. The PAR methodology may use diverse methods, both qualitative and quantitative, to further these ends, many of which will derive from vernacular (often oral) traditions of communication and dissemination of knowledge. (Reason 1994a, 329)

In general, methodological issues are examined within a context that goes beyond the sterile debate over the relative merits of quantitative and qualitative methods. While neither of these methods is viewed as a priori unacceptable, the tendency toward qualitative methods seems to reflect a desire to be coherent with the ontological and epistemological positions discussed above. The connection between objectivity and subjectivity, the active involvement of participants, and the objective of capturing the depth and complexity of the particular situation under study may very well explain the favoring of qualitative methods. Moreover, most PAR researchers do not concern themselves with the limited ability of qualitative methods to produce universal facts since the immediate problem is usually the primary concern.

Therefore, the positivist methodological tools in terms of design, concept formation, measurement, validity, relevance, and so on take second place to the emphasis on establishing processes of collaboration and dialogue that aim at empowering participants and establishing community solidarity. Thus, expressive forms such as sociodrama, plays, dance, drawing and painting, and other "engaging activities encourage a social validation of 'objective' date that cannot be obtained through the orthodox process of survey and fieldwork. It is important for an oppressed group, which is often part of a culture of silence, to find ways to tell and thus reclaim their own story" (Reason 1994a, 329).

Accordingly, a key methodological feature distinguishing PAR from other social research is dialogue, which is different from traditional interviewing in several aspects. As Sohng (1996, 85–86) remarks, "interviewing presupposes the primacy of the researcher's frame of reference. It offers a one-way flow of information that leaves the researched in the same position after having shared knowledge, ignoring the self-reflective process that the imparting of information involves." Moreover, in the dialogic approach, the researcher shares his/her perceptions, questions, and reflections in response to the participant's account and puts forward different theories and date. This sharing invites participants to engage in explicit reflexivity. It is also conducive to the creation of an authentic, two-way relationship between researchers and participants, in which learning involves self-examination from a new, critical standpoint.

The foregoing review of PAR values and ideology clearly reveals the similarities between PAR and critical theory;[5] the traditional distinction between ontology and epistemology is challenged by virtue of the belief that what can be known is created by the interaction between the researcher and the researched. Furthermore, as is the case with both critical theory and constructivism, the methodological question in PAR is approached with a great deal of dialectical sensitivity. Dialogue and the dialogical relationship between the researcher and the researched are perceived as dialectical in nature, producing tension conducive to a more informed and aware consciousness. Varying personal constructions are elicited and refined through interaction between the researcher and the researched, and are compared and contrasted through dialectical interchange.

PAR values and ideology also converge with moderate strands of postmodernism, such as "constructive postmodernism," (Reason 1994b, 1994c) "resistance postmodernism," (Kincheloe and McLaren 1994; Lane 1999) and "affirmative postmodernism" (Rosenau 1992) with respect to difference, relativism, subjectivity, concentration on process, and cultural sensitivity. However, there still remains a basic difference between PAR tenets and those of postmodernism, namely, PAR still strongly holds onto the idea of human rights as being fundamental to all people, regardless of culture, nationality, race, gender, and so on (the humanist project). Ife (1999, 216) argues that postmodern skepticism of universal principles has resulted in the construction of a relativist concept of human rights that can be used to justify the oppression of minorities in different parts of the globe, and by the same token "has not been helpful to human rights activists (including social workers) seeking to protect the basic civil, political, economic, social, cultural, and environmental rights of vulnerable individuals, communities, and populations." Nonetheless, Ife (1999), along with Leonard (1997), Pease and Fook (1999), and Healy (2001) maintain that critical social work and development can still benefit from the insights of postmodernism without jeopardizing the claim to social justice on which their foundations rest.

As we will see, this convergence of PAR with critical theory and postmodernism has led critics of PAR to develop high expectations of its promises, which, admittedly, hinge on representing PAR as a sort of panacea.

Let us now turn to the difficult issue of the limitations of PAR.

The Limitations of Participatory Action Research

To facilitate the discussion of the limitations of PAR, I have grouped the major elements covered in the literature under three headings: the ideological foundation; the role of the researcher; and the nature of participation. In reality, the issues discussed under the different headings are interrelated. In the discussion below, I draw attention to missing elements in the literature and attempt to further problematize the limitations of PAR in a more holistic manner.

Ideological Foundations

Many PAR researchers designate social change as the research objective. In so doing, they adhere to an ideology in which *power* is a central notion. They argue that by critically analyzing institutionalized power and by constructing knowledge (research) as well as action strategies (mobilization, education and training, pressure groups, setting up action projects, and so on), more power can be acquired. Unmasking the myths imposed by the power structure, creating popular knowledge that prevents those in power from maintaining a monopoly on determining the rights of others, and reinforcing the organizing potential of the base group are some of the main mechanisms that are conducive to the acquisition of more power.

But power for whom? Vaillancourt (1981, 69) soberly reminds us that PAR *"est située quelque part dans les rapports sociaux, soit du côté des forces sociales dominées, soit du côté des forces sociales dominantes . . . [elle] peut être faite pour promouvoir les intérêts des classes populaires dominées, soit des classes capitalistes dominantes."* In other words, PAR is not intrinsically conducive to acquiring power for the benefit of the powerless; the risk of appropriation is always there.

While Freire's notion of 'conscientization' refers to a process by which self-awareness is raised through collective self-inquiry—dialogue and reflection in opposition to indoctrination—there are many traditional processes of knowledge transfer that falsely attribute to themselves a liberatory Freirean approach (McTaggart 1991, 171; Rahman 1991, 17) Selener (1997) points to the paradox often observed between the researchers' intentions, claims, and desires for dialogue and the actual effort made to convince participants of the value of the researcher's view and method, thus, paradoxically producing the very effect that they want to avoid, that is, the 'indoctrination' of the other that is, the uneducated.

Hall (1981, 1992) maintains that unless adequate control is placed over the PAR process and results, abuse can result in further empowerment of those who are already in control. PAR provides researchers with insights and views which are not otherwise readily accessible and which they can sometimes use to accrue more power for themselves within the academic status quo (Hall 1981, 15). This raises the ethical issue of the use and ownership of PAR results, which, if left uncontrolled and/or not addressed, can lead to manipulation and abuse.

Groulx makes the same critical remark regarding the use of qualitative research (including PAR) in social work:

> Est-ce que cette démarche méthodologique produit des connaissances renou-vellant l'intervention et l'analyse de la réalité sociale ou ne participe-t-elle pas plutôt à la construction de l'identité du travail social en agissant comme discours de légitimation sociale? (Groulx 1997, 64)

The argument advanced by Groulx is that qualitative research in social work has two functions. Qualitative researchers believe that knowledge production based on their research methodologies promotes disciplinary autonomy and democratic processes. The emphasis on the subject as actor, the attention paid to context, the replacement of control of variables by reflection-in-action, and the replacement of social determinism by the logic of action have led to the emergence of a new, inter-subjective rationale. This orientation has contributed to the construction of a new discourse in social work, one that renews the intelligibility of social work practices within an autonomous intervention discipline. However, Groulx (1997) argues that the re-appropriation of qualitative methodology in social work can also be viewed as an ideological strategy to establish a distinctiveness *vis-à-vis* concurrent discourses and practices in the disciplinary, professional, and administrative arenas. As such, the hypothesis of disciplinary renewal can be substituted by a corporatist hypothesis aimed at the acquisition of more authority (Groulx 1997, 65).

Deconstructed by the corporatist hypothesis, the qualitative discourse, according to Groulx (1997, 66), can be shown to be harmonious with recent state policies regarding decentralization and partnership with innovative practitioners using creative practices. The attention paid by the qualitative discourse to the subjective lived experience of clients, to action strategies, and to community networks, coupled with the critique of institutional dependence, can be used to legitimize the current disengagement of the state. Groulx's conclusion is that despite the different, if not contradictory hypotheses that one can have about the role of qualitative research in social work, it has nonetheless generated new categories for understanding social problems (Groulx 1997, 67).

Role of the Researcher

The role of the researcher is often perceived ideologically:

> *Le chercheur est amené à s'engager non seulement intellectuellement mais également affectivement et socialement, c'est à dire avec ses valeurs, ses idéologies, ses croyances et tout son être . . . Le chercheur ne peut donc prétendre à la neutralité: y prétendre serait un leurre.* (Amegan et al. 1981, 47)

Also, the role of the researcher is often described rather humbly as a 'co-learner' and 'participant.' Yet the researcher is also engaged actively in 'educating,' 'building capacity,' 'awareness raising,' 'enabling,' 'managing conflict,' and making other contributions that would not only make him/her less of an outsider, but also lead to the 'emancipation' of both the individual and the community.

Healy (2001) remarks that all of these activities, including the initiation of the research itself and the promotion of participants' involvement, illustrate research workers' power, an issue that often receives insufficient attention. She highlights a certain culture of silence, an occlusion of power issues, reinforced by a "radical egalitarian stance," an "edict against the explicit use of power," and a "power aversion rhetoric" that are responsible for the "dissonance between the claims of PAR and its actuality." This situation, she argues, stems from the fact that PAR workers do not reflect on the positive (liberatory) as well as the negative (constraining) effects of their own power. She maintains that this kind of reflection is necessary if one wants to attend adequately to PAR limitations. In her critical appraisal of PAR, Healy uses insights from postmodernism, arguing that PAR workers can themselves gain from such a perspective by acknowledging the different forms of power intrinsic to their work and by questioning their claims and practices.

The fact that researchers are often from outside the social milieus or communities in which PAR is conducted provokes little critical reflection in the literature. This issue is usually dismissed by resorting to Gramsci's notion of 'organic intellectuals,' according to which the authentic and practical commitment of the researcher and the collective pursuit of social, educational, and political practice prevent the creation of permanent hierarchies.

Very few writers address the contradictions and conflicts that arise when researchers from academia become involved in activist PAR type of research, and they become the main producers of PAR accounts in the literature. Cancian (1993) contends that when researchers with academic careers develop strong ties with community groups in PAR undertakings that are strongly oriented toward community empowerment, they are likely to be the least successful in academia—a combination of activism with an academic career requires going against an academic mainstream that focuses on research products rather than on the research processes; on regular publication in academic journals rather than in publications for laypersons; and on accountability to academic standards rather than to activist standards.

Cancian's own experience with PAR as an academic researcher allows her to draw a conclusion regarding the ideal that the empowerment of oppressed community groups is the single legitimate *raison d'être* of PAR:

> I now believe that this ideal does not fit people like myself who value their membership and standing in academia . . . Another departure from the ideals of participatory research stems from my observation that most non-researchers are not interested or skilled in many aspects of academic research; therefore, I plan to separate some of my academic research from the participatory components of the project, and retain control over the research process, although part of the research agenda will be collectively controlled. (Cancian 1993, 97)

For Petras and Porpora (1992, 109), two sociologists from academia involved in PAR, the 'action' component in PAR is conceptualized as 'service' rendered to the community by academic researchers keen to "reciprocate for the time, tolerance, and confidence provided by community leaders and activists." As such, the tension created when academic researchers become involved in PAR undertakings with community groups is a tension between service and scholarship. The service, according to these two writers, could take the minimal form of providing documentation and special publications to community groups and their members. Academic researchers can also assist the groups to build strategies that help them to confront their opponents effectively, to develop models and typologies based on successful PAR undertakings, and to acquire a variety of technical skills. This minimal form of PAR, coined by the writers as the "parallel process model," is the means by which academic researchers who are sympathetic to community concerns can respond to the community's needs while keeping control of their scholarly questions and research regarding the community group's immediate agenda.

In the same article, Petras and Porpora analyze another model of participatory research, that of the institutional engagement of an entire university (as opposed to individual researchers from within a university) with the community. They report on the experience of the University of Central America (UCA) in El Salvador as a model for an entire university establishment to be fully and organically engaged with oppressed groups and communities, a commitment which cost the lives of six faculty members and two co-workers in 1989. However, the writers do not seem to favor the UCA model:

> Our academic identity should not be disparaged . . . . For all our sympathies with the poor and oppressed, for all our willingness to engage in social activism in other capacities, when it comes to our research, many of us will opt for some of the parallel process rather than for the mutual engagement or UCA models. (Petras and Porpora 1992, 121)

This position seems to stem from Petras's and Porpora's belief that universities ought not to be the voice of the poor but rather its "theoretical reason" (Petras and Porpora 1992, 123).

I would like to end this brief discussion of the role and problematic of academic researchers involved in PAR by quoting other sociologists, Stoecker and Bonanich (1992, 9), who wrote the guest editor's introduction to a special volume of *The American Sociologist* on participatory research:

Now we need to recognize with cold clarity that PR (participatory research) is not going to win us many friends among the wealthy and powerful, and in that sense it can be threatening to our own well-being. Doing PR, at least in its purist forms, is antithetical to climbing the ladder of professional success. PR is revolutionary sociology. It is not business as usual . . . [and] puts forward a compelling moral challenge. It raises the question: Who are our universities for? Are they for faculty, for the students, for the power elite, or should they be for those who are most hurt by the system?

Nature of Participation

Ideally, PAR seeks the active and collective participation of people concerned in all research activities, including research design, data collection, processing, analysis, and interpretation. If the research involves a large number of people, it is usually accepted that the natural leaders or 'peoples' cadres' represent the group in the research process.

Finn (1994, 28) attenuates the passionate rhetoric of PAR's tenets. She argues that although participation is reflected in the philosophical commitment of the researchers, its scope is often limited by practical realities. Rather than a dichotomy between orthodox and participatory research, there is a continuum with varying degrees of meaningful participation in and control of the process and products of research by the participants. Just as the process of 'citizen participation' in the planning of public social programs has often been co-opted or made routine, Finn maintains that similar risks of co-optation face participatory research as the concept gains political popularity.

For Sohng (1996), forging an egalitarian relationship between researchers and community members is no easy task. Disenfranchised groups often internalize the negative connotations of the stigma imposed on them by a dominating structure, which may reinforce subordination to outside researchers. The latter may find it difficult to relinquish the role of expert and tend to impose their own views and ideas. These tendencies can be countered, according to Sohng, if there is a clear commitment to implement mechanisms in the PAR process for explicit reflexivity and for scrutinizing interactions and unexamined assumptions of authority and expertise.

Hall (1981, 11) prefers to see the problem of how collective a participatory research process may be as a key methodological issue. He recognizes that under the guise of participation and strategies for 'involving' the people, outside interests may attempt to manipulate communities for purposes of domestication, integration, and exploitation. He believes, however, that manipulation can be explicitly rejected if enough zeal is employed in keeping control and learning in the hands of the people.

Lastly, Reason (1994a) recognizes a sort of inevitable tension between the ideal of participation as presented in PAR discourse, and the practical demands for effective leadership. For Reason, this tension is a "living paradox, we have to live with, to find creative resolution moment to moment" (Reason 1994a, 335).

However, the participation issue is even more complex; some issues I discuss here, and others I address in the commentary section below. Firstly, the concern for participation is well justified in the eyes of its critics, given the emergence of an escalating number of practices in both social work and international development arenas that claim to espouse PAR ideals, whereas in fact they reinforce the status quo of power differentials. It is indeed ironic to see that the writings of people like Paulo Freire (1970, 1973, 1982) and Ivan Illich (1976, 1990), whose writings were perceived as revolutionary and threatening until not long ago, have now entered the mainstream and have been accepted by the development establishment, notably the World Bank (Francis 2001). The World Bank's motivation for adopting an ostensibly radical rhetoric regarding participation is a question that merits active analysis but is beyond the scope of this book. Suffice it to say that its endorsement of participatory methods in 1998 triggered the emergence of structured participative technologies based on formulaic prescriptions that have helped strip the concept of empowerment of its political potential (Cooke and Kothar 2001).

Secondly, in addition to the question of who does, and who does not participate, the nature of participation itself needs to be explained. There is a tendency to label any activity along the continuum of participation (from information-sharing to consultation to participation) as 'participation.' Information-sharing and consultation occur more frequently than participation in decision-making or implementation.

Thirdly, the social in the participatory discourse emerges as a heightened sense of 'community' and 'empowerment.' For the most part, it is viewed in terms of process, consultation, and partnership. However, 'community,' when used to refer to homogeneous groups as equally disempowered and disenfranchised, glosses over social and power differences within these same groups. The appearance of consensus may be deceiving. PAR researchers cannot simply, by fiat, wish, or otherwise, create a participatory stance, one enabling them to lead the community, bringing it to rise above historically rooted issues related to gender, factions, class, and so forth.

The preceding discussion of the limitations of PAR reveals the existence of some putative PAR practices that are not always consistent with PAR values and assumptions. Furthermore, there is a strong tendency to consider these divergent practices as a manifestation of the co-optation of PAR, both as a discourse and as a methodology. In my view, the co-optation issue merits further problematization. Let me mention three elements that can provide material for a deeper critique. First, the predominant representation of recent PAR co-optation as a 'risk' ignores the fact that the co-optation process has been in operation for a long time, that is, since the instrumentalization of PAR in organizational development practices shortly after Lewin's death, and can now be said to be fully fledged. The fact that PAR has already been co-opted is not acknowledged in the debates, and the overemphasis on the continued risk of co-optation creates confusion that needs to be clarified.

Secondly, radical practitioners and thinkers are often unduly concerned about the *risks* and *dangers* of co-optation. Over the years, the prevailing capitalist mode of production in Western societies has displayed a formidable ability to co-opt the discourses and methodologies of progressive/radical movements that question its premises. The commodification of the youth and sexual liberation movements are two outstanding examples. In short, co-optation is part of the game, and it needs to be addressed within this context by dissecting (deconstructing) its mechanisms and revealing the interests that are involved and often occluded.

Third, by hastily associating all divergent PAR practices with some form of co-optation, critical practitioners and researchers not only fall into the trap of the 'who is more radical' syndrome, but also, and more importantly, fail to discern different types of divergence. For in addition to the type of divergence that is part of the co-optation mechanism (use of technical instrumentalization supported by formulaic prescriptions), there is another type of divergence that is not necessarily a sign of co-optation. The divergence from the utopian ideals of PAR may stem from the fact that they are precisely *utopian*, that is, they are to be pursued regardless of whether they are attained. Thus, appraisals of PAR cannot simply be reduced to measuring the attainment of ideals. Instead, the focus of appraisals and evaluations should be on the PAR process undertaken to pursue these ideals within a specific local context and on the quality of reflexivity that informs and directs the process. I develop this issue further in the commentary section below.

Summary of the Literature Review

Let me summarize the main points in the foregoing account. Kurt Lewin, originally a specialist in Gestalt psychology, is generally acknowledged to be the father and inventor of the concept of action research. His innovation resides mostly in his suggestion that the best way to learn about social systems is to try to change them through action. The AR tradition developed by his students and followers after his premature death has for the most part been associated with organizational development, and therefore underemphasizes the wider implications of Lewin's insight.

In the early 1960s, PAR emerged in the Third World in the context of organized resistance to intellectual colonialism by the Western social research apparatus and its hegemony over the Third World development process. The imported development agenda and technology were accused of promoting the economic and political interests of First World power brokers and local elite at the expense of the less powerful. PAR was born out of this resistance; its proponents advocated increased local participation and recognition of the value of local knowledge and popular wisdom. In short, PAR in the South has challenged the expertise of Western science in order to foster the research capabilities of the disenfranchised, who as knowing actors can define their reality, describe their history, and thereby transform their lives.

Throughout the turbulent 1960s and 1970s in the North, there was harsh criticism of the supposed value-neutral character of social scientific knowledge, long associated with positivist epistemology. Many scholars and thinkers attacked the control functions of professional expertise and demonstrated how the link between knowledge and power was intrinsic to social science methodologies and how these only served particular power interests. Critiques of this kind challenged the claim that only one scientific solution to a given social problem could exist and emphasized the failings of established social theory, which, they argued, derived from its inadequate account of prevailing socio-cultural conditions and inability to bring about social change.

In response to the escalating criticism of the positivist epistemology, a number of social scientists have attempted to advance a participatory approach to knowledge production by which social theory is readjusted in order to address the problems of contemporary society more effectively. In this approach, the relationships between scientists, practitioners, and citizens are geared toward the requirements of democratic empowerment.

PAR, as one of these participatory approaches, subscribes to the basic tenets of critical theory. It seeks to link theory and practice through an understanding of praxis that occurs across both the personal and the political. PAR questions dualistic modes of thinking and adopts a dialectical perspective, suggesting that creative change can emerge in the tension between binary oppositions. PAR further asserts that knowledge and action cannot be separated and that the dialogic method developed by Freire is the best way to integrate them. In the dialogic method, researchers, workers, and participants engage in relationships of mutual education within an overall context of reflexivity. Lastly, PAR focuses on the production of knowledge that can help disadvantaged groups articulate and meet their needs.

However, different conceptions of PAR have led to the emergence of 'appropriated' and 'co-opted' PAR practices that do not conform to these ideals and assumptions. This state of affairs, coupled with PAR promises that sometimes tend to represent it as a panacea, seem to have made PAR critics, especially those inspired by postmodernist/poststructuralist perspectives, focus on issues of power at the expense of dismissing other important issues, as is discussed below.

Reflective Commentary
The Need to Demystify the Promises of PAR

My review of the critiques of PAR provoked a mixed reaction on my part. It was very interesting, comforting, and encouraging to find many of my own criticisms in the literature. Given my constructivist orientation, I was particularly attracted by critical poststructuralist/postmodernist perspectives. My curiosity and frustration, elicited by an overabundance of references to Foucault, and especially to his notion of power as related to knowledge production,[6] led me to review Foucault's writings and some of their postmodernist interpretations. I quickly became irritated by the postmodernist insistence that the fact that Foucault himself denied being postmodernist did not really matter; Foucault's concept of power remains a foundation for the postmodernist paradigm. As my frustration mounted, I chanced upon an interview with Foucault conducted only a few months prior to his death in 1984, following the publication of the second and third volumes of his *The History of Sexuality*. In this interview (*Magazine Littéraire* May 1984),

Foucault's extended answers to the well-informed and astute interviewer were very enlightening regarding his own trajectory. Equally important, Foucault's answers also revealed a contradiction in the postmodernist discourse, which I will address later.

Returning to my mixed reaction, after much wrestling and agonizing, I managed to identify the source of my frustration with poststructuralist/postmodernist critiques of PAR, despite my agreement with the basic premises of these perspectives. These critiques seem to add to the confusion that arises when PAR ideals are represented as attainable objectives if only one sticks to PAR principles. This made me realize the need for PAR accounts to demystify PAR promises, which this book attempts to do.

Prototype definitions of PAR describe it as research initiated by a community of oppressed people who get together and decide to do something about their situation. Somehow, an external academic researcher or two become affiliated with this community and lead its members in studying and researching their situation in a participatory (democratic) manner. In this way, everybody participates in the specification of the research questions, data collection, processing, analysis, and interpretation. Accordingly, the group enters "into a living process, examining their reality by asking penetrating questions, mulling over assumptions related to their everyday problems and circumstances, deliberating alternatives for change, and taking meaningful actions to improve the situation and empower the group members" (Smith 1977, 173).

Understandably, this prototype definition of PAR, which represents it as a sort of panacea, tends to generate very high expectations among its critics. It is quite legitimate for these critics to strive to attenuate the passionate rhetoric in PAR. However, when PAR promises paradoxically come to be viewed as specific objectives to be measured only in terms of attainment or non-attainment, without paying due attention to the process that culminated in their realization or non-realization, there is a danger of falling into the trap of dogmatic puritanism. In other words, when the ideals that are supposed to be the guiding principles in PAR processes become rigid criteria in the construction of critical appraisals, we run the risk of becoming 'utopist' instead of remaining 'utopian.' The trap here is also one of conceptual confusion stemming from the myths perpetuated in some PAR discourses. Let me elaborate.

As mentioned above, one common claim in the PAR literature is that PAR processes are usually initiated by a group of oppressed individuals who come together with a view to undertaking actions to improve their situation and become more empowered. Reason (1994a, 334) acknowledges that "many PAR projects could not occur without the initiative of someone with time, skill, and commitment, someone who will almost inevitably be a member of a privileged and educated group." Yet Reason refers to this fact as a "paradox . . . [with which] PAR appears to sit uneasily," and Healy (2001, 96) quotes him to strengthen her argument with regard to the necessity for researchers to recognize their power in PAR structures. Notwithstanding the validity and pertinence of Healy's and other writers' pleas, it would seem appropriate now, after decades of PAR practice and documentation, to recognize the fact that the majority of PAR undertakings are initiated by outside researchers and/or practitioners, keen to develop solidarity ties with oppressed grassroots communities or groups. This recognition can pave the way for divesting PAR discourse of the utopist claim and ambition that the initiation of the research process itself comes or should come from members of the oppressed communities or groups. Many oppressed groups have neither the abilities nor the resources to initiate a PAR process.

Another PAR promise that needs to be demystified concerns the ideal of democratic participation. PAR researchers and practitioners are often confronted with the participation issue, and are reproached with the fact that participants do not assume a primary role in the research process. Once again, these criticisms assume that egalitarian participation should be the normal state of affairs in PAR, whereas in reality there is a great deal of evidence that points to the contrary. As already mentioned, researchers do spend a great deal of time promoting participant involvement by facilitating meetings, raising consciousness, fostering activist attitudes, and conducting other mobilizing activities. Again, recognition of this active role played by researchers can serve to dismiss another myth about PAR related to democratic participation. When people from different cultures enjoy varying levels of power, status, influence, and facility with language come together in a PAR undertaking, the notion of participation becomes so problematic that it needs to be incorporated into the research process as an objective to be continuously addressed and reflected upon. In other words, democratic participation, like other PAR promises, is an ideal toward which researcher and participants strive in a PAR process.

As an open-ended process, PAR undertakings cannot be expected to be exemplary models of participation, where power issues are acknowledged and subjected to effective mechanisms of democratic control. PAR promises are utopian ideals that guide the process. Whether these ideals can actually be achieved is another matter. Those involved in PAR ought to be asked what they do to elicit more participant involvement, how they approach obstacles to increased participation, and how they deal with power differentials. PAR researchers should account for their efforts in transmitting knowledge and skills: have they been able to demystify research, and have participants and workers acquired critical analysis and research skills? Have researchers themselves been able to develop and refine their methodologies? In short, the challenge for PAR is to strive for the attainment of its promises through a monitored and reflexive process so that the emphasis is less on achievements and more on the processes that facilitate them.

Another element that contributes to my frustration with PAR criticism is the fact that many of my concerns, like those of other PAR practitioner-researchers, are only addressed superficially in the literature. PAR literature remains predominantly research-focused and/or biased despite significant efforts to include demonstrations from the field. In particular, the ethical dilemmas that arise in day-to-day PAR practice are presented mostly in terms of protecting participants from exploitation by 'powerful' researchers, which is quite a legitimate concern. However, the focus on the protection of participants is often at the expense of dismissing from the debate other, equally important and more complex, ethical dilemmas that PAR and street work practitioners face by virtue of the proximity and familiarity with excluded groups. Indeed, these practitioners often become involved in situations that are value laden, ambiguous, complex and uncertain, and for which established academic knowledge is of limited use, and which in addition often require an immediate response. In general, the literature neither addresses such issues nor does it dwell on the fact that practitioners often need to rely on their own experiential knowledge based on the spontaneous and intuitive *savoir-faire* that they deploy in the field.

Another day-to-day practice concern that does not receive due attention in the literature is that of leadership. Yet, as mentioned above, leadership is vital to initiating a PAR process, and it often comes from the ranks of intellectuals by virtue of their privileged economic and social status. I would hasten to add that this leadership's input is often necessary to sustain the process as well. There is an implicit expectation in the literature that leadership skills and responsibilities and, by the same token, the power associated with them, have to be rapidly disseminated in order to facilitate the emergence and establishment of genuine participation (democracy).

Moreover, leadership that does not strive for the distribution of its power is either viewed as abusive of PAR or in need of being sensitized. Once again, the ideal of participation is either praised or criticized without a more profound reflection on the underlying problematic. While diffuse leadership is certainly desirable and a goal toward which PAR leaders should strive, it is important to realize that in practical terms, the concrete demands of effective leadership require a wide range of abilities, including personal, intellectual, political, and moral commitment, as well as interpersonal, group management, and data management skills, in addition to a capacity for self-awareness and reflexivity.

Some elements of the leadership issue not addressed in the literature include the following:

1. The transmission of skills and knowledge in a PAR process is not simply a technical question. It takes place within a liberatory pedagogical framework and process that needs to be respectful of the participants' pace and the material conditions of their daily lives, which tend to be harsh and strategically oriented toward survival mechanisms. Accordingly, the pedagogical pace tends to be slow, often delaying the full sharing of leadership. This raises the question of the necessity, not to mention the paradox, of PAR initiators maintaining leadership for longer than is implied by PAR promises.

2. Given the existence of individual differences, especially in large groups, it is naïve to think that all participants will simultaneously acquire similar levels of leadership skills and knowledge to enable them to participate. In effect, in PAR undertakings with large groups, only a small group of participants become 'full' participants. This issue is handled in the literature rather superficially by maintaining that when working with large groups, it is not essential for everyone to participate. While this assertion may be comforting, it dismisses a wide range of related problems from the analysis. When, for example, a number of participants become actively engaged in daily PAR activities, ambiguous reactions are elicited among their peers. The latter, even if not so keen themselves to participate more actively, nonetheless resent and resist the assumption of leadership roles by peers. As such, participants who may be ready to assume leadership roles and responsibility have to cope with this resistance. This is no easy task for an emerging leadership of participants who, for good reason, are usually concerned about not jeopardizing their relationships with peers.

It is sometimes argued in this connection that natural leaders do exist in communities of oppressed groups, and the problems discussed here may not be all that thorny. But this argument is not consistent with the fact that natural leaders frequently do not associate closely with PAR promoters (the outsiders); it is, rather, the less powerful community members who work exceptionally hard to reciprocate the efforts of promoters and thus run the risk of being 'othered' by their peers.

3. Even when some of the natural leaders of a community become more active within PAR activities, the others do not automatically accept them in their newly assumed responsibilities. They often express their resentment and resistance by reminding the natural leaders that their behavior and values are not consistent with their new role.

4. As Schapiro (1995) notes, situations of this kind are more complex when the emerging participant leaders gain greater authority and begin to focus their efforts on maintaining this newly acquired power.

5. Another element that further compounds such situations is the fact that all too often there are two sets of participants: those who belong to the disadvantaged group, and those who are the practitioners within the community organization in which the PAR process is initiated. This differentiation is notoriously absent in the literature and, consequently, its problematization is dismissed.

6. By challenging oppressive political and social arrangements, PAR leadership is often positioned in opposition to dominant and mainstream forces, which often elicits charges of subversion and repression from governments and various vested interests. While issues of this kind are sometimes mentioned in the literature, they are seldom problematized.

Associated with the leadership issue is that of training and education, also notoriously absent from the literature. It may be that the overemphasis on the researcher as a co-learner has prevented any acknowledgment of the fact that PAR leaders do assume an important role in training and educating their co-workers, as well as the participants. To overlook this fact is to help perpetuate a conception of egalitarianism confounded with identity (similarity) that does not recognize differences within the heterogeneous group of actors in the PAR process. By insisting that we learn both together and from each other, we dismiss the whole problematic issue related to the encounter between different types of knowledge. For while it is true that in PAR all knowledge and wisdom (of researchers and participants alike) are equally valued, they nonetheless remain circumscribed by a dialectical tension that requires further analysis.

Two Different Conceptions of PAR

Reflecting on the reasons for my frustration with PAR literature, I asked myself the following difficult question: Could the conceptual confusion and the dismissal of the problematic associated with the simultaneous articulation of the three components of PAR be related to the fact that a great deal of PAR literature is produced by researchers in academia who have had 'encounters' with PAR solely through association with a community activist group, over a limited period of time?

Without disputing the necessity and value of such encounters, I would like to suggest that when PAR is implemented in this fashion, it is frequently characterized by: researchers whose professional affiliation lies elsewhere than in the community group itself; a timeframe limited to the duration of this collaboration; and researchers who report the results to colleagues and in academic literature. Such a model of PAR operationalization may explain the bias in the literature toward a more research-oriented treatment of PAR issues. More importantly, the problematic related to other models of PAR operationalization is not addressed in the literature. Here, I am referring particularly to the model of PAR operationalization in which researchers are professionally affiliated with activist community organizations as 'practitioner-researchers,' that is, they are part of the organization's framework. This second model is characterized by the following three factors: the research activity is incorporated into the everyday operational activities of the community group; consequently, it is not limited in time, but constitutes an ongoing activity in the context of an open-ended process; and lastly, the results are not published in the literature. The implications of these two different models of PAR operationalization raise the following question: To what extent is the first model responsible for maintaining the traditional gap between theory and practice? Similarly, to what extent is the second model of PAR operationalization bound to remain underrepresented in academic literature?

It seems to me that these two different models of PAR operationalization (for the sake of convenience, I will call the first model the 'detached-researcher' model, and the second the 'engaged-researcher' model) may reflect different conceptions of PAR.[7] When PAR is conceptualized as an open-ended process, the research activity must be incorporated into the everyday practice of the activist community organization (as opposed to research being carried out on the side or in a parallel way). This in turn requires that the organization's staff, or at least some of them, have the skills and knowledge required for PAR to be undertaken. The presence of a practitioner-researcher, that is, a practitioner who is also a PAR researcher, among the organization's staff, as found in the engaged-researcher model, can facilitate the introduction of a PAR approach in practice. The sustainability of the latter within an open-ended process is possible only if staff and beneficiaries join in the undertaking, acquire PAR skills and knowledge, and approve the adoption of the methodology.

In the detached-researcher model, the activist community organization wants to initiate a PAR process (either willingly or because of a donor request) but does not have the necessary knowledge and skill. As such, it requests the help of an outside researcher, usually from academia. Sometimes, outside researchers themselves propose undertaking a joint PAR venture to activist community organizations. The partnership thus developed between outside researchers and grassroots communities is usually restricted by time limits, by virtue of the grant that has made it possible or by the researchers' other career commitments. This detached-researcher model raises many questions.

First, PAR entails a long process requiring sustained commitment and involvement; it is usually intense and laden with tensions and risks. As such, time is a critical element for the success of a PAR undertaking. Accordingly, researchers need to ask themselves whether their input and collaboration within the specified timeframe can realistically be conducive to instituting a PAR approach in the organization's practice. I am raising this issue because in my view the incorporation of a PAR approach *in practice* is the essence of PAR itself and the safeguard against reducing it to a mere research activity.

Second, by joining a pre-existing activist community organization, researchers encounter at least two sets of actors. The first is composed of the cadres who are responsible for running the organization, that is, the practitioners who, like the researchers, are often from outside the disadvantaged community group. The latter constitute the second set of actors encountered by researchers. In addition to the fact that these two groups of actors, the activists and the community, are not usually homogeneous groups, outside researchers walking into the setting of pre-existing organizations are bound to encounter institutionalized modes of operation reflecting values that are often different, even the exact opposite, of those promoted by PAR promises and ideals. Such situations are not uncommon and leave outside researchers, often wearing the hat of PAR advisers, overwhelmed by the obstacles preventing the institution of democratic processes of practice and research.

This raises an important third question: is it worthwhile initiating a PAR undertaking with community groups that have been in operation long enough for a top-down management to be rather firmly instituted, as well as mechanisms for maintaining power differentials? Many such organizations exist and their motivation to espouse a PAR approach is driven by an escalating tendency among donors to make funds and grants conditional upon adopting a participatory methodology. This situation has led to the emergence of much misuse and abuse of PAR, deplored loudly in the literature. In such situations, we are likely to witness the adoption of formulaic prescriptions for participation that are presented as full democracy, although they seldom go beyond consultation.

Power, Resistance, and Foucault

A fourth question is related to the strategy adopted by PAR critics who are informed by poststructuralist/postmodernist insights. Healy (2001, 97) rightly observed that the claim of a radical egalitarian stance by many PAR researchers not only produces "power aversion rhetoric," but also seems to encourage researchers to claim the realization of democratic processes of participation "even in the face of considerable contrary evidence." This prompts me to ask whether such attitudes denote a certain resistance, and if so, how it can be dealt with. It seems to me that insisting on using Foucault's notion of power, as do Healy and other critics inspired by poststructuralism and postmodernism, may only fuel the "power aversion rhetoric" and intensify practitioners' resistance to 'post-' theories that are increasingly charged with being paralyzing and nihilistic, as Healy and others acknowledge.

The notion of power is easily confused with that of domination, and it is understandable that it creates aversion among activists, who often prefer to have a purer image of the self. While it is important to challenge this, it is equally important for educators not to rock the boat so violently as to produce the contrary effect. For in addition to the resistance elicited by the power discourse, the present global context seems to be one of disillusionment with the possibilities of change. This disillusionment has lately been intensified by the aftermath of the September 11th event, which has clearly led to significant losses of individual freedom and setbacks to civil society's struggle for democratic participation. The rapidity and ease with which many democratic rights have been suspended points to the fragility of these 'acquired' rights. This tendency is all the more dangerous when, as we are currently witnessing, a war is declared to save Western democratic values from the threat of 'evil' forces. In this light, we can expect that further confusion, if not chaos, is likely to occur with regard to the democratic ideal.

The point that I am making is that in cynical times like the present, action strategies, to the dismay of revolutionary activists and theorists, cannot be designed with the sole aim of acquiring more power for the oppressed. Instead, whether we like it or not, action strategies will need to focus on minimizing further inevitable losses with a view to saving the essentials. Even achieving this objective is not going to be an easy task, given that the current corruption of many political systems, in the North and in the South, is bound to impinge further on local realities (the trickledown of corruption). Resistance then becomes the primary issue that ought to be in the forefront of PAR researcher and practitioner concerns.

The fact that Foucault himself abandoned the use of the notion of power in his last two books (Foucault 1984a, 1984b) does not seem to inspire post-structuralist/ postmodernist critical perspectives. On the contrary, Foucault's emphasis on ethics in his last two books is either dismissed, or neglected, or acknowledged merely in order to lend "credence to a view that it is not appropriate to locate him within postmodernism (a location he himself contested)" (Fawcett and Featherstone 2000, 17). Beyond the concern for situating Foucault, what is hidden and muted by dismissing his last writings are the reasons for his shift from focusing on the concept of power to that of the 'ethics of government' (including 'government of self' and 'government of others'). Foucault recognized that in his earlier works, including Volume 1 of *The History of Sexuality*, he had maintained a focus on the 'government of others,' whereas in the following two volumes he focused on the 'government of self.' He also acknowledged that this shift came as a surprise, if not a disappointment, to his readers, who were expecting, in accordance with his work plan announced in the first volume, a history of sexuality modeled on his famous history of madness, emphasizing the role of repressive mechanisms and institutions. However, Foucault explains that in undertaking this shift, he was only being faithful to himself and to his belief that intellectuals should strive to shed their fondness for themselves by trying not only to change the thought *(pensée)* of others but also their own: *"Qu'est-ce que l'éthique d'un intellectuel—je revendique ce terme d'intellectuel qui semble aujourd'hui donner de la nausée à certains—sinon cela: se rendre capable de se déprendre de soi-même"* (*Magazine Littéraire* May 1984, 22).

In conclusion, I am inspired by Foucault to ask whether in light of mounting resistance to postmodernism and the acknowledgment by many scholars inspired by it of a nihilistic tendency in some of its extremely relativist positions, is it not now time to let go of one's fondness and persistent referral to it and to its 'fatal attraction,' while keeping the essence of its insights (criticizing the status quo, certainty, and oppositional identity categories; rejecting imposed artificial uniformity and the privileging of technical rationality and experts' knowledge; emphasizing difference and focus on process), which, after all, are not that new. And in light of mounting aversion to power rhetoric observed among activists, it is important to ask whether the ethics with respect to the government of self and of others might not be a better entry to elicit the critical reflection necessary for producing social emancipatory change.

2

Street Work

I was introduced to street work in the early 1980s in Montreal through my participation in the design and implementation of *Le Projet d'Intervention auprès des Mineur(e)s Prostitué(e)* (PIaMP), sponsored by *Le Bureau de Consultation Jeunesse* (BCJ). By design, the PIaMP project employed both street work and action research (AR) as basic methodological tools. In 1993, in Cairo, I incorporated street work into the design of a participatory action research (PAR) project—the subject of this book—with street children and youths, which was implemented over a period of eight years.

In the early 1980s, when the PIaMP project was initiated in Montreal, there was almost no literature to consult; the transmission of knowledge and techniques of street work took place orally, relying on the experiences of a few surviving street workers. Since then, an escalating number of projects and programs using street work approaches and methodology have emerged in both industrialized and developing societies throughout the globe. These undertakings, mostly within the non-governmental sector, have attempted to address the social problems associated with marginal and excluded children and youth populations that fall through the cracks of the government network of social services. However, the rapid development of street work practices over the last twenty-five years has not been matched by similar developments in widely published documentation and theorization. Most relevant writings are by groups of individuals associated with street work projects and organizations, and, as we will see, are published and debated within the context of study groups emerging out of an international network of street workers initiated in early 2000.

As a practitioner-researcher interested in the phenomenon of marginal youth, I have had the opportunity to visit many street work projects in

Quebec, Ontario, British Columbia, California, Costa Rica, Egypt, India, France, Lebanon, and Turkey. I have also maintained a collegial relationship with *l'Association des Travailleurs et Travailleuses de Rue du Quebec* (l'ATTrueQ) since its foundation in 1993. In 1997 Jacques Pector, researcher and trainer at l'ATTrueQ, and I put together the initial design for a PAR program intended to be used in the ongoing training and education of street workers, members of l'ATTrueQ. The program was subsequently named *'Action–Recherche–Réflexive–Formative,'* and has been in operation since 1999 (Pector 1999). Through international networking activities, local versions of this program have been adopted by other non-governmental organizations (NGOs) in fifteen countries since 2000. A coordination committee made up of representatives of the NGOs has been monitoring progress made locally, and organized The First International Conference on Street Work in Brussels, November 25–28, 2002. At this conference it was agreed to further promote PAR as the general framework for the street work projects implemented by the network's member organizations, to sustain the activities of the coordination committee and to hold a yearly international conference to allow for exchanges of experience and expertise as well as to increase advocacy for critical street work.

This privileged position has allowed me access to very enriching exchanges with street workers and researchers as well as to a number of documents published by various street work organizations in different countries. Both the documentation and literature reviews reveal the existence of different conceptions and practices of street work that are only briefly addressed in the literature. In this chapter, I highlight and analyze two major conceptions of street work that have characterized it since its emergence. I specify their values and assumptions as well as the theoretical perspectives that inform and shape their discourses and practices. I start with an overview of the development of street work since its emergence in the United States and its subsequent transplantation to Canada, France, Belgium, and Switzerland. I then examine the major parameters of street work practice before discussing the underpinnings of the current situation in street work.

The major focus in this historical overview is on the United States, where street work first emerged and was already characterized by a polemic regarding its goal and methodology, one that is still vigorous in contemporary debates surrounding street work. Another, but less intense, focus on Quebec reflects my own biography and the fact that it was in Quebec that the first effort to document what had until then been an oral tradition got underway. It was also in Quebec that the twinning of street work and PAR was first implemented in the West after the Egyptian experience, the subject matter of this book.

Historical Overview

Inasmuch as it refers to solidarity ties and comradeship among people sharing misery and destitution, street work can be said to have always existed. The Socratic Method presented in the work of Plato may have been one of the earliest forms of aid delivery. Having devoted his life to the poor and needy, Socrates spent a great deal of time in street markets and may be considered the prototype of the street worker of his times.

The modern philanthropic movement, which dates from late eighteenth century, started to adopt a more scientific approach toward the end of the nineteenth century with the emergence of social work as a profession and, later, as a discipline. These early forms of social intervention were characterized by the practice of 'immersion' in the living milieus of targeted urban poor populations. Indeed, the escalating industrialization in the West at that time resulted in massive migration from rural regions to large cities where the working and living conditions of the masses of workers were becoming increasingly precarious. Children, youths, and adults were resorting to the street to make their living and were perceived as a threat to urban organization. It is in this context that some pioneers of social work, like Jane Addams, decided to live and work in poor neighborhoods in order to share the lives of the poor, to help them, and to advocate for structural reforms to remedy the social injustices that perpetuate poverty (Brieland 1990).

However, this philosophy of 'being with' the poor and disadvantaged that characterized the early history of social work practice did not last for long. The ensuing, rapid 'scientific' development was articulated along a 'case work' perspective that held the poor themselves "at fault for their condition," (Germain and Hartman 1980, 326) and who, so it was claimed, needed "personal rehabilitation" (Franklin 1986, 508). It was only in the context of the late 1920s in the United States (during the Great Depression and escalating fascism), when community organizing was given legitimacy within the discipline and profession of social work, that the call to reach out to and be with the marginal re-emerged. It is in this context that Kurt Lewin, as described in the previous chapter, established the foundations of action research, and called for academics to go out and try to change problematic social situations. It is also in this context, as will be described below, that the street work tradition emerged in the United States.

U.S.A.

According to many contemporary street work organizations, street work first emerged in the 1920s as a new practice. Reference is made, without much elaboration, to Saul Alinsky, the famous American organizer, as well as to two sociologists of the same period, Shaw and McKay at the University of Chicago, who supposedly undertook innovative research and worked on the delinquency of marginal youth gangs (Maurer 1992; Schaut and Van Campenhoudt 1994; l'ATTRueQ 1997). In this section, I provide a detailed review of the work of these protagonists. My purpose here is to add to the meager body of street work literature some historical elements, which, in addition to their significance to today's debate on street work, can consolidate the rather marginal status of contemporary street work practice.

A review of the literature reveals that the phenomenon of 'street youth gangs' in the 1920s in the United States was a cause for great concern:

> One of the most disturbing aspects of the problem of crime in America is the fact that such crimes as burglary, robbery, and larceny, which comprise a numerically important place among the total crimes for which persons are committed to reformatories and prisons, are to a very great extent a phenomenon of youth. The large number of youthful offenders in our prisons comprises one of the critical problems confronting the American people. (Shaw and McKay 1942, vii)

This excerpt is from the foreword by R.H. Brandorn, Director of the Department of Public Welfare in the State of Illinois, to Clifford R. Shaw and Henry D. McKay's 1942 book. In addition, in the book's introduction, Ernest W. Burgess from the University of Chicago describes Shaw and McKay's work as

> a magnum opus in criminology . . . [that] has been in progress for twenty years . . . [it] covers twenty cities, includes cases of thousands of juvenile delinquents, and is the product of the collaboration of several investigators with a field staff and clerical assistants. (Shaw and McKay 1942, ix)

Like that of other sociologists of the Chicago School, Shaw and McKay's work adopted an ecological perspective that considered society as a living organism (Shaw and McKay 1942, 5; Rémy 1990). The notion of 'social disorganization' is essential to this ecological conception of urban settings.

In this light, juvenile delinquency is perceived as a deviant subculture and a sign of social disorganization. The delinquent, in this perspective, is diagnosed as suffering from faulty socialization.

I propose to dwell further on the work of Shaw and McKay in order to shed light on the main assumptions of the ecological approach to juvenile delinquency. These assumptions continue to underlie several discourses.

Interpreting the data gathered throughout their studies, Shaw and McKay formulated a general conception of juvenile delinquency, incorporating both the structural determinants and the subjective experiences of youth. With regard to structural determinants, the writers strongly view the material conditions of life in the slums as the major cause of social disorganization (physical deterioration of housing conditions, lack of space—except the streets—for children to play, poor infrastructure, unemployment, and so on). Poverty and precarious living conditions are not conducive to healthy organization, and lead to deviations from traditional conventional values promoted by the family, the church, and school (Shaw and McKay 1942, 440).

At the subjective level, the writers insist that social disorganization does not necessarily reflect an aversion toward conventional values; these are present, albeit suppressed, even in communities having the highest rates of delinquents. Three case studies (life stories) of juvenile delinquents are reported to highlight the fact that children growing up in the slums are exposed to competing value systems, including both conventional and delinquent values (Shaw and McKay 1942, 166). Thus, delinquent behaviors, within the same community, may be defined as right and proper by some groups and as immoral by others. Accordingly, a career in delinquency and crime is one alternative for youth growing up in the slums. Moreover, because it develops in the form of a social tradition inseparable from the life of the local community, juvenile delinquency needs to be understood within the context in which it emerges:

> From the point of view of the delinquent's immediate social world, he is not necessarily disorganized, maladjusted, and anti-social. Within the limits of his social world and in terms of its norms and expectations, he may be a highly organized and well-adjusted person. (Shaw and McKay 1942, 436)

Shaw and McKay's studies advance new conceptions of the phenomenon of juvenile delinquency and of how it should be approached. The innovation may reside in their insistence on viewing juvenile delinquency as a group rather than as an individual, phenomenon:

> Year after year, decade after decade, large cities—and especially certain areas in large cities—send to the courts an undiminished line of juvenile offenders. Year after year, decade after decade, likewise, society continues to organize or construct new agencies or institutions designed to reduce the number of these offenders and to rehabilitate those who have already offended against the law. Perhaps the unsatisfactory results of these treatment and prevention efforts have been due, in part at least, to the fact that our attention has been focused too much upon the individual delinquent and not enough upon the setting in which delinquency arises. (Shaw and McKay 1942, 446)

To remedy this 'century-long,' faulty approach, a collective perspective is advocated:[8]

> If juvenile delinquency is essentially a manifestation of neighborhood disorganization, then evidently only a program of neighborhood organization can cope with and control it. The juvenile court, the probation officer, the parole officer, and the boy's club can be no substitute for a group of leading citizens of a neighborhood who take the responsibility of a program for delinquency treatment and prevention. (Shaw and McKay 1942, xii)

The call for community organizing in the slums in American cities was thus voiced by the Chicago School. In 1932, in Chicago, Shaw and McKay designed and supervised the implementation of 'The Chicago Area Project,' a mega-urban project that took the neighborhood as the unit of operation (Burgess, Shaw and Lohman 1939). A committee composed of local residents (including members of churches, labor unions, business groups, and others) was set up in every targeted poor neighborhood. These committees functioned as boards of directors, and assumed full responsibility for the sponsoring, planning, and management of all aspects of the community project. The employment and training of local leaders was a major feature of the project. The input of professional workers was sought but not glorified: "While there is much that the lay resident can learn from the professional, it is equally true that the professional can learn from the lay resident" (Shaw and McKay 1942, 442).

Interestingly, the Chicago scenario was played out again in the period following the Second World War, this time in other major American cities in which several "area mega-projects" were designed and implemented, with "area committees" to supervise and a team of "area workers" to reach out to street youths and gangs (Klein 1995; Spergel 1976). The New York City Youth Board Project was initiated in 1950, and grew to include some eighty street workers who had contact with more than a hundred street gangs throughout the city (Klein 1995, 142). In Boston, between 1954 and 1957, The Boston Roxbury Project reached out to some four hundred youths, members of twenty-one street gangs (Klein 1995, 144). In Chicago again, The Chicago Youth Development Project, implemented between 1960 and 1966, reached over five thousand youths within a geographic area of one thousand square miles in downtown Chicago (Klein 1995, 144). Other area projects were implemented in Philadelphia, Los Angeles, San Francisco, El Paso, Seattle, and San Antonio.

The practitioners who implemented these mega-community organizing projects in the United States were referred to as 'street workers,' 'street educators,' 'outreach workers,' and 'detached workers' (Klein, 1995). Regardless of the terms used to designate them, these workers, many of whom were professional social workers, did go out into the streets, yet with a predominant conception of community organizing that informed and guided their practice. This conception was built on a simple assumption: if youths *elude* the institutions that are supposed to contain them, then the institutions should reach out to them in order to reinsert them into the mainstream. Broadly speaking, this is how juvenile delinquency was to be treated. No wonder, then, that these mega-projects were generously funded by private foundations and a wide range of religious organizations; the disturbing phenomenon is defined in rather simplistic terms, and the prescribed solution is *functional* and *pragmatic*.

By dismissing the political dimension of community organizing, and by endowing it with a set of formulaic prescriptions, these mega-urban projects succeeded in reducing it to a mere technique for controlling deviancy and disorganized neighborhoods. As we saw in the preceding chapter, this is quite similar to what happened to Lewin's insight, that is, the instrumentalization of action research. The overemphasis on group and interpersonal dynamics, common values, and social integration was as prominent in the co-opted community organizing discourse. Furthermore, this discourse was given a radical nuance by appropriating principles of 'citizenship' and 'civil society' such as access to public services, defense of rights, participation in collective actions, democracy, education, and the like.

It would be unjust if we allowed the glamor of these mega-urban projects to dominate our historical overview, and failed to acknowledge less well-known local street work practices in the United States which subscribed to other, more humanistic, and often critical conceptions. While most of these critical street work practices remain in the shadows, one notorious exception was the person and practices of Saul Alinsky (1907–1972), perhaps the last of the American radicals. Commonly known as the 'radical organizer,' the 'revolutionary,' the 'genius of social reform,' and the 'radicals' radical,' Chicago-born Alinsky referred to himself using these designations and added some of his own, such as the "irreverent" and the "survivor of the Joe McCarthy holocaust." Yet the designation he preferred the most seems to have been "the rebel," to which he proudly responded by quoting Tom Pain: "Let them call me rebel and welcome. I feel no concern from it; but I should suffer the misery of devils, were I to make a whore of my soul" (Sanders 1970, 38).

Aside from the rather sensationalist media representation of Alinsky, his innovation resides in the use of conflict as a vehicle for advocating and promoting more rights to disadvantaged and poor social groups, black people and immigrants in particular. As such, he represents a school of thought and action in community organizing that is quite different from the consensus social theory approach of the Chicago School presented above. Equally interesting is the fact that Alinsky, himself a Chicagoan, was community organizing in the slums of Chicago around the same time 'The Chicago Area Project' was implemented under the supervision and guidance of Shaw and McKay and other sociologists from the Chicago School. Alinsky's work and thoughts not only represent a different conception of community organizing, but also carry a provocative critique of the Chicago School. Indeed, his writings reveal an impressive capacity for reflexivity and critical analysis. Moreover, Alinsky's discourse, as we shall see, is quite similar to that of present-day proponents of street work who resist, as he did, the reduction of street work to a mere tool for implementing the technocratic model of community organizing.

In the remainder of this section, I provide a detailed review of Alinsky's history of organizing, covering his background, philosophy, discourse, and some of his criticism. Since there is little awareness of it among contemporary street workers, and in light of the fact that it has been largely overlooked by academia, it is important for the sake of the street work tradition to document the legacy of Alinsky's organized activism. While contemporary street workers in both North America and Europe take pride in asserting that they follow Alinsky's heritage, they seem to be unaware of the context within which Alinsky laid the foundations of radical community organizing, one that was politically positioned on the side of the oppressed and disadvantaged. Alinsky's *Rules for Radicals* (1971), written in a didactic style, is the only reference contemporary street workers mention, and without much elaboration at that. There would thus appear to be a need to supplement the historical documentation of street work with more details and analysis with regard to Alinsky's heritage for contemporary street workers to gain a better understanding of the full meaning and implications of this rich legacy, which contains much of significance in today's context.

Alinsky's Organized Activism

In a tape-recorded conversation with a friend of his, Alinsky relates that he was born to Jewish and very orthodox Russian immigrant parents in one of the worst slums in Chicago: "As a kid I remember always living in the back of a store. My idea of luxury was to live in an apartment where I could use the bathroom without one of my parents banging on the door for me to get out because a customer wanted to get in" (Sanders 1970, 12).

Alinsky describes the period of his youth as one of "upheaval and massive dramatic change, with the collapse of many accepted values . . . [of] security, work, and money as the way to 'happiness' . . . [in] the great crash of 1929" (1969, viii). This seems to have entailed certain disillusionment in the young Alinsky that shaped his irreverent attitude: "Disillusionment's child is irreverence, and irreverence became one of my major heritages from an angry, irreverent generation" (1969, ix). However, irreverence for the mature Alinsky meant being neither unruly nor aggressive; it was political in the sense of giving oneself a basic democratic right: "I believe irreverence should be part of the democratic faith because in a free society everyone should be questioning and challenging" (Sanders 1970, 56).

This kind of irreverence is particularly clear in Alinsky's determined rejection of the claim to objectivity made by academics:

Objectivity, like the claim that one is non-partisan or reasonable, is usually a defensive posture used by those who fear involvement in the passions, partisanships, conflicts, and changes that make up life; they fear life. An

'objective' decision is generally lifeless. It is academic and the word 'academic' is a synonym for irrelevant. (Sanders 1970, 56)

Alinsky was quite familiar with academia. In 1926 he attended the
University of Chicago, majored in archaeology, and took many courses in
sociology that did not leave a profound impression on him:

> In the sociology department it was a cardinal sin to make a categorical state-
> ment. You qualified everything you said; then you qualified the qualifiers
> and added some footnotes so that the final conclusion had more escape
> hatches in it than a loan shark's mortgage contract. (Sanders 1970, 14–15)

He graduated in 1930 as the Depression was hitting, could not find a job, and
had to face hunger. Much to his surprise, the University of Chicago awarded
him the Social Science Graduate Fellowship in Criminology despite the fact
that he had not taken any courses in criminology. As a graduate student,
he had the assignment of gaining insight into crime. After several failed
attempts, he managed to infiltrate the ranks of Al Capone's gang. However,
two years after starting graduate studies, he was offered a job with the State
Division of Criminology, which he accepted and, consequently, dropped out
of university. Alinsky's dismay with academia stemmed from the fact that he
found himself "dependent on foundation grants, on university trustees, and
on public authorities. You're not supposed to get involved in controversy or
public issues or you will become known as a 'trouble maker' or as someone
who has 'personality difficulties'" (Sanders 1970, 25).

In his new job, Alinsky once again managed to infiltrate a rather hardcore
gang of Italian youth. Known as the "Forty-two Gang", this gang was responsible for 80 percent of automobile theft in Chicago at the time: "It was much
harder than getting in with the Capone gang because these children were very
suspicious . . . [But] I was lucky and we got to know each other as people"
(Sanders 1970, 22). In his next job, as a criminologist at the state prison
in Joliet for three years, Alinsky learned more about human relationships.
However, working for state institutions made him feel equally alienated: "you
get institutionalized-callous. You stop thinking" (Sanders 1970, 24). After
three years of working in the prison, he quit and never returned either to
academia or to working with state institutions, refusing many tempting offers;
his decision was clear: "I decided I'd do the organizing myself" (Sanders 1970,
30). He then embarked on a long journey of what can be called 'organized

activism,' still circumscribed within the emerging methodology of community organizing but politically positioned on the side of the oppressed and disadvantaged populations and aiming at more economic and social justice. When Alinsky first became involved in organized activism in the 1930s, he was very critical of the community organizing model advocated by Chicago School sociologists. Although this model was founded on the recognition of both structural and subjective determinants, the latter received undue focus at the expense of the former:

All the experts agreed that the major causes of crime were poor housing, discrimination, economic insecurity, unemployment, and disease. So what did we do? We went in for supervised recreation, camping programs, something mysterious called 'character building.' We tackled everything but the actual issues. Because the issues were controversial. (Sanders 1970, 25)

Indeed, in their appraisal of the impact of 'The Chicago Area Project,' Shaw and McKay (1942, 444) acknowledged that the changes regarding the improvement of housing and sanitary conditions as well as the creation of job opportunities were modest.

Alinsky was also very critical of approaches to youth problems in which the young individual was viewed as a composite of "separate problems to be addressed through separate and different interventions" (Alinsky 1969, 57). This critique still holds today among critical street workers with respect to the numerous community projects that are implemented with a 'prevention' mandate specific to one particular problem, like drug abuse, reproductive health, social exclusion, housing, unemployment and so on. This approach fragments the totality of the individual youth into separate problems, which are addressed through correspondingly separate prevention projects.

'Uncertainty' may be a weak word choice in reference to the 1930s, a period marked as much by the Depression as by the rise of fascist groups in America and abroad. Although he was appalled and knew that it would be tough, Alinsky was not deterred from organizing in 'The Back of the Yards,' Chicago's most notorious slum, situated behind the gigantic stockyards, and which inspired the title of Upton Sinclair's novel *The Jungle* (Doering 1994, xviii). Reflecting on his adventure there,[9] Alinsky says:

When I went into 'Back of the Yards' . . . this was not the slum from across the tracks. This was the slum across the tracks from across the tracks. Also, this was the heart, in Chicago, of all the native fascist movements—the Coughlinities, the Silver Shirts, the Pelly movement. Lots of people can tell you what was in mind at the time. Boy, there are pages in criminology textbooks on my philosophy of 'grassroots holism.' I don't know what that is. I went in there to fight fascism; delinquency was just incidental, the real crime was fascism. If you had asked me then what my profession was, I would have told you I was a professional anti-fascist. (Sanders 1970, 30–31)

The Back of the Yards Council, set up under the tutelage of Alinsky, was successful in mobilizing the population of poor immigrants living in the 'nightmare' of this slum. They were able to create an efficient local organization that involved the local population and determined to fight against all forms of discrimination and exploitation. They achieved their goal and were able to establish local services (housing, public health, social welfare, and others), to the extent that their neighborhood became a national model of successful local self-organization.

In the wake of this success, Alinsky rose to national prominence. Among other prominent figures, Alinsky drew the attention of the wealthy Marshall Field III, who offered funding to set up a foundation that would provide him with a modest salary enabling him to continue to implement his ideas and methods. After ensuring that his freedom of action would not be jeopardized, Alinsky accepted the funding, established The Industrial Areas Foundation, recruited a small staff and began to work as a freelance professional organizer in turbulent cities (riots and mobs) around the country. During numerous visits to local jails, Alinsky was able to write the first draft of *Reveille for Radicals*, which in 1946, the year of its publication, became the number one non-fiction bestseller, received wonderful reviews, and was hailed as the 'Common Sense' of today (Doering 1994, 24).

The Alinsky Heritage
When Alinsky died in 1972, he had already observed the retirement of American radicals, whom he felt were in a deep sleep within "the cradle of organized labor" (Alinsky 1969, 24). He felt that the passing of the activist "torch" had been aborted:

Few of us survived the Joe McCarthy holocaust of the early 1950s and of those there were even fewer whose understandings and insights had developed beyond the dialectical materialism of orthodox Marxism. My fellow radicals who were supposed to pass on the torch of experience and insights to a new generation just were not there. (Alinsky 1971, xiii–xiv)

At the time of his death, however, his fame and reputation (and as he claimed, the "torch") had already crossed into Canada and into Europe. His book *Rules for Radicals* (1971), translated into French in the same year,[10] profoundly inspired an emerging generation of street workers in Canada, France, Belgium, Germany, Holland, and Switzerland, who were concerned about the situation of an escalating number of youth joining the ranks of marginality.

In his writings, as well as in his recorded conversations and correspondence with friends and supporters, Alinsky not only prescribed rules for the new generation but, more importantly perhaps, he vividly described his values and assumptions and their unequivocal embrace of the 'humanist project.' A summary of the major assumptions and values included in the Alinsky heritage is warranted here.

First, the social theory of consensus is refuted:

Talk about politics being a matter of accommodation; a cooperative search for the common good; . . . consensus . . . this is typical academic drivel. How do you have consensus before you have *conflict*? There has to be a rearrangement of *power* and then you get *consensus* [author's emphasis]. (Sanders 1970, 61)

Second, oppressed people are not offered power; they work and struggle for it: "people don't get opportunity or freedom or equality or dignity as a gift or an act of charity. They only get these things in the act of taking them through their own efforts" (Sanders 1970, 45).

Third, the lived experience of people is valued: "It should always be remembered that a real organization of the people, one in which they completely believe and which they feel is definitely their own, must be rooted in the experiences of the people themselves" (Sanders 1970, 78). Further, the organizer becomes deeply involved in people's reality: "When I go into a community, I suffer and resent with the people there, and they feel this. It's a big thing in my relationships" (Sanders 1970, 14).

Fourth, community organizing is people centered, and democratic participation is central: "There should not be too much concern with specifics or details of a people's program. The program items are not too significant when one considers the enormous importance of getting people interested and participating in a democratic way" (Alinsky 1969, 55). In addition, the "substance of democracy is its people and if that substance is good—if the people are healthy, interested, informed, participating, filled with faith in themselves and others—then the structure will inevitably reflect its substance" (Alinsky 1969, 56).

Fifth, Alinsky questions the claim to objective knowledge made by experts and academics in relation to defining ordinary people's problems and the decisions that affect their lives. He therefore values people's knowledge: "It is impossible to overestimate the importance of knowledge of the traditions of those people whom it is proposed to organize" (Alinsky 1969, 76).

Sixth, reflection is an intrinsic component in community organizing:

> Through action, reflection, study, testing, and synthesis I have learned to distil experience from living. Experience is the integrating of the actions and events of life so that they arrange themselves into meaningful universal patterns . . . I have learned to search for laws of change, to discover for myself such simple truths as that *the real action is in the reaction* [author's emphasis]. (Alinsky 1969, ix)

Seventh, "popular education"[11] is conceived as an intrinsic part of the overall participatory process of organizing, and is the ultimate objective of organizing (Alinsky 1969, 155–59). It enjoins organizers to create conditions that favor participants' learning where "[it] is no longer learning for learning's sake, but learning for a real reason, a purpose" (Alinsky 1969, 173). Furthermore, knowledge is viewed as "an arsenal of weapons in the battle against injustice and degradation" (Alinsky 1969, 173).[12]

In concluding this review of the Alinsky legacy, I would like to raise the following important question for contemporary critical street work practitioners and for activists in general. As we have seen, Alinsky's mode of organizing is more confrontational and conflictual than today's activism, which largely conforms to procedures of claims-making activities circumscribed by a consensus ideology, and which under the guise of democratic rhetoric (partnership and dialogue), all too often serves to dilute and even mute the claims of excluded populations. In light of the escalating conservatism, if not fascism, that has been witnessed in recent history, it is legitimate to ask whether it is still appropriate to keep to methodologies of soft advocacy and claim-making activities when democratic procedures are violated by the majority of political regimes, including the American superpower with all its claims to being the guardian of democracy.

Let us turn now to examine the development of street work after it crossed the American border to Canada, onto Europe and many countries to the south.

Canada

It is in Quebec that street work first landed after crossing the Canadian border. Indeed, the practice of street work that appeared there in the late 1960s was inspired by Alinsky (l'ATTRueQ 1997, 11). This was the era of the hippie and feminist movements, the sexual revolution, and the use of the Pill as a contraceptive; and of the rise of the Quebec nationalist movement, the Quiet Revolution, and the rapid disengagement of the clergy and religious communities in the areas of health and social services, social work, and education. The end of the 1960s was also marked by new problems stemming from the discovery and consumption of psychedelic drugs and cannabis. To address these problems, alternative approaches to intervention were undertaken through the creation of 'street clinics' that incorporated street work as part of their function (Lamoureux 1994).[13]

Street work, which emerged as part of the function of these clinics, was experimental and concerned with being as close as possible to the realities of the drug consumption milieus. For this reason, according to Lamoureux (1994), ex-drug addicts and even users who maintained a non-problematic relationship with drugs were engaged as full members within many teams working in these clinics. These street workers were better suited not only to meet with their peers in order to ensure them adequate support, but also to help their 'professional' colleagues to identify different drugs, the methods of consumption, as well as the resulting short- and long-term effects.

These street workers undertook an interpretation of youth realities, which quickly became 'in demand.' In particular, their active presence in the milieus of drug consumption was valued.

As a result, many street workers were assigned to the social affairs network (L'ATTRueQ 1997, 14). Gradually, the technocratic mode of operation gained the upper hand and street workers lost contact with the milieus of consumption, even as they maintained contact with their colleagues in the community sector.

The beginning of the 1980s confirmed the crisis in traditional social work vis-à-vis youth, social, and cultural phenomena. It is within this context that the tradition of non-institutional street work emerged for a second time, and a large number of NGOs were set up throughout Canada during the 1980s and 1990s to meet the new challenges arising from heroin consumption, the emergence of AIDS, and the start of a rapid escalation in the number of school drop-outs (BCJ 1994). However, this time the state did not take over as it did before, in the mid to late 1970s, when it integrated street workers into the structures of government social services during their reorganization. Instead of integrating street workers into expensive jobs, it was viewed as more cost-effective for them to continue their practice in the community sector, an approach that fit well with the discourse of the 'complementarity' and 'plurality' of practices,[14] the promotion of community involvement, and the disengagement of the state. All this might appear rather progressive. In one sense, this policy recognizes new social vocations practiced in a complementary fashion, in partnership with or alongside the official state network. Nevertheless, while it is true that the state apparatus, which manages the budgetary envelopes destined for the community sector, does not explicitly appear to interfere in the affairs of community organizations, street work in Quebec (or elsewhere) finds itself in an increasingly precarious situation because of insufficient funding and the fragmentation of the reality of youth through so-called preventive measures that address one problem at a time (drug addiction, STDs, AIDS, homelessness, school drop-outs, prostitution, unemployment, and others).

As always, the takeover by the technocratic apparatus does not erase all resistance, and many street workers in Canada continue to advocate a form of street work that has an emancipatory, politically positioned vision.

Europe

In Germany, France, Great Britain, Switzerland, Norway, and the Netherlands, street work was developed in the late 1960s and was sustained primarily by isolated people or associations, few traces of which remain today (De Boeve 1997, 50).

In Belgium, street work made its entry toward the end of the 1970s when some communities that were aware of the emergence of street work in Quebec, established contacts with their Quebec counterparts and began a first street work experiment.

Only toward the middle of the 1980s did other street work initiatives begin to occupy more space in the field of social intervention, though in a marginal way. The 1991 'riots' in Brussels made many people aware that the collective and spontaneous expression of social malaise, which was thought to be limited to French suburbs, could also occur in Belgium. As a consequence, public authorities were given a social defense mandate: to anticipate and prevent rioting in order to defend, secure, and reassure society and its citizens. This defense was supposed to occur in the streets since it was there that the riots had taken place.

Significant new budget resources were made available, and 'street social work' *(travail social de rue)* was rapidly developed through new projects established at the institutional and the community group level alike (Schaut 1994). There then appeared the infamous security contracts under the auspices of the Federal Ministry for the Interior: the police engaged street workers, and their mandate was clearly placed in a perspective of social control. Nevertheless, street workers from community groups continued to resist and maintain a political outlook for promoting the rights of youth and their emancipation (De Boeve 1997, 48).

In France, street work practice, already in existence for fifty years, was institutionalized in 1972 under the rubric of *prévention specialisée*. Particularly targeted were, above all, the suburbs of big cities, where immigrant populations resided. In 1992, during the largest assembly of street workers in Toulouse, it was proclaimed that the values and the references of street work, which had characterized it in the 1970s, had been overwhelmed by an increasingly technocratic, administrative logic. However, this affirmation did not incite a large-scale resistance movement since apart from several exceptions, street work in France remained limited to socio-cultural activities, with neither vision nor political agenda (Legault 1994).

In Switzerland, a project called '*Gassenarbeit*' (street work in German) was launched in 1980 in Basle (Maurer 1992) It was premised on the conviction that considerable potential for forces of emancipation lies within society and the individual. This potential, it was argued, should be supported, developed, and reinforced by means of street work. Some of the initial ideas came from a critique of most of the social institutions, which were viewed as being limited to *administering* people who lived on the margin by methods that were becoming increasingly refined and concerned chiefly with the maintenance of the social machinery. The Basle experiment report stressed the importance for social work to maintain its non-institutional character. Ironically, this report was published at precisely the moment when street work was institutionalized in Switzerland. The report's authors feared that with the institutionalization and the professionalization of street work, certain essential principles could no longer be guaranteed (Maurer 1992, 11). Their fear was well founded: presently, these principles are observed only by a handful of workers, who operate outside the grip of institutional bodies.

To conclude this European historical survey, it is worth noting that many street work initiatives have been started in recent years in Russia and a number of other European countries that emerged after the collapse of the Soviet Union, in order to face a growing number of children and youth who take to the streets in order to survive very precarious socio-economic conditions.

Elsewhere

In many countries to the south (Brazil, Columbia, Chile, Morocco, Egypt, Sudan, Kenya, India, the Philippines, and others), the street children phenomenon was at the origin of a panoply of intervention projects and programs, which use street work methodology, often with a non-formal educational· scope, to face this ever-increasing phenomenon. The majority of these projects and programs are carried out by local social development NGOs. Despite the wealth of innovation and creativity that characterizes many of these programs, they remain as marginalized as the street children with whom they work.

As we have seen, since its emergence in the United States in the 1920s, street work has been associated with two different conceptions. The first is concerned with 'standardizing' social situations that are off course, while the second is more concerned with enabling excluded youth to use their agency in a process of emancipation. In the presentation of street work's parameters that follows, I refer to this second conception, which I call 'critical street work.'

The Parameters of Critical Street Work

In this section, I attempt to illustrate the practical and theoretical elements that characterize critical street work and which will help, I hope, to provide a better definition of this little-known and rarely acknowledged practice. I maintain a favorable judgement with respect to the rich potential that street work represents, in terms of both 'action' with marginal groups and of the 'reflective research' that goes hand in hand with such action with the aim of making it more efficient and, as such, more emancipatory.

In following the different stages in street work, my objective is to shed light on the concrete nature of this practice. At the same time, I will establish links with theoretical and methodological premises that appear to me to be pertinent to each of these stages. My objective is to underline the affinity between street work and methodological perspectives of critical, engaged action and research.

Street Work as Street Ethnography

The first task of the street worker is to develop a strategy of 'social infiltration' into the living milieus of targeted youth. In so doing, the street worker, like every ethnographer, must turn to observation and participant observation.

Infiltrating the living milieus of youth takes place by means of a gentle process, which is well moderated and supervised. This demands considerable tact and talent from the part of the street workers in order not to perturb daily routines or the regular course of things. Indeed, street workers must demonstrate numerous qualities, a partial list of which includes: sensitivity; knowing how to observe and listen; the ability to make connections and to take time to understand; belief in the capacities of the youth and in his or her potential; acceptance of differences in language, values, and culture; respect for the youth and those surrounding him/her; an ability to establish their own limits and recognize their own strengths, weaknesses, and fears; availability; and a spirit of initiative.

Initially, it requires a great deal of observation to familiarize oneself with the context, the movements, the activities, the faces, the spatial and temporal dynamics, and so on. Next, and very gradually, the participation dimension becomes more active after the street workers have identified points of entry. Street workers thus begin to initiate and develop contacts, to identify key people/informants and friends, which allows them to start decoding and better understanding the language and the culture of the milieu they are attempting to infiltrate. The initial contact with youth on the street and the construction of relations of confidence and solidarity with them and their surroundings demands not only that street workers have a great deal of sensitivity and *savoir-faire*, but also that they adopt a working methodology scrupulously developed and supervised, which enables a non-intrusive and progressive approach into street groups, in such a way as to avoid being rapidly excluded. Throughout this approach, street workers must observe three rules. First, they must abstain from making moral judgements concerning the lived experiences and realities of the youth. Second, they must not situate the youth in the role of victim, nor in one of a recipient of help. Lastly, they must help youth groups and collectives to claim their rights.

As participant observers, street workers must maintain a sustained presence in various areas of the youths' lives. This sustained presence in the street constitutes, in effect, the basis of street work. It signifies a sharing of day-to-day existence by mixing oneself into the life of the group, by participating in diverse activities and by making the effort to understand them from the perspective of the attitudes and behaviors judged to be important. It is, therefore, a matter of personal engagement; that is to say, not only is the objective of distancing impossible (and undesirable), but every attempt by a street worker to maintain an external stance will limit the process of accompaniment.

In sum, the first step of street work consists of gentle infiltration into the milieus of youth groups to make contact, to become accepted, and to win their confidence and esteem. This stage is developed following an ethnographic methodology. Indeed, the three principles, which, according to Edgerton and Langness, lie at the heart of contemporary ethnographic inquiry are observed throughout the infiltration process (1974, 2–5). The first of these, the emphasis on participant observation methodology—reflecting the concern that ethnographers live intimately in the societies under study—is ensured by meaningful and sustained interactions (that is, sharing in day-to-day activities) between the street workers and the youth and their surroundings. The second principle is that the culture under investigation must be considered from the viewpoint of the people whose lifestyles are being studied. This is usually accomplished by being acutely attentive to the lived experiences from the viewpoint of the youths themselves, viewed as social actors and self-reflecting individuals able to interpret their own realities. Lastly, by developing an "intimate familiarity" (Blumer 1969) with the social fabric and dynamics of street milieus, street workers act in accordance with the principle of holism, that is, the contextualization of human conduct by reference to the setting in which it naturally occurs.

It is important to note here that the ethnographic inquiry inherent to street work derives from 'street ethnography.' The use of street ethnography for the investigation of deviancy is amply documented in the literature. According to Gigengack and Van Gelder (2000, 11), this tradition's foundations were laid by W.F. Whyte in *Street Corner Society* (1943), in which he studied the social structure of an Italian slum. However, C. Shaw's *The Jack-Roller* (1930), in which Shaw depicted the day-to-day situations that street children encounter may very well be considered its foundation. But it was only in 1977 when R.S. Weppner edited a collection of selected studies under the denominator 'street ethnography' that this kind of work came to be recognized as "a respectable academic activity" (Gigengack and Van Gelder 2000, 11).

Lastly, I would like to note that unlike street ethnography, which typically seeks to understand deviance and to contextualize deviant behavior, street work, as further elaborated below, does not claim to be neutral. It sides with the excluded groups of youth to transform personal problems into collective advocacy for inclusion and a greater stake in the public good. As such, street work can be conceptualized as street ethnography that is *engaged* and *critical* (Kincheloe and McLaren 1994).

Street Work as Action Research

There are many similarities between participant observation and action research. Both come within the scope of the day-to-day existence of individuals and groups and both have a scientific and social objective. In addition, besides the universal scientific goal of understanding the operation and realities of social groups, these methods aim to elucidate social problems, to evaluate innovations, and to draw attention to marginalized groups.

In their daily work, street workers are engaged *de facto* in a process of action research. The term 'action research,' as a compound noun, expresses its double aim well: to produce knowledge, to resolve a problem, or to contribute to the achievement of projects. In other words, action research refers to field action closely related to a form of research activity, which, in an interactive process, enables one to sustain, orient, and consolidate the action. It is, therefore, not a matter of theoretical research, but of instituting a constant process of collecting, analyzing, and interpreting data, not only to enrich our own knowledge, but also, and above all, to better define the field action with the youth concerned. For this reason, the concept of an alternative approach for youths who refuse to integrate into institutional networks becomes possible.

Between action and research, 'reflection' nourishes and enriches the experience of the street workers who are at once a subject and an object in this approach: street workers place themselves in the group being studied in order to understand it more thoroughly and to grasp its real-life experience, all while maintaining the distance of observation. Thus, street workers are situated both as insiders and outsiders *vis-à-vis* the group. In being both observers and participants, street workers have recourse to a dialectical approach that leads them back and forth from practice to theory, and from the observing subject to the participating subject.

Street Work as Action Science

Whoever is involved with action, research and reflection is necessarily situated in the domain of 'action science,' a body of work developed over the last two decades primarily by Chris Argyris (Harvard University) and Donald Schön (1931–1997) (MIT) (Argyris 1980, 1982, 1983; Argyris and Schön 1974; Schön 1983, 1987, 1995). Interestingly, Argyris and Schön view their effort to promote action science as a renewal of the action research tradition initiated by Kurt Lewin in the 1940s in the domain of social psychology. It is beyond the scope of this chapter to present in detail the parameters of action science. I present here a broad overview with some emphasis on the 'reflective' approach developed by Schön.

The starting point for Argyris and Schön was the crisis of confidence in the profession and the decline in professional self-image that started early in the 1970s. They argued that the crisis was not only the result of bureaucratic pressure for increased efficiency; professional knowledge produced by the positivist epistemology of practice had increasingly been "mismatched" to the changing character of professional practice and increasingly entailed complex problem solving involving "indeterminate zones of practice characterized by complexity, uncertainty, instability, uniqueness, and value conflicts" (Schön 1983, 14).

The gap between research and practice characteristic of the traditional scientific model of applied sciences accounts, according to Argyris and Schön, for the fact that professional practitioners were not finding the answers to their dilemmas in the prescriptions drawn from research results. This model is based on an epistemological principle, which asserts that knowledge should come before efficient action. Accordingly, the methodological rules of this model, which consistently dissociate the practitioner from the research process (or associated only as an experimental subject), are viewed by the founders of action science as systematic errors responsible for producing results irrelevant to actual situations encountered by professionals in their day-to-day practice. This dominant model of production of practice knowledge ignores the fact that it is the practitioner who is best placed to grasp the givens and the totality of the situation under study (Argyris 1980; Schön 1983).

Moreover, by limiting the power of problem definitions and prescriptions of solutions to the domain of fundamental sciences, positivist epistemology promotes a perspective of 'technical rationality,' which reduces practitioners to mere consumers of scientific products. By the same token, professional practice is reduced to a process of problem solving, which thereby evacuates the definitional process of 'problem setting' with respect to decisions to be made, ends to be achieved, and the means to be chosen:

> In real-world practice, problems do not present themselves to practitioners as givens. They must be constructed from the materials of problematic situations which are puzzling, troubling, and uncertain. In order to convert a problematic situation to a problem, a practitioner must do a certain kind of work. He must make sense of an uncertain situation that initially makes no sense. (Schön 1983, 39–40)

This awareness of the limits of technical rationality made Argyris and Schön depart from the dominant discourse according to which theoretical knowledge is considered the generative basis of knowledge production and should precede the action for it to be efficient. Rather, they advocated the opposite: action itself is a source of valid knowledge, and this paved the way for the emergence of a new epistemology.

'Knowing-in-action,' 'reflection-in-action,' and 'reflection-on-action' are the three operational concepts in action science, which are used to produce a deliberate overlap of action and reflection in the context of a spiral process in which every cycle is composed of fact finding, analysis, conceptualization, planning, implementation, and evaluation (Schön 1983).[15] Accordingly, knowledge that emerges from an action/practice, that is experiential knowledge, is 'constructed' through a continuous process of 'reflection during action and on action.'

If, as the proponents of action science maintain, it is true that every professional innovator often has recourse to knowledge stemming from his or her own practice—to a greater degree than disciplinary or curricular knowledge, or from professional training—when he faces uncertain, unique or ambiguous situations, that is, the social *par excellence*, then this is the case to an even greater extent for the street worker who works in the territory of the 'client.' Indeed, for street workers, reflection is an indispensable means of continuous self-education. Two spaces of reflection are necessary: individual supervision and group reflection. It is within these two spaces of reflection that the continuing education of street workers is enriched through the problematization of the link between theory and practice.

Before concluding this section, it is important to note that the great majority of street workers do not use the notion of ethnographer/researcher to refer to their work, and even less the notion of action science to describe the theoretical framework of their practice and education. Nevertheless, they would agree with the general process described above. The conceptual attributes I have advanced are formulated in order to illuminate the potential within the street worker's practice, a potential that is little or poorly known.

Street Work as Accompaniment Practice

The practice of street work is located directly within the field of the social, and is essentially a practice of 'accompanying' youths, to whom numerous stigmas and prejudices have been attached (dropout, runaway, from the street, in the street, itinerant, junkie, homeless, 'I don't give a damn-ists', at risk, lost, problem kid, beyond redemption, and even victim and/or delinquent). These youths are often excluded as being non- or anti-conformists.

The notion of accompaniment is borrowed from *acompañamiento*, which means 'accompanying the process,' and is used by "Latin American development workers to describe a relationship with communities, groups, and individuals that fosters mutual support, trust, a common commitment, and solidarity" (Bradbury and Reason 2003, 162). In accompaniment work, encounters with participants are followed by the building of meaningful relationships based on recognition of the *other* in whatever s/he is and whatever s/he lives as *actor-subject* of his/her history. It is this fundamental recognition of the other that ascribes a symbolic scope to the meaningful relationship, permitting in this way, through interaction and in a relational rapport, the emergence and construction of sense and meaning.

··The practice of accompaniment is achieved through a 'process' in which street workers engage themselves as subjects and bearers of their own history, culture, and values. By involving themselves as subjects guided by the desire to be in contact and to communicate with youth, street workers, in adopting a reflective approach at both personal and professional levels, learn to know, understand, and recognize the culture (or cultures) of youth without letting themselves be carried away by the relational proximity to such an extent that they create identity confusion by a strong desire to be an insider rather than an outsider (over-identification). In other words, the street worker is continually led to set a clear relational boundary between the private and the professional. These more or less permeable boundaries are intended not to engender rigid professional distance, but a position simultaneously enabling sufficient involvement and necessary distance.

A more in-depth exploration of the practice of accompaniment reveals that the creation of meaningful relationships with youth favors a response to their fundamental needs: a contact, a bond, someone who listens, understanding, empathy and, at a symbolic level, recognition, consideration, witnessing, and respect. These attributes are fundamental in a relationship of help and are taken for granted in social science discourses.

While the therapeutic dimension in the relationship between youth and street worker is often omnipresent, it is not a matter of clinical therapy from a medical perspective. Rather, it is a question of a therapeutic approach that might be described as awareness raising and as being centered on the subject-actor. It is as well an eclectic approach guided by a humanist ideology and borrowing, among others, the principles of 'active listening' and 'empathy' from the Rogerian method, the notion of 'liberatory dialogue' from the Frierean methodology, as well as the notion of 'social accompaniment' from clinical sociology. This means that the therapeutic dimension in street work is expressed in the daily practice of accompaniment in a similar fashion to the one that takes place in field interventions within the methodology of participatory action research. In effect, street work is in many senses, and could be even more (if recognized and consolidated), one of the most interesting and efficient forms of participatory action research, since this type of community action relies essentially on the availability of the practitioner-research implicated in the day-to-day experience of the target groups. Street workers occupy a very privileged position in this respect.

Lastly, in accompanying street children, street workers are often called upon to mediate between the children and their families, the police, the school, social workers, and a variety of other individuals and instances. This mediatory dimension of accompaniment work is not without contradiction. The mediator role requires that street workers invest in their authority at the risk of being perceived by the children as 'all powerful.' Obviously, this can entail problematic transfer issues that can be taxing if not attended to. Such situations point to the fact that despite all conscious efforts from the part of street workers to downplay and control power differentials in their pursuit of egalitarian relationship with the children, the affective perceptions of the latter are bound to raise power issues that must be addressed. It is then that the street workers become aware of their "longing for innocence and purity" (Flax 1993) when they represent their work as mostly educational and devoid of any social control function.

Street Work as Socio-cultural, Non-formal, and Collective Education

Eventually, in the practice of social accompaniment, the street worker is asked by youths to help them 'carry out a project' that interests them. Whether it is to stage a theater play, produce a video, go on a trip or any other activity, this request opens the door for articulating and raising the 'educational' component of street work. It thus becomes a matter of orienting these activities within a non-formal context corresponding to the realities of youths who have dropped out of the 'formal.'

It was in the late 1960s that non-formal education appeared in the international discourse on education policy as an alternative to the escalating "world educational crisis" (Coombs 1968, 1985). Formal education alone could no longer respond and adapt to rapid and constant technological, social and economic changes; non-formal education, it was claimed, was necessary and complementary to formal education and particularly relevant to the needs of disadvantaged groups (UNESCO 1972). As a concept, non-formal education was constructed using notions drawn from the works of John Dewey (Dewey 1916, 1938) on democratic education, Ivan Illich's notion of 'deschooling' (Illich 1976, 1990), and Paulo Freire's 'liberatory dialogue' (Freire 1970) and 'critical consciousness' (Freire 1973). There is not enough space here for an exhaustive discussion of the parameters and underlying theories of non-formal education. I will, however, briefly discuss some of its basic principles, drawn from the works of these writers and educators (Graubard 1972; Hern 1996).

Mainstream notions of education are typically articulated solely around its social function—little attention is paid to the learning process, and learning and creativity are generally viewed as distinct processes. In contrast, non-formal approaches to education seek to dissolve this distinction. In these approaches, learning is not merely the addition and accumulation of knowledge and skills; rather, it involves integration and disintegration, construction and deconstruction, creating new wholes, and going beyond limits and opening the door to a limitless horizon of possibility. In this view, there is no such thing as a distinction between learning and creativity.

In non-formal education, learning is viewed as emancipatory inasmuch as it involves reinterpreting and giving significance to one's experience of the present. As such, education is neither passive nor neutral. It contains the possibility of being a vehicle for expression, for creativity, in a dynamic relationship with action in and on the environment.

When the act of learning helps to define and form relationships with the environment, it becomes possible for individuals to redefine and reconstruct their material environments, which include power relations between human subjects. In this view, social change, at the individual and group levels, is intrinsic to the experience acquired in the process of socialization and education. In other words, in non-formal education, change is the natural result of a voluntary and emancipatory educational process.

Consequently, when youths ask to carry out a project of their own, it is an ideal occasion for street work to become group accompaniment work in a collective undertaking of carrying out projects. Voluntary involvement in this type of activity allows youths to have a multitude of experiences in a real and concrete moment, one that requires decision-making, participation, negotiation, and organization. The very process of completing a project becomes the vehicle for very enriching interactions and exchanges because it is necessary to struggle with the meaning of notions such as responsibility, cooperation, solidarity, engagement, democracy, motivation (or its absence), tolerance, respect, criticism, justice, and many others. The role of educator assumed by the street worker is one of moderator, coach, host, informant, and participant who obviously takes part with the others in creating and constructing the meaning of their communal existence and their project.

Street Work as Ethical *Savoir-faire*

In the foregoing description of the parameters of critical street work, I highlighted the familiarity with the realities of excluded youths that street workers develop by placing themselves in the living milieus of these youths. This 'intimate familiarity' and proximity with the excluded inevitably gives rise to a multitude of ethical issues and dilemmas to which critical street workers devote a great deal of thought and discussion. These deliberations, carried out individually, with peers and with the children themselves, constitute the vehicle for promoting a 'critical reflection' that is the pre-requisite for emancipation (Fook 1999, 2004).

In adopting what may be called an 'ethical attitude,' street workers are continuously engaged in problematizing the different realities they encounter in their practice, even when these seem obvious. As such, an ethical attitude strives to raise questions without a priori conceptions modeled according to established morality, codes of ethics and laws that are enacted with a view to dictating behaviors. In other words, an ethical attitude enables the actors to participate in the ongoing interrogation and construction of what is *just* and *human*.

It is this ethical attitude of continually interrogating the obvious and problematizing issues that makes street workers able to cope with situations of 'ethical uncertainty' in the "indeterminate zones of practice characterized by complexity, uncertainty, instability, uniqueness, and value conflicts" (Schön 1983) so characteristic of intervention with marginal and excluded children. The experiential knowledge that is constructed in conjunction with living in and reflecting upon such situations of ethical uncertainty can very well be named ethical *savoir-faire*.

The above descriptions of the ideology and values in the radical discourse of street work are almost identical to those underlying the Southern (Freirean) school of participatory action research (PAR) presented in the previous chapter. Indeed, the convergence of the values and assumptions of these two methodologies has facilitated their combination into the same program. Many street work organizations in different countries are in the process of incorporating PAR into their programs. In addition to a contribution to action theory constructions, when PAR becomes part of everyday practice, that is, when action is constantly subjected to participatory reflection and analysis, the tasks of monitoring and evaluation are assumed collectively and in a timely fashion. Similarly, the ongoing process of action and reflection ensures the continuing education of street workers.

Underpinnings

Since its origin in the United States in the 1920s, street work has been associated with juvenile delinquency and community organization. Two conceptions that are difficult to reconcile have marked in a general way the development of street work as a social practice since the end of the 1960s. According to the first conception, street work is above all a method of intervention, even a simple technique of approaching, of making contact with deviant populations—who escape the institutions that are supposed to contain them—with a view to controlling and reproducing a specific social order that is not challenged. Thus, a perspective of 'social defense' characterizes the first conception, the primary objective of which is the standardization, if not the control and repression of individuals and groups who are a menace to society due to their asocial behavior.

The second conception of street work, which I call critical street work, comes within the scope of another political and social philosophy. It proposes a reading of social life that penetrates the lived realities of actors in precarious situations. This reading begins with the assumption that problems posed by deviance are above all social in nature. In this light, the priority is the fight against exclusion, relying on the reinforcement of natural systems of socialization. Policy with regard to criminality is not a favorable instrument for mobilization; on the contrary, it should remain in the background as much as possible. In this second conception of street work, the emphasis is placed on the protection and emancipation of excluded individuals and collectivities and not on the potential danger they represent. It is thus a perspective of 'social inclusion.' This perspective rests entirely on the ability to construct a relationship of mutual trust with those excluded, a relationship that nothing should be allowed to compromise. If this approach ultimately contributes to the fight against deviance and violence, this contribution is only an added feature, not the primary objective.

Obviously, each of these two conceptions will orient the analysis of the situation and the practice in very different ways. In a conception based on a perspective of social defense, the predominant vision of the young deviant is often that of the 'lost sheep,' who must be recovered from the street and redirected onto the proper path. This vision rather explicitly suggests that the street is a place of ruin, and its influence on the people who live in it can only be bad. Moreover, the idea of the deviant, the lost sheep, implies that a certain adaptation must have occurred before the aberration or deviance. The stakes here are based on the supposition that the deviants, despite everything, carry conventional societal values within them—as Shaw and McKay argue—and that a little resilience on their part and help from the interveners will suffice to get them to rejoin the flock. As for those who are not resilient enough to leave the street, they will still be offered condoms, syringes, and advice; and if they become uncontrollable, they will be incarcerated.

This vision of the baneful street into which young sheep go astray excludes any approach which would attempt to grasp the meaning and significance of the lived realities and experiences of youths other than as ill-fated and negative. Youths are therefore supposed to dissociate themselves from street life, if not completely disavow their street experiences, since they have no positive value.

This analysis of deviance is very different from the one advocated by critical street work. Here, the street is no longer perceived solely as devastating; it is also educating and socializing in ways that can be rewarding. By appropriating public spaces in the street and transforming them into spheres of work, production, relations, innovations, adventures, leisure and consumption, youths search and create a place, an identity; make their existential choices; experience recognition and solidarity with their peers; share their fears, their anxieties, their revolt, and also their friendship and love. For them, the street is a place where they can have a certain amount of power over themselves and their environment. In taking to the street, their agency emerges in a state of re-action, that is, in 'action.' According to this conception of life in the street, it would neither be conceivable to ask youths to repent their entry into the street nor to uphold leaving the street as the primary objective of intervention. On the contrary, the street workers attempt to understand the cultures of the street and to co-construct with youths a sense of their lived experience in order for them to be able to reappropriate it and subsequently direct themselves toward becoming responsible and autonomous.

Throughout this chapter, the opposition between two conceptions of street work has been accentuated in order to place in relief the traits of each of these poles. However, these two conceptions each have their legitimacy, and the contrast between them echoes the omnipresent tension between what Alain Touraine (1992) calls the pole of "rationalization" and the pole of "subjectivation." All actors, including the proponents of the two opposing conceptions of street work, are inhabited by the tension between these two poles. The primary issue rests on the ability and willingness of actors to transcend this polarization. This can happen if the actors make room for a dialectical sensitivity to concede that reality is a concrete totality in movement and agitated by contradictions that necessarily remain open. As such, it is from these very contradictions that the possibilities for new meaning and innovative actions may emerge. In this sense, the primary issue here is one of democracy. A political system that favors one pole to the detriment of the other and which does not envisage any kind of dialectics is a form of totalitarianism that only recognizes what lies along the straight and narrow line of normality. Similarly, activist groups that do not acknowledge the inevitable defense dimension in social matters will remain prisoners of their longing for innocence and purity.

For the promoters of critical street work, another dilemma emerges from the pressures exerted by the sponsors—essentially the state and its different bureaucratic apparatuses—for a quantifiable street work that does not escape control. Does one thus want to attempt to better formalize and structure this practice (its methodology, objectives, statute, and so on) at the risk of locking it into a form of institutionalization, or of losing its originality and of distancing it from its target public, the excluded? Or on the contrary, does one not wish to attempt to formalize it at the risk of maintaining it in its marginality, reinforcing in this way the mistrust of authority and its lack of recognition?

It is interesting to note here the similarity between this dilemma and the one which street youth often encounter when they contemplate disengaging themselves from their street career. For both street workers and youths, this sort of dilemma poses a rather difficult choice between a precarious, unstructured, and autonomous way of existence and institutionalization and loss of creativity. The autonomy that critical street workers enjoy in their work often elicits the envy of those working in institutions of social work. Indeed, critical street workers feel that their mandate comes neither from the organization with which they are affiliated nor from their employer or the sponsor, but, rather, from their public, that is, those on the street, the excluded, whom they view as ineluctably engendered by the socio-economic system (Moreau 1990). In addition, street workers do not maintain client files, as nothing is allowed to compromise the relationship of confidentiality they have with their public.[16]

Thus, contrary to professionals who work in institutions, who are constrained to follow bureaucratic rules of the administration and who are often situated far from strategic decisions, street workers enjoy a comparative advantage that allows them to have considerable autonomy. Nevertheless, just as for the youths they accompany, this autonomy must be paid for. Street workers often find themselves in situations of precarious work, and their work itself receives little recognition, or is even denigrated as amateur and non-professional.

In this context, the promoters of critical street work recognize the need to produce, implement, and assert within the political sphere a viable project involving a structure of operation, purposes, and appropriate and efficient methods. Indeed, this may have even become more essential in order to face an increasing instrumentalization of street work, which is implemented through a variety of new initiatives (street police, street nurses, doctors, and psychologists) better equipped with resources and eventually able to monopolize existing street workers and those who are available for this type of involvement. The general framework of 'participatory action research' with which many street work organizations have been experimenting should, to my mind, facilitate better recognition of street work, which after all is necessary since it responds to situations of exclusion which are beyond the limits of the institutions of social work.

However, a perspective of this kind would not be possible unless the state first developed a genuine interest in providing financial support for activities that are accountable to it while escaping its direct control. The principle is not new. It already directs relations between, for example, the state and justice, medicine, and university research.

Concluding Commentary

In this first part of the book I undertook an historical review of two methodologies of social action/practice and research: participatory action research (PAR) and street work. This review reveals that for each of these two methodologies, there are two opposing conceptions along a continuum stretching from radical/critical/objective to instrumental/control/subjective. The review also reveals that the polemic around these opposed conceptions has consistently featured in the debates around these two methodologies since their emergence in the 1930s (street work) and the 1960s (PAR) respectively. In addition, it reveals the fact that both methodologies, in their radical/critical version politically positioned on the side of the excluded, have occupied a marginal status both in academia and in the field. Indeed, the Southern Freirean tradition of PAR and critical street work share a common ideology that values the participation of excluded individuals and groups in the decisions affecting their existence as a means to acquiring more empowerment. This common ideology, as well as the insistence on being with participants in their own milieus, has inspired the eclectic combination of PAR and street work within programs that target excluded and marginalized youth populations.

Lastly, the historical review reveals that the Southern tradition of PAR and critical social work, each with its particular history of action with grassroots communities, not only share a common philosophy, but they have also both been co-opted and instrumentalized within technocratic structures. Nevertheless, the tradition of activism that has carried these emancipatory methodologies of social action has survived even though its substance and strategies may have changed according to place and time. It is interesting to note here—in reference to what I described in Chapter 1 as an undue concern with the issue of co-optation—that accepting co-optation as an inevitable part of the game reflects neither a pessimistic nor a fatalist view. It is always refreshing and comforting to identify in history a common thread of *resistance* to many injustices that have prevailed in all societies over a long period of time. This thread seems to have survived the perpetual co-optation of activists' discourses and methodologies.

In the following chapters, I narrate the PAR process undertaken with street children and youths in Cairo spanning eight years of fieldwork, which eclectically combined street ethnography, street work, and action science. If this work permits a better understanding of the specifics of PAR and critical street work and a better definition of the conditions of their success—autonomy, the necessary relationship of confidence with those excluded and duration—it might also help to prevent these methodologies of social action from becoming totally distorted or from losing their substance through instrumentalist use.

Part 2

The Story

In this second part of the book, I reconstruct the story of the participatory action research project that targeted the street children of Cairo, Egypt between 1993 and 2001. In this part I am very keen to highlight the processual nature of the undertaking in order to demystify some of the promises alluded to by some PAR discourses. Specifically, my intention is to demonstrate that it is naïve to assume that by simply wishing ourselves into a 'participatory stance,' we, as PAR practitioners, will be able to lead the community in transcending historically and culturally rooted differences and conflicts. Both subjective and structural impediments to democracy need to be attended to in a PAR process and this, in my opinion, is the essence of PAR itself. As such, I strive to demonstrate here that democratic participation, like other ideals of PAR and international development work in general, cannot from the outset constitute a fixed feature and mode of operation. Instead, they are to be actively, dialogically, ethically, and dialectically pursued as medium- and long-term objectives in an open-ended process of ongoing action, reflexivity, and adjustment.

In this part of the book I am also keen to demonstrate that for a PAR process to be emancipatory, it is necessary to dwell and critically reflect on the various and complex ethical issues and dilemmas that arise by virtue of the contradictions inherent in the very intention of promoting a democratic process of action and research. Through continually problematizing day-to-day practice situations and questioning their ethical attributes at both the individual and collective levels, the story of PAR that unfolds here is indeed one in which methodological and ethical issues merge in the organization of work.

One last, but certainly not the least, concern I had in writing the following chapters was with respect to the concept of emancipation that is increasingly becoming a catch-word. I demonstrate here that the concept of emancipation, insofar as it denotes, as aptly noted by Fook (1999, 201–202), the development of "a consciousness which is able to imagine the transformability of current arrangements" and "the capacity to analyze social situations and to transform social relations on the basis of this analysis," must be applied to all the actors who are involved in the PAR process. I reject the all too often implicit assumption that emancipation defined as such is the goal reserved mostly for the participants from the 'oppressed' group, often represented with 'false consciousness.' In what follows, I demonstrate that the claim of 'emancipating the other' is flawed if it does not involve the emancipation of those making the claims themselves. The practitioners and researchers in the PAR reported here certainly had a lot to gain from interactively constructing what Fook calls "emancipatory knowledge," by continually trying to position the different intelligence and *savoir-faire* of the actors on an equal footing.

This second part of the book consists of four chapters. In Chapter 3, I analyze both the international and the Egyptian contexts with respect to the phenomenon of street children. I then describe how the PAR process with Cairene street children, the subject matter of this book, was initiated, and the technical and political tasks that needed to be performed in conjunction with the launching of street ethnography to conduct research into some of the realities of the phenomenon in question. The analysis of the data observed and collected through street ethnography was used to develop a conceptual framework that informed the construction of the PAR process. This framework is presented in Chapter 4, before resuming the re-construction of the PAR story in Chapter 5 with the opening of the drop-in center and the launching of non-formal education and advocacy activities, which sought to empower and emancipate the participants.

Lastly, in Chapter 6, I highlight and discuss the changes and impact we observed at the individual and the group level, as well as changes with respect to Egyptian policy regarding street children. I then summarize and discuss the methodological features that characterized the PAR process presented in this book, before ending with a discussion of some of the unresolved issues.

3
The Beginning

I n this chapter I narrate the beginnings of eight years of action and participatory research both *on* and *with* Cairene street children. This exploratory
and preparatory beginning phase required the accomplishment of both technical and political tasks. These included the design of a PAR project to be
implemented in developmental stages; the recruitment of individuals; training and educating them in street ethnographic work with a marginal and
highly skeptical population of children and youth; the initiation of observation work in the streets of Cairo to identify localities where street children
are found; and the covert infiltration of some of the children's milieus in
order to gain a better grasp of the realities and context of their lives on the
street through participant observation. Furthermore, the awareness that the
project was to be implemented in a rather conservative and repressive context of state surveillance—practiced by an inflated and corrupt technocratic
machinery—necessitated the development of an institutional and political
framework that was acceptable to government officials, even if they did not
completely approve of it.

I start by specifying both the international and local Egyptian contexts
with respect to the street children phenomenon and by highlighting some
of the conceptual underpinnings.

The Context
International Context
Since the early 1980s, the social phenomenon commonly referred to as
'street children' has been of increasing concern to policy makers, researchers,
and development planners in both the North and the South. A substantial
number of publications have been produced since then to describe street

children and their lives on the streets and to suggest possible interventions (de Moura 2002). Many programs have been designed to intervene with street children, including the provision of services and the adoption of both rehabilitative and correctional measures (Bemak 1996).

Despite the widespread concerns and the numerous intervention programs, the street children phenomenon continues to escalate throughout the world, and there is still confusion surrounding the definition and conceptualization of these young populations living and surviving in the street environment.

Street Children: A Problem of Definition

Obviously, the formulation and definition of a social phenomenon create the cast that shapes all subsequent organizational intents and actions: the wording of policy, the choice of solutions, the political and moral responsibility for reform, and the design of programs, including the selection of personnel and the identification of assessment criteria and the scope of research.

'Street children' is the generic term used to refer to groups of children, adolescents, and young adults who develop a special relationship to the street, whereby they make it a living space.[17] Glauser aptly remarks that "the frequency of its use seems to suggest that such a group exists as a homogeneous phenomenon in reality" (1990, 139). At first glance, they do indeed resemble one another. Their clothing is shabby and they do odd jobs or just wander around, seemingly aimlessly. This overall appearance leads outside observers to identify them as street children. On the other hand, they have different family characteristics, and different experiences, trajectories, and futures. A number of researchers have come to problematize the term 'street children,' arguing that it lends itself to a misleading view of these children, namely, that they are all alike, dwelling in the street in identical ways and for identical reasons (Cree et al. 2002). In recognition of this, scientists and policy-makers have made several attempts to divide street children into subgroups that differ in key characteristics. However, this has resulted in the production of broad, ambiguous, and often contrasting definitions that have not added much clarity to the phenomenon (de Moura 2002).

One definition that is still to be found in most of the literature to date was put forward by UNICEF. It divides the street child population into two categories. The larger category consists of working street children, or 'children on the street.' These are children "who work on the streets during the day and often return home to their families at night. These children may attend school part time and have limited access to health and other social services" (UNICEF Executive Board 1986, 1). The second category consists of 'children of the street,' that is, children "who work and live on the streets, maintaining mimimal ties with their families but essentially living on their own" (UNICEF, Executive Board 1986, 2).

Although the two categories do have the word 'street' in common, the street also acts as a differentiating element between them. This differentiation is made according to the type of relationship that exists between the child and the street as well as between the child and his family. Living at home with one's family and working in the street is opposed to living in the street away from one's family, suggesting a basic, but implicit, dichotomy between home/family and street.

The underlying concept of the UNICEF definition serves to classify street children as 'children at risk.' The risk factors are assessed along two dimensions. The first is a physical dimension, measured as a function of the degree of permanence in the street. The second is a social dimension regarding the degree of contact with family. Together, these two dimensions actually propose a linear theory of causality based on the degree of family connection, which continues to be a major reference in the literature on street children (de Moura 2002).

The operational value of the UNICEF definition, which is based on drawing a distinction between children *on* and *of* the street, has been seriously challenged by the majority of research and practice findings concerning street children over the last twenty years (Aptekar 1994; Lucchini 1996a; Koller & Hutz 1996; Rizzini 1996). These findings have clearly demonstrated that the situation of many children does not fit easily into either category. Some children spend the night on the streets for reasons related to how they make their living. Some go back to their homes in the morning, while others only do so every few days. Others remain on the streets during the weeks, returning home only on the weekends, while others work the weekend and return home during the week. Still others stay out on the street when the weather is warm and return home during cooler periods, with the result that there are more children sleeping in the streets during the summer than in the winter. Given this wide variety of ways that children use the streets, it is difficult to decide just when a child becomes *of* the street rather than merely *on* it.

The second operational difficulty regarding the UNICEF definition is linked to the fact that many so-called children *of* the street do not live continuously on the street. They may spend months at a time in institutional settings before going back to the street. Others leave the street for varying periods of time, living with family or relatives in an effort to re-establish themselves. They may also live with someone who takes care of them for one reason or another. What they share, however, is the fact that they all eventually return to the street. The third difficulty concerns the operational measurement of the degree of family contact, which does not depend so much on the mere amount of contact between the child and the family as on the quality of this contact. The painful reality of many street children is that their lives on the street are healthier, both physically and emotionally, than at home.

The UNICEF definitional approach has been refuted by ample empirical evidence showing that the vast majority of street children are in fact neither homeless nor abandoned, and that although most have homes to which they could return, many end up essentially living on the street (Aptekar 1992, 1994; Lucchini 1993, 1996a).

Recognizing the difficulties with the definition of 'children of the street' versus 'children on the street,' some definitional attempts have led the way in grouping together all working children—whether working on city streets or elsewhere—and using the term street children to refer to the *smaller* number of largely abandoned children for whom the city streets are home (UNICEF Program Division 1989). Obviously, this has not helped to clarify the confusion regarding the nature and definition of the phenomenon.

The debate around who the street children are has led to the realization that this phenomenon is typical of many complex, multifaceted social issues for which no simple, agreed-upon definition exists. The multi-causal and diverse nature of the phenomenon needed to be dissected and elucidated.

Street Children: Conceptual Confusion

The problems surrounding the definition of street children may stem from conceptual confusion over how to represent this population. For the most part, these children are depicted as either victims or deviants (de Moura 2002; Cree et al. 2002).

The representation of street children as victims takes all responsibility off their shoulders. They could not have played a more or less active role in the process that led them to the street. They could not have chosen to be on the street. Rather, they are on the street because of circumstances beyond their control. In other words, any agency on the part of the children is dismissed by the victim discourse. Furthermore, the representation of street children as 'victim children' naturally assumes that their own interests are at stake by the mere fact of spending most of their time on the street (Glauser 1990). Children and adolescents are expected to be at home or attending school and not to be spending most of their time on the street, where they are exposed to different kinds of dangers: pollution, accidents, exploitation, sickness, abuse, and so forth. Equally hazardous is the fact that they work or live without being supervised by their parents. This is viewed as inadequate and contrary to their interests since the prevailing view in most cultures is that a child ought to grow up with his biological family, that is, in the presence of at least one of his parents. Even when physically separated from the family, a child is supposed to be under the supervision and protection of a responsible adult or group of adults. Thus, according to the victim conceptualization, the term 'street children' seems to point to a group of children and youth who are found in situations considered inadequate for them for reasons that they cannot help. The coining of the term responds to the need to take action on their behalf to rescue them.

When street children are represented as deviant, the concern is more about society's interests, which are perceived as threatened (Glauser 1990). The use these deviant children make of the street defies accepted norms. Instead of using the street as a channel for getting from one point to another, they openly make it their main habitat, where they make a living, eat, sleep, and engage in all sorts of reprehensible behavior. Furthermore, in appropriating a public place such as the street, they are perceived as a physical menace. The common belief that these children would do anything for survival, including committing acts of violence and assault, justifies the call for protecting the public. While some of the children's behavior may seem aggressive on an individual level, it is their very existence *in the open*, living in ways that contradict what is regarded as normal which, disturbingly, questions social and cultural patterns. Ultimately, this seems to be what is at issue, according to the deviant representation. Street children are deviations from the norm, and confront the mainstream values of society, threatening its major interests. It becomes clear, therefore, that society should take necessary measures to express public concern.

Both representations of street children, as victims and as deviants, dominate the discourses on street children and the scope of conceptualization that they elicit is obviously quite narrow. Social norms and needs, especially the need to prevent disruption of normality and mainstream interests, color the formulation of the concept of street children in both the victim and the deviant representation. As such, the dominant discourse in the literature on street children can be seen as conforming to the 'social defense' perspective presented in the previous chapter.

This reductionist conception of street children pointed to the necessity of enlarging the scope of conceptualization of street children. Early in the research undertaking, therefore, we assumed that street children could justifiably be represented as social actors who play a more or less active role in the development process of their situation and are capable of participating in the making of decisions affecting them.

Egyptian Context

In Egypt street children are viewed by mainstream society as immoral and as perpetrators of serious social violations. Their visible presence contradicts the state's ideological discourse on family values, public order, and safety. Such transgressions justify the periodic 'cleaning up' of children from the streets, arrests, imprisonment, institutionalization, and torture (Human Rights Watch 2003). Street girls are doubly marginalized in that they are viewed as blatant violations of femininity in mainstream discourse. The formal system of juvenile justice in Egypt operates under the Child Law (Act No. 12 of 1996), which defines the acts committed by youths under the age of 18 which constitute criminal offenses. These acts include begging, vagrancy, prostitution, drug use, having no stable living arrangements, mixing with other delinquents, running away from a reform institution, rebelling against parental authority, sleeping in public areas, having no legal source of income or reliable source of support, or being mentally ill. Clearly, a street child, from the legal viewpoint, is a criminal offender and a threat to social order and should be treated as such.

The Child Law provides for a wide range of court dispositions for street children, who are described as children "vulnerable to delinquency," including referral to mental health and social services, probation, and release into the custody of parents. However, the outright release of children (often to the street) or their institutionalization is the most common disposition (Bibars 1998; UNICEF 2002).

In 1993, when the PAR reported here was first initiated, officials in the Egyptian Ministry of Insurance and Social Affairs and the Ministry of the Interior did not recognize it as a phenomenon worthy of study or interest.[18] The concern expressed by certain international organizations like UNICEF and the The International Labor Organization (ILO) was trivialized in an apparent attempt to dismiss it altogether. According to the officials, there were only a limited number of children and youth to be found roaming the streets of Cairo; they were well known to security officials and the situation was under control. Many of these officials advised us not to adopt the concerns of *foreign* organizations, which they viewed as intent upon defaming Egypt.

Yet street children constituted then (and even more so now) a global phenomenon observed in large cities around the world, and Cairo was no exception. This is no surprise given that even a very conservative estimate would indicate that one in every three urban residents in Egypt lives below the poverty line. This means that in Greater Cairo, five million people are poor, and 50 percent of them are children under the age of eighteen, that is, 2.5 million children live below the poverty line and constitute a pool for generating a street children phenomenon. In Latin America the number of street children is calculated as more or less equivalent to 10 percent of this pool. Accordingly, the number of street children in Cairo could be estimated to be around 250,000.

Despite the official denial of the phenomenon, there seemed to be a general consensus that the number of street children was escalating. Yet confusion existed as to the nature and definition of this phenomenon. Futile debates around the UNICEF definition mentioned above were paralyzing roundtables and study groups. While no official definition had yet been developed, juvenile crime and/or drug abuse, child abandonment, school dropouts, child labor, poverty, domestic abuse, modernization trends, including rural/urban migration patterns, and changing family structures had all been listed as causes for the existence of street children. Each of these differing explanations indicated a distinctive response: correctional or punitive measures, rehabilitative programs, or fundamental changes in educational policies and practices, for instance.

Therefore, it was a crucial moment in Egypt in 1993 as we were on the threshold of constructing definitions and concepts regarding the phenomenon. It already seemed that social norms and needs, especially the need to prevent disruption of normality and mainstream interests, were coloring the formulation of the concept of street children.

Egyptian Research Context

Conducting any type of field research in Egypt requires an official permit, which is issued by the Central Agency for Public Mobilization and Statistics

(CAPMAS). Applicants are requested to present a research proposal, including all questions and questionnaires to be administered. In normal situations, it can take between six to twelve months before the permit is issued. Permits are not issued to individual researchers who are not affiliated with a recognized research institution.

The 'permit' is the tool used by the state to control field research. The need for control may stem from an avalanche of field research being undertaken in Egypt and other developing countries that may exceed the amount of research conducted in developed countries (after all, ethnography started in the colonies). Most of the field research undertaken for the last twenty-five years has been associated with the socio-economic development enterprise generously funded by the international community. Conducting some kind of field assessment/appraisal in order to identify needs is now incorporated as a necessary initial phase of most social, health, and economic development projects. Many of the researchers who conduct this kind of research are expatriates working or studying in Egypt.

The Egyptian state apparatus has a strong aversion and suspicion toward anything 'foreign.' This trend developed under the socialist regime of Gamal 'Abd Al-Nasser, and has been constructed within a nationalist discourse. The bureaucrats who use this discourse today are generally not motivated by ideological conviction. Instead, they exploit it as a means to usurp different profits.

More dangerously, the suspicion of the 'foreign' has been adopted and amplified by right-wing religious militants. They have developed a discourse that ascribes much of the blame for Egypt's problems to the imposition of foreign Western values on the country with the active cooperation of a corrupt regime. These values are portrayed as antithetical to Islamic values.

It is in this local context of trivialization of the phenomenon and the global confusion with respect to its definition and conceptualization that I, with others, attempted to 'do something about' street children.

How It Started
Spring 1993, Cairo

I was introduced to Dr. Samia Said, a sociologist by training and president of Social Development Consultants (SDC), a private consultancy firm. One of Dr. Said's main achievements is an action research program she instigated with the objective of organizing street food vendors in one of the major cities in Upper Egypt. We met to discuss a possible collaboration. Going over my curriculum vitae, her attention was drawn to the AR program, in which I had participated in the early 1980s in Montreal, regarding the phenomenon of juvenile prostitution. She asked me if I had thought of 'doing something' regarding the phenomenon of street children in Cairo. Dr. Said mentioned that a counterpart working for ILO had informed her that his organization wanted to deepen its understanding of the phenomenon. The 'working children' phenomenon, a priority item on the agenda of the ILO, seemed to be confused with that of street children, hence the need for a better understanding and analysis. I also learned from Dr. Said that UNICEF was also interested in street children in Egypt, as being part of the population that the organization defined as 'children at risk.' UNICEF had observed that the 'street children' phenomenon was on the increase in Egypt, and believed that the issue needed to be addressed. In short, according to informed international observers, there was a need for both understanding and action regarding a worrying and escalating social phenomenon, that of street children perceived as children at risk.

I became excited and told Dr. Said that I would be very interested in trying to do something about the phenomenon. We both agreed that an understanding of a phenomenon such as that of street children could not be developed according to traditional methodologies. A participatory action research (PAR) approach, to be applied by means of a street work methodology, struck us as a plausible option. However, I needed some time to verify the plausibility of undertaking street work in a city like Cairo.

Verification of this kind meant first identifying prospective street workers in a context in which this kind of community organizing did not exist. This, in turn, meant that street workers had to be recruited and trained. I started thinking of the young men I knew and tried to imagine which one could be qualified to go down the streets of Cairo, link up with street children, befriend them and gather information about them and their world. To my mind it had to be a young man since I was already anticipating the necessity of working odd hours, especially late evenings and nights.

It did not take long time to identify Samir as the street-worker-to-be. I explained the basic idea of street work to him, and soon we were going down the streets of Cairo on observation trips, laughing about our 'mad' idea of infiltrating the street world.

I met again with Dr. Said and started working on a tentative PAR design. In our mind it was clear that the 'action' component of PAR, in terms of achieving social change, could only be adequately conceived through the process of getting to know these children and through their increasing participation. Accordingly, the action of bringing about social change was not predetermined but was intended to be developed 'as we went along' and as our understanding of the social realities with which we would be engaged deepened, and after a comfortable level of trust was attained with individuals and groups from the street communities. Therefore, we designed a PAR project to evolve in developmental stages, with the overall objectives of:

- Penetrating street children's milieus and establishing a meaningful participatory presence, using a street ethnography methodology.
- Understanding the magnitude, underlying factors and conditions, and persistence of the street children phenomenon.
- Developing community-based alternatives to institutionalization with the individuals and groups concerned.

Our next hurdle was to obtain a permit from CAPMAS, which, as we knew, had the discretion to conclude that certain research proposals address what are commonly referred to, in the language of Egyptian officials, as "sensitive issues." In such situations, CAPMAS asks the applicant to obtain preliminary approval from the City Governor and the State Security Intelligence Department. Not surprisingly, officials labelled the question of street children as "sensitive." Fortunately, the SDC umbrella facilitated rapid acquisition of these preliminary approvals. Otherwise, the application process might have been very lengthy and might have ended with refusal.

Upon our return to CAPMAS we were asked to produce a questionnaire including all the questions that we intended to ask the street children. Our informants explained to us that CAPMAS normally reviewed research proposals that used traditional methodologies. A questionnaire, in the mind of the bureaucrat, is essential to every field research proposal. A methodology involving going into the streets, linking up with street children, establishing relationships of trust, and thus gaining an understanding of the situation of street children would be far beyond the officials' tolerance level for innovation.

It was thus deemed useless to present a research proposal articulated around street ethnographic work. Instead, Dr. Said and I decided to present a typical research proposal in which we stated that three researchers would administer a questionnaire to about 180 children. A questionnaire containing thirty-five questions was developed. Aside from demographic questions, which later helped to draw profiles of family background and places of origin, the remaining questions revolved around some of the themes and issues we thought were linked to the three research topics that we were pursuing:

- Factors that push the children out from home.
- Factors that pull them to the street.
- Factors that sustain them in the street.

Although we knew that the permit would not be issued until a year later, we decided to start work immediately. The fact that we had obtained preliminary permission from the relevant Egyptian security officials convinced us that major problems were unlikely to occur. In any case, we had agreed to conduct a kind of initial covert infiltration work, in which there was no need to introduce ourselves as researchers. We certainly had no intention of administering the questionnaire, which would serve instead as a set of guidelines for themes and issues to be investigated in an informal way.

Street Ethnography
Preliminary Observation Work

The main objective of preliminary observation work was to identify street localities where substantial numbers of children were hanging around and to find potential points of entry. The work consisted primarily of roaming around the streets of Cairo at different hours of the day and night. In our search, we followed our own prior observations and knowledge, as well as following the children in the streets. Friends and colleagues who knew of our undertaking passed on information and told us that they were surprised to observe that there were many more children on the streets than they had initially thought. The fact of keeping an open eye made us all see better.

Twenty-seven street localities were identified over a period of three months. They included strategic busy street corners, bus-stops and terminals, railway stations, public squares, markets, commercial streets, vacant lots, areas around mosques, garbage dumps, spaces under bridges, and overpasses. However, in the course of identifying these localities, we also observed a wide variety of individuals and activities. The street localities looked like living social milieus with numerous interactions, transactions, and activities, many of which we were unable to discern or grasp. In some localities, the children seemed to be actively engaged in some type of work, such as helping in a street food vending set-up, shoe-shining, or peddling goods such as paper tissue boxes to drivers at traffic lights. In other instances, the children seemed to be just wandering around, or sniffing glue, or participating in some group activity that was difficult to identify with precision. Some localities were empty by night time, whereas some children were still to be found in other areas late at night and even slept there. A review of the literature on Latin American street children had drawn our attention to the polemic surrounding the definition of a street child. We started to wonder whether some children went back home at intervals. Furthermore, many of the interactions between street children and their surroundings were incomprehensible to us. Who were these youths and the adults often found in the immediate vicinity of street children and who seemed to be involved in some kind of relationship with them?

In short, we were unable to tell on many occasions what exactly was going on. We had to contend with the fact that the answers to many of the questions and puzzles confronting us could only be revealed once we managed to infiltrate some of the street milieus.

Getting in

Faced with the question as to which street locality to use as an entry point, we decided on a place that was most familiar to the street worker Samir. It was situated in the neighborhood where he had been brought up, and where he still had good relations with influential and ordinary people alike.

The chosen street locality was strategically situated at the beginning of the Pyramids Boulevard, a major commercial thoroughfare, at the end of which are the famous Giza Pyramids. The area also harbors many hotels, as well as one of Cairo's most active red light districts (Appendix 2: Zone 1, Locality B).

We had noticed that many children hung around this locality and seemed to have relationships with the store owners in the area. One of these shops, a small grocery store, belonged to a friend of Samir.

It was planned that Samir would pay more frequent visits to his friend at the store. Hanging around and having informal exchanges with his friend and the neighboring milieu of store owners was a convenient means of conducting close covert observation of the children in the area.

A few weeks after Samir started intensive observation at this street locality, Ranya, a female street worker, was recruited and prepared to embark on a similar venture, targeting a community of street girls and women whom we had noticed in our preliminary field observation. The street locality where Ranya started working was in the busy vicinity of the Giza railway station, where children running away from Upper Egypt disembark from the train. This is a key street locality that groups of street people have been occupying for many years. This locality had the added advantage of being close to Ranya's workplace (Appendix 2 : Zone 1, Locality A).

Ranya started by approaching female sidewalk vendors, who make tea and sell flat cakes and cookies that they purchase from nearby bakeries. Buying cookies and exchanging greetings with the girls and women on a daily basis, Ranya gradually became a well-known, friendly figure.

From Observation to Participant Observation

The main objective of this preliminary phase was infiltration and establishment of relationships of trust with some street children. Conceived as 'a process of learning and acculturation,' participant observation concentrated on observing routine activities, social organizations, behavior, conversations, and events, and on identifying values, norms, power structures, and patterns, as well as learning the language of the street.

To facilitate the building of relationships of trust, Samir and Ranya were instructed not to be too inquisitive, but to display interest, care, and humor, and to create some kind of complicity over trivial matters. In short, the strategy consisted of seducing the children while leaving them eager for more of the street workers' company.

In his observation work at the grocery shop, Samir noticed that there were relationships between the shop owners and the children. Cleaning the sidewalk in front of the shops, bringing tea from a nearby café or going to change a large bill were some of the petty tasks that the children occasionally did in return for a little money. In this way, Samir started to establish contact with some of the children by asking them to buy him tea.

Being a professional athlete, Samir quickly became a sort of idol and a great deal of his early exchanges with the children revolved around sports. Ranya, being a mother herself, started sharing with the street mothers concerns and problems regarding child rearing and parenting. She noticed that the girls were interested in the way in which she applied make up and so, picking up on it, she started to give them some hints and advice.

As noted by Prus (1996), the move from observation into participant observation adds a new and vital dimension to ethnographic work as researchers come much closer to the lived experiences of the people they are studying. Thus, after several weeks of these rather superficial participation activities, some children and mothers started to tell their personal stories, interests, concerns, complaints, and problems to Samir and Ranya. The street workers became a kind of 'buddy' for some and a 'big brother/sister' for others. Some children and mothers started to compete for the street workers' attention, to the extent of secretly telling them about the 'bad' behavior and 'strange' stories of peers. From then on, participant observation started to develop toward its full potential for revealing the specifics of street life, the cultures and norms of its inhabitants, and the viewpoints and practices of the children themselves.

In accompanying the children through their everyday living in street milieus, Samir and Ranya capitalized on the use of the self as a powerful tool for mutual trust building. However, the genuine interest and care they displayed with regard to the children were accompanied by disturbing emotions that the street workers needed to manage, as will be discussed in the commentary below.

Finally, while Samir and Ranya were accessing these two street localities, observation work was also being undertaken in other areas. The children befriended by Samir and Ranya facilitated subsequent access to many of the other localities. That is to say, once trust and mutual respect had been established with the children, they became the guides to other street localities.

Reflective Commentary
Initiation of the PAR Process by 'Outsiders'

The present PAR was initiated by Dr. Said and me, two outsiders from the street milieus who had developed an interest and experience in working with marginal street populations. As already mentioned in the review of PAR literature in Chapter 1, the common claim that PAR processes are usually initiated by a group of oppressed individuals, who come together with the aim of taking action to improve their situation and to become more empowered, is a flawed claim. Actually, the majority of PAR undertakings, like the one presented here, are initiated by outside researchers/practitioners who are keen to develop ties of solidarity with oppressed grassroots communities or groups. Recognition of this reality helps to divest the PAR discourse of the utopian claim and ambition that the initiation of the research process itself comes or should come from members of the oppressed communities or groups. Many oppressed groups, including street children, have neither the capacities nor the resources to initiate a PAR process.

The association with Dr. Said and her consultancy firm SDC was also strategic. As I already noted, researchers cannot undertake field research in Egypt individually unless they are affiliated with a recognized and politically approved research institution. SDC was such an institution. Moreover, the credibility of the research itself was more likely to be accepted if at least one of the researchers had a Ph.D. Dr. Said had the additional advantage of being a researcher who was open to innovation and risk taking. Her work with street food vendors had certainly been daring and had adopted an action-research methodology that culminated in the creation of an NGO administered by the street food vendors themselves. Equally important was the fact that under the patronage of SDC it would be easier to apply and obtain grants for sustaining the process.

Recruitment and Education of Street Workers–Researchers

Many researchers have highlighted the difficulties encountered when conducting research with street children (Bemak 1996; Lucchni 1996; Kefyalew 1996). Bemak, in particular, strongly believes in the non-applicability of traditional research methods. He puts forward a new paradigm for research with street children in the specific culture of the street. Introducing the concept of 'street researchers,' Bemak (1996) calls for the integration of ethnography into the training of researchers to enable them to enter the culture of the street as novices eager to learn about street children in their natural milieu. The characteristics of the street researchers outlined by Bemak are essentially those of skillful ethnographers whose research can be used subsequently to inform the design of intervention programs.

Although I fully agree with Bemak regarding the value of including ethnographic skills in the training of street researchers, it does not in itself constitute a new paradigm. Bemak's main concern is for the integration of practice and research, which he views as a "formidable task" (Bemak 1996, 147). He recommends that street researchers assume responsibilities not only as research agents but also as "social change agents." The latter role involves a clear explanation of the research findings, their implications, and their practical application. For Bemak, the social change that can be produced by street researchers resides in their ability to produce and interpret results that can be helpful to program administrators and policy makers (Bemak 1996, 155). Notwithstanding the importance of informing and influencing policy making, we are still within the boundaries of traditional research paradigms and policies that are formulated in a top-down fashion.

The approach advocated in this book regarding research and work with street children is different, in both form and content, from the paradigm presented by Bemak. Instead of viewing research as an activity that takes place prior to the design of practice/intervention programs and where street children are the research subjects, the plea made here is to involve the children themselves, not only in the research process, but also in the design and administration of intervention programs. In my view, many of the methodological difficulties and challenges mentioned by Bemak cannot be overcome as long as the children perceive that they are subjects in a research project over which they have no control and from which they do not receive any immediate benefit. The numerous occasions on which the children described to us their frustration and anger with researchers and journalists who approached them for the sole purpose of gathering information, lends credibility to the plea for a genuine participation by the children themselves.

In recruiting and training Samir and Ranya, and later the other members of the team of street workers, it was clear in my mind that they were to assume both street work and research tasks. Hence, they were to be equipped with both intervention and research skills within a PAR framework.

All these considerations, as well as the lack of a street work tradition in Egypt, made us aware of the importance of carefully recruiting, training, educating, supervising, and coaching street workers. Indeed, the selection of street workers itself required a great deal of caution. Many people volunteer for this kind of work because they feel sorry for street children and want to help them. Individuals who have such feelings often encounter problems once they start working. Depression is the most common consequence, as workers become overwhelmed when they imagine how sad and desperate they themselves would feel if they had to face the adversities of the streets. Well-meaning individuals who do not understand and control their feelings may actually harm the children they wish to help by strengthening the children's feelings of exclusion and making them feel helpless. At the other end of the spectrum are individuals who perceive street children as outcasts or juvenile delinquents, rather than as social actors who are surviving under very harsh circumstances. Individuals who view the children as criminals do not last long on the street. Their fear or disregard for street children prevents them from working effectively. I had previously experimented with recruiting laypersons and training them to assume the same tasks as professional development workers. Over a three-year period (1990–93) I was responsible for designing and implementing a comprehensive training program in 'Methodologies for Community Organizing and Community Development' in four governorates in Upper Egypt. The idea of this program was to strengthen local development work, not through the traditional manner of parachuting in foreign/outsider development experts, but through identification, recruitment, and training of local leaders. Their training started by promoting their increasing involvement in their own communities in taking the lead to identify, in a participatory fashion, a community concern that needed to be addressed.

While participants were involved in fieldwork under my supervision, regular meetings with the large group (participants from the four governorates) took place to share experiences and analyze problematic situations that had been encountered. In these meetings, the focus was on sharpening the participants' critical analysis skills while injecting theoretical references corresponding to the issues and concerns they had encountered in the field. Their lived experience in the field made it easier for them to relate to theory in a critical manner and thus avoid the trap of 'going by the book,' a mistake which is characteristic of so many development programs. Not only were the participants able to be critical of development theories, but they also, and more importantly, felt free to innovate and experiment. In a sense then, they developed their own practice research and theories.

At the time, I was not then aware of Donald Schön and Chris Argyris' work, who strongly argue that research and theory need not necessarily precede practice in a linear and deductive fashion (Argyris & Schön 1974; Schön 1983, 1987). Instead, they maintain and demonstrate that people's practical experience can be used to produce theories inductively through a process of reflecting on that experience. It was only in 1997 that I discovered their work, when I first registered in the doctoral program. I was pleasantly surprised to recognize the similarity between the reflective and experiential learning approach that they make a plea for and the one that I used with the rural local leaders and, subsequently, with the street workers. The cyclical process in which systematic 'reflection on-action' and 'in-action' attempts to integrate theory and practice was quite similar to the method that I used in the regular group meetings. In discussing and analyzing uncertain and complex situations they had encountered in the field, participants were actually engaged in identifying contradictions and theoretical assumptions implicit in their work, in dissecting the various perspectives for interpreting situations in their field context, and in articulating the basis for their intuitive actions, their meaning and impact, as well as the inevitable ethical dilemmas that they raised.

Paradoxically, when I started making reference in 1997 to the reflective approach developed by Argyris and Schön, my own experimenting with training community and street workers became more credible in the eyes of many scholars, researchers and practitioners, though not in the eyes of the bureaucrats at the Egyptian Ministry of Insurance and Social Affairs (MISA). They insisted that intervention with street children should be implemented by accredited social workers. The street workers' lack of professional accreditation was one of the main justifications provided by MISA for dismantling the program in 2001.

Lastly, I want to specify that, starting with Samir, the recruitment of street workers relied on informal networks. Samir was the son of one of my friends and I had numerous occasions to observe him in different settings. Likewise, it was Samir who introduced Ranya into the project, and through snowball recruiting both of them subsequently introduced additional street workers. The recruitment procedure included a voluntary (unpaid) period of two to three months during which the candidates were observed by me and their peers in actual street work situations. The main criteria used for the selection included the following:

- Tact, manners, and general attitude favoring the establishment of contact and developing relationships.
- Aptitudes and non-judgmental attitudes favoring the involvement with street children in an empathic fashion.
- Familiarity with and/or having access to some street milieus.
- Motivation for street work.
- Self-confidence and the ability to be self-critical.
- Ability for active listening, clear expression, functioning in a group, negotiating, advocating, and dealing with authority.
- Ability to have a critical view on social realities and issues.

I have frequently been asked why I recruited laypersons and invested in educating and training them to become street workers and researchers instead of resorting to accredited social workers. In both Montreal and Cairo it was difficult to identify social workers willing to go down the streets and link up with children in their life settings. It seems that for a great majority of social workers, this kind of activity is not consistent with a professional view of what social work is.

The Children's Manipulations and the Workers' Acculturation

On a practical level, it was necessary to appreciate the physically and emotionally demanding nature of direct, day-to-day street work. The workers were relating not only to the children, but also to their surroundings and the street community as a whole. These included a wide variety of street adults who, in some capacity or another, influenced the daily existence of street children: natural leaders, police informants, street food vendors, tea makers, security agents, street employers, grocery and coffee shop owners, shoe-shiners, commercial sex workers, and others who were part of the children's surroundings in the streets. Although many children were forming attachments with individual workers, the workers began to realize that such gratifying relationships could also be very taxing if they were not adequately managed.

Further complicating the situation was the tendency of the children to manipulate. Presenting untrue, well-rehearsed stories about experiences, family background, current situation, age and reasons for leaving home is often well integrated into the behavior patterns of street children. This misrepresentation seems fundamental to survival and is related to an ability to manipulate the environment. The street worker becomes another facet of the environment that the children must successfully maneuver in order to survive. There are other reasons why the children manipulate information: it allows them to get back at a society that devalues them. Falsified information also serves to keep society from knowing the details of their lives.

Consequently, street workers had to learn to accept a degree of 'healthy manipulation' from the children, who were seeking to maintain a sense of control. This also facilitated the development of a relationship between the child and the street worker based on the child's terms and not just the worker's.

Moreover, there is a delicate balance to be observed by street workers, who not only have to maintain professional integrity and identity, but also to be versatile enough to move comfortably in the street child's domain without trying to become one of the children. There is a danger of 'false acculturation,' whereby street workers over-identify by assuming cultural characteristics that are unnatural for them. All of the above required the maintenance of a high level of engaged support and self-investment.

Infiltration and Ethics

Maurice Punch (1986, 1994) maintains that 'infiltration' is a key skill in field research methods, despite the fact that this concept/technique is fraught with negative connotations and associated with police and espionage techniques. At many of the public presentations I have given over the last ten years on our work with street children, objections have been made to the use of the term 'infiltration' to describe the strategy of accessing the street milieus. Disdain has often been expressed at the analogy between a scientific endeavor and an intelligence methodology, one that is viewed as being one of the uglier aspects of repressive state conduct. Upon closer verification, the objection is often based on ethical and moral concerns that argue against deception and for the fully informed consent of the research subjects. The objection is even stronger in PAR where subjects are supposedly viewed as participants/partners, thus "to dupe them in any way would be to undermine the very processes one wants to examine" (Punch 1994, 89).

The issue here is whether *covert* research is ethical or not. The debates over the covert-overt issue in the literature are far from conclusive. While some writers totally reject covert participant observation, others argue that without it many street-style ethnographies would be practically impossible to undertake. In my view, the choice of when and how to resort to covert participant observation has to be consistent with the research objectives and the methodology used, and must always be guided by principles related to the dignity and privacy of individuals, the avoidance of harm, and the confidentiality of the research data. In other words, "sound ethics and sound methodology go hand in hand" (Punch 1994, 95).

I would like to elaborate on this covert-overt dilemma using the example of the PAR presented here. Had Ranya or Samir from the outset revealed to the children that they were involved in some kind of research aimed at understanding their situation, it would have been impossible for them to establish relationships of trust with the children. Although it may sound contradictory to say that the establishment of trust necessitated concealment of the research agenda, this was the case in this particular situation. Continually harassed by security agents and passersby, regularly picked up and maltreated by police, and always suspected of different crimes, street people are understandably cautious and suspicious of inquisitive intruders. Introducing oneself as a researcher or data collector would have elicited enough mistrust to subvert the establishment of a meaningful and sustained relationship with the children. Furthermore, most street children are not spontaneously enthusiastic about telling their *true* stories to outsiders. These stories are sometimes the unique thing over which they may have some control. Understandably, they do not wish to readily relinquish this control to satisfy those questioning them.

Furthermore, in the case of PAR presented here, the concealment of the street workers' identity, both as practitioners and researchers, was necessary in light of the uncertainty regarding the development of the PAR enterprise. During this initial phase, there was no guarantee that we would be able to identify and obtain the necessary funds that would have enabled us to make the switch from research *on* street children to action and research *with* them. Indeed, we were eager not to elicit unrealistic expectations on the part of the children; had we not been able to move further in the work, the promises of PAR presented to the children would have been the source of major disappointment.

Invisible Others: The Gatekeepers

Prior to infiltration work, we had hypothesized that street children did not live on the streets in a bohemian or individual way. Rather, we assumed that in order to survive, most children would join some kind of group or street organization in which the leaders might not welcome outsiders poking their nose into their affairs. As such, we expected that the children contacted by the street workers were being observed and had to inform their peers, as well as the leaders, about what was going on. A non-obtrusive form of infiltration was deemed necessary in order to avoid a rapid rejection by the milieu, providing another reason for being covert.

This hypothesis required the street workers to be very careful about how they presented themselves, the impressions they gave and the questions they asked. The leaders had to be neutralized. In addition, the state security agents and informants, who were bound to be mingling with the children and their surroundings, had to be taken into account. They, too, had to feel that we were benign for them to let us proceed with our work.

These 'invisible others' were thus the 'gatekeepers' who had to *authorize* and not hinder our access to street milieus. Being invisible meant that our messages to them regarding who we were and what we were doing had to be conveyed indirectly through the children and the street individuals with whom we established contact and relationships.

Managing Emotions
Fear and Prejudice

During early participant observation work, our fear had to be acknowledged—fear of violence, of being ridiculed by the children, or of looking stupid, and certainly the fear of being unable to handle sensitive situations that might suddenly arise on the street. We realized that many of our fears originated in the stereotypical mass fantasy about the wildness and havoc of street life and the belief that street children would readily, for the sake of survival, commit violent acts. We had to remind ourselves constantly not to let these prejudices exaggerate our fears and unduly immobilize us.

Later, as the work progressed, many of these prejudices were challenged. Most of the violence takes place in-group and is directed against members of the group, seldom against outsiders. The crimes committed by street children are of a petty nature; for example, stealing hanging laundry and goods in marketplaces. Contrary to widespread belief, over the eight-year duration of the program, no evidence emerged tying these children to terrorist groups, as is often assumed.

We also needed to come to grips with the repugnant appearance of many of the children. Barefoot, wearing shabby and dirty clothes, most had black dirt on their faces, arms, feet, and on every exposed part of their bodies, which were often also covered with scars. Their fingernails were quite long and full of dirt. It was difficult not to feel unnerved after shaking hands with them, and as the closeness of the rapport with them increased, so did the physical closeness so characteristic of Middle Eastern societies, which further intensified our feeling of discomfort.

However, this initial apprehension dissipated gradually as the development of a closer rapport with the children made us less disturbed by their physical appearance. Subsequently, we found out that most of them enjoyed and appreciated personal cleanliness. Access to water and washing facilities were indeed some of their main problems. Interestingly, we also learned that the black dirt on some children's bodies was self-administered, using mud. They resorted to this practice while they were begging, hoping to elicit enough disgust among prospective donors so that they would contribute some change hurriedly in order to get away from these 'filthy young monsters.' Furthermore, we came to appreciate that long fingernails are kept for defending oneself against assault.

Later, when the drop-in center was opened, the street workers felt no hesitation about helping some of the younger children to shower. Periodic hairdressing of all the children and application of medicated lotion became a regular practice in order to minimize hair lice.

Witnessing Destitution

During this early participant observation work, one of the most tormenting issues that we had to handle was our feeling of being incapable of providing much help regarding some situations of utmost destitution and misery facing young children. I still recall one late winter night when we met two girls holding hands and going around parked cars trying to identify a convenient sleeping spot. The older girl, who was seven or eight years old, told us that they had to sleep under a car so that they did not get picked up by the police. Under her arm, she was holding a piece of cardboard to use as a mattress for her and her younger sister, who was crying desperately. "She is very tired and wants to sleep," said the older sister, who looked exhausted and pale herself. She nevertheless made the effort to explain to us that they had fled from a police raid on nearby 'Ataba Square earlier in the evening, where their mother had been arrested. We knew that an urban upgrading plan was about to be implemented in the area of the square. This, as is often the case, was accompanied by the eviction of street people, who had managed to eke out a living and make a kind of habitat around this busy square for many years, surviving by selling tea, soft drinks, and food to travellers waiting for buses at a main terminal located in the vicinity of the square. The dilemma for the older sister was that she did not really trust sleeping under a car. She was worried that she might not notice if the car started moving and that it might run them over. It was getting late and cold when it occurred to us to ask the doorman of an apartment building if he would let the two girls sleep in the building entrance hallway for a few hours. To our relief, he agreed.

Later, in my warm bed, I was thinking of the strong desire that I had felt to bring these two girls home, to make them safe and comfortable and to accompany them to look for their mother the following day. Such situations occurred repeatedly afterwards, and we had to learn to acknowledge the limits of our ability to help.

Concluding Commentary

The action research with Cairene street children was initiated by two researchers who had previous experience of action research with street populations. The preliminary/preparatory phase encompassed the following:

- Establishing an alliance and association with a like-minded researcher, Dr. Samia Said, and the institutional framework, SDC, which she headed, in order to bring support, credibility and legitimacy to the projected PAR.
- Designing a PAR that would evolve in developmental stages. The design needed to be easily adjustable to be able to respond to the evolving analysis of the situation 'as we went,' and as the emergence of new data, and the increasing participation of different actors fed into the process.
- Recruiting individuals and training and equipping them 'on the job' with the skills and knowledge necessary to carry out an ethnographic investigation of Cairene street children.

- Working out the intricacies of how to obtain approval for our activities from the relevant Egyptian authorities in a context that did not encourage the undertaking of such research.
- Conducting observation work in the streets of Cairo in order to identify street localities where street children were to be found in substantial numbers.
- Covertly infiltrating, researching, and establishing a meaningful and sustained presence in several identified street localities.
- Overcoming our fears and prejudices.
- Resisting the discouragement of colleagues, friends, and families who warned us that we were embarking on a 'difficult and dangerous' mission.

It took over two years to accomplish the above, to acquire an adequate understanding of the phenomenon of street children and to establish a comfortable level of complicity between the children and the street workers. The acculturation required to achieve this necessitated a long-term self-investment.

This beginning phase of the PAR can be seen as street ethnography undertaken with a view to preparing the ground for a PAR to develop progressively. As such, this phase consisted of research *on* street children. The participation dimension was focused on educating and enabling street workers to become practitioners-researchers and, consequently, increasing their participation in the design, implementation, and monitoring of the different activities. The explicit participation of the children was not possible as long as the work was being conducted covertly. As we shall see, the progressive participation of the children started when we 'came out' to them and revealed our hidden interest in supporting them through a PAR process aiming at their empowerment. I will describe the evolution of this process in Chapter 5. But before continuing the story, I propose first to present in the next chapter the conceptual framework that I developed with the group by analyzing the data observed and collected through street ethnography.

Introduction to carpentry at the drop-in center. Photograph by Naji Zahar.

Many of the children, including girls, are interested in sports and athletics and display a marked sense of body awareness. Photographs by Naji Zahar.

Music, singing, and dancing are
constant features of street culture.
Photograph right by Naji Zahar.

Access to clean water, hygiene, and health services at the drop-in center are greatly appreciated. Photograph left by Naji Zahar.

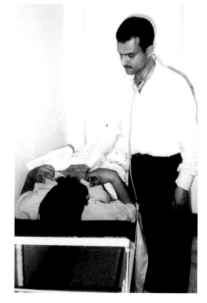

4

Conceptual Framework

I present here the sense we made out of the data gathered through observation and participant observation, which constituted the bulk of ethnographic street work that was implemented over the beginning phase of the PAR process described in the previous chapter. The collection and analysis of the data recorded in field notes and critically reflected upon, culminated in the formulation of what is tantamount to a conceptual framework that informed the orientation of the PAR presented in this book. Obviously, given the processual nature of this PAR, this framework, once formulated, did not become a rigid structure. On the contrary, it had to maintain certain flexibility in order to accommodate the new data and new perspectives that kept feeding into the process as we went on. Indeed, observation and participant observation were ongoing activities throughout the project's eight years as we moved into new street localities and as we came to establish a rapport and relationships with additional children and individuals in the new settings. However, after more than two years of street ethnographic work and before the opening of the drop-in center, we were able to formulate the essentials of the framework presented below.

Who is a Street Child?
Street Children: A Diverse and Heterogeneous Phenomenon

When I ran away, I ended up in Ramses square in the middle of crowds of so many people. I was very afraid and I kept going around the railway station looking at people selling all sorts of things. Time went by very quickly and suddenly it was night. I was getting hungry, I had no money. I was standing close to a beans sandwich stand when suddenly I felt the hands of two other boys on my shoulder. I knew they were 'sees'[19] and they were my age or a little older. They asked me what I was doing there. I told them my story and I found good buddies in them; they brought food and we sat and ate together and we became good friends.

(Male, 12 years old)

I take the pills and sniff glue so I can live in another world and don't want to remember anything. The other day I swallowed a big amount of pills. I hurt one of the children with a broken bottle right in his eyes because he takes the money the other children make; and many times I hurt myself so that policemen let go of me.

(Male, 13 years old)

Sometimes I feel there isn't any need for me in the world, and that the people like me must die because the others always make us feel that we are dogs, not human beings.

(Female, 11 years old)

I feel that I will always be 'sees,' I will not change. Nobody will stretch his hand to me and tell me to go and work with him. People are afraid of me, of the way I look and of my clothes. I am nineteen now, no work and no place to live; how shall I be when I reach fifty?

(Male, 19 years old)

I am unlucky in this world. If I had good father and mother, I would be like the other girls; but I feel I am less than other people.

(Female, 15 years old)

I am good because I help my mother and father and brothers with the money I make from begging. It is better that I work instead of my mother taking to the street.

(Male, 10 years old)

Thank God I consider myself good person. I go back home when I feel like it, and I don't need money from my parents. I know how to talk to anybody and my friends love me.

(Male, 14 years old)

I feel I am better than all others. I look nice and am very happy living in the street.

(Female, 14 years old)

One of the early lessons learned from participant observation was that the term 'street children' is deceptively simple and conceals enormous variations in the lived experiences of the children, who spend most of their time in street environments. Indeed, the 'street children' phenomenon does not encompass a homogenous group of problem children with the same essential characteristics. The fact of being on the street over an extended period of time is certainly an important criterion that distinguishes the street child from other children. However, this shared condition is insufficient to distinguish street children as a particular social category.

Individuals included under the street-child rubric display a great diversity. They range in age from new-borns to eighteen-year olds of both sexes; they are often intermingled with young adults of both sexes. In some cases it is the parents who send them into the street to make money for the family's upkeep, and in others they work alongside their parents in the street. Some are forced into the street by parents who cannot afford to support them, while others leave on their own to escape abusive treatment by their parents, stepparents, or the owners of the workshops in which they were forced to work. Some children beg or do menial work; others work in the informal economy. Some live almost full time on the street whereas others are there for varying periods of time. Some have dropped out of school, and others resort to the street to make money during school breaks. Some are of rural origins, others are from urban settings. Some are relatively sedentary, knowing little of the outside world, while others move from place to place, from city to city. Intelligent and mentally healthy children live alongside those with a variety of disabilities. This mix is made even more heterogeneous by the presence of different personalities, life trajectories, bodily characteristics, gender, family, and cultural backgrounds.

This apparent diversity led us to pay less attention to the production of a universal definition and/or identification of categories and subcategories, the major concern of policy makers and many academics. We realized that efforts needed to be directed toward capturing the diversities within the phenomenon in order to avoid an approach that defines street children *ipso facto* as problems. As with many problems related to marginality, what is visible does not correspond to what really is the case. An in-depth understanding of an issue such as street children needs to be 'dug out' in all respects, moving from a superficial analysis based on mere numbers and descriptive data to an analysis of what goes on in the lives of street children and in their surrounding environment.

Notwithstanding this diversity, homelessness and street life share a number of important features. Living on the street, a public place *par excellence*, not only strips individuals of their right to private and personal space, it also exposes their miserable life conditions to the public gaze, arousing pity, disgust, horror, and/or disapproval. Ultimately, street populations risk becoming viewed as the epitome of social degradation (de Moura 2002, 353). Furthermore, survival on the street requires a presentist attitude and the abandonment of any orientation toward the future. When survival concerns become a moment-to-moment reality, dividing and ordering time to plan for a future comes to be viewed as a futile exercise. And the multiple facets of the mechanisms developed for survival (that is, how people learn to live with minimum resources) do not in the least attenuate the fact that street children are confronted with conditions of life and existence that are often very painful and which endanger their psychosocial development.

> I think I am a good person. The problem is with people who look at me in a bad way because I wipe cars and sniff glue. What can I do? I sniff glue precisely to forget the way they look at me.
>
> (Male, 16 years old)

Capturing some of the Diversities

The street ethnography experience confirms the inadequacy of definitions of street children limited to presence in the street and absence of rapport with the biological family (as is the case with the UNICEF definition). Indeed, the bi-dimensional definition of street children fails to take into account many other factors such as age, sex, and factors directly related to the family of origin, (for example, its composition, mode of organization, the quality of family ties, and economic conditions), as well as factors directly related to the street. Let us examine some of these factors more closely.

Age

Misconceptions and confusion arise when the population in question is homogeneously referred to as 'children.' Indeed, in addition to children, it also includes adolescents and young adults. Obviously, the need to distinguish between different age categories is important in many respects. For example, the vulnerability associated with living in the street differs in degree and form according to age. The comparative advantage and survival mechanisms enjoyed and elaborated by a street child differ from those of a street adolescent or adult. For example, begging and eliciting people's affection are easier for younger individuals.

Furthermore, the reaction of families of origin to their runaway children often varies according to the age of the runaway. Likewise, mainstream society's view of the street individual varies according to age: children may be perceived as victims whereas adolescents and young adults are more likely to be categorized as deviants, delinquents, or criminals. Lastly, from a legal perspective, the age of the street individual determines the way in which he is treated when arrested by the police.

Gender

Last week I saw a girl sitting in the nearby garden. She was crying. I asked her what was the story. She told me she had just run away from home because her mother's husband beats her, maltreats her and wants to marry her to someone she does not want. I walked with her and introduced her to other girls who hang around in the vicinity and asked them to take care of her, I left and as I walked down the street a taxi driver who had been observing us approached me and told me he had a nice place where we can take the girl and share her for the night. I refused of course because this is not what I do; all I wanted was to help her.

(Male, 16 years old)

While there are many fewer street girls than street boys, their numbers are not negligible. We did not observe much difference in the deviant socialization patterns to which boys and girls are exposed in the street. Drug consumption, group rituals, and violence are not the preserve of males. Even commercial sex activities, which are commonly believed to be the girls' means of survival, are witnessed among males as well, though perhaps to a lesser degree. Furthermore, boys who do not act tough are often ridiculed by peers. It is the risk of pregnancy that distinguishes the situation of many girls when they first become sexually active. The specific vulnerability associated with unwanted pregnancies is particularly hazardous in traditional societies like Egypt.

The very human existence of female children is negated by conflating them with prostitution. This assimilation often serves bluntly to dismiss the existence of street girls altogether and has been observed in different countries (Beazley 2002; Van Beers 1996).[20]

Length of Time in the Street

The length of time of being in the street varies a great deal among street children. We met with individuals who were trying to make a habitat out of the street for the first time, others who had been in the street for a few weeks or months, and many others who had spent most of their time in the street for many years. There seemed to be no clear correlation between the length of time in the street and the decision to end a street career. Furthermore, we met with individuals who decided to quit street life many times, returned to their families of origin and/or found a regular job, only to return to the street a few weeks or months later. There seems to be no precise rule governing this movement, which may depend on opportunities and coincidences, rather than prior planning. However, this does not mean that street children are incapable of striking a balance between the advantages offered by the street and its alternatives.

Nature of Ties with Family of Origin

My parents divorced and they both remarried. My father used to beat me up all the time. So did his wife and she used to send me to buy things for her. I started begging and gave the money to my father's wife. This made her very happy and she would leave me alone for a while . . . I left my father and went to live with my uncle who used to send me out begging saying he has no money to take care of me . . . I then went to live with my mother but her husband did not want me there. When I went back to my father, he beat me with an electric cable. I ran away and have been in the street since then.

(Female, 16 years old)

Many of the children we met came from families where both parents had divorced and later remarried to spouses who also had children from a previous marriage. The children did not live permanently with one family member but alternated between their mother's new family and their father's new family, and sometimes lived with a grandparent. The lack of space, an often conflictual relationship with stepparents, as well as harsh economic conditions, often caused the child to disengage gradually and join the street. In other words, the lack of a stable residence following the divorce of the parents, maltreatment by the stepparents, fights and jealousy with half-siblings, and the fact that the child became a source of dispute between the parents of origin all contributed to the child running away to the street.

Many other children belonged to single-mother families, where the father had divorced the mother and remarried, was in jail, had died, or had just disappeared. Usually the mother had not remarried and had several children. She often encouraged and arranged for some of her children to work as apprentices in workshops or just go to the street to beg or hold menial jobs in order to increase the household income. In other cases, the mother herself went to the street with some or all of her children in a desperate attempt to make a living. As the children grew up, they gradually became independent of their mother and the street became their major habitat, even if they continued to visit and/or bring some income to the family.

It is my mother who forced me to work at the workshop because we are poor and have no money. My father left my mother many years ago and there is no contact between them. If I don't obey my mother, she beats me up.

(Male, 11 years old)

My mother made me work in a leather workshop where I used to work from nine in the morning till seven at night. The owner of the workshop used to beat and insult me. He gave my mother LE15 every two weeks. But now I wipe car windows, make LE15 per day and nobody bosses me around.

(Male, 15 years old)

The nature of ties with family of origin plays a major role with respect to the prospect of ending street life and returning home. We found that the vast majority of the children who disengaged from street life temporarily or permanently entertain more or less good and healthy ties with at least one of their biological parents, especially the mother. It was quite rare for street children to return to homes where a stepparent lived.

Patterns of Working in the Street

In the street, the day is mine. Nobody beats me and I smoke cigarettes and take pills freely and I make good money from begging and wiping car windows. When we wake up and have some money with us, we go right away to have breakfast. If we have no money left from the day before, we go begging to get the money for food. After that we go to the coffee shop for tea and watch videos. Around sunset, we go by microbus to buy pills and when we get back we take them and have fun together and go around the places we feel safe.

(Male, 14 years old)

After breakfast, each one of us takes off to make some living begging or wiping cars. Some bring back food, others bring cigarettes and glue. And sometimes we go under the bridge by the waterfront to bathe and then we make good money by harassing young, loving couples so they buy flowers from us.

(Male, 13 years old)

We observed two broad categories of street children, differentiated accord-ing to patterns of income-generating activities. The first category consisted of those who were runaways and engaged irregularly in income-generating activities. For these children, work and play were closely linked. Work was not an obligation but usually a choice made by a child individually or by a small group of children. Periods of inactivity on the street alternated with periods of sudden intense activity in which children took chances or created opportunities. For the majority of these children, the street seemed to be a source of liberty. It enabled them to take initiatives; it was stimulating and a place of apprenticeship in which they could learn about people, social life, and behavior. However, many of these children also had ambivalent feelings about street life. Although the street is appropriate for all kinds of activities, street life is sometimes repetitive, boring, a source of danger, or the target of adult criticism.

For a second category of children, income-generating activities are a daily and regular part of their street life. These youngsters arrive in the street not as runaways, but are forced out into the street by their parents or guard-ians to work in order to increase the family income. Once again, there are significant differences in the realities of these children. Some work in the street under the supervision of one or both parents. More often than not, it is a mother who resorts to the street with a group of her children in order to make a living by begging or itinerant selling. At the end of the day or night, some families may return home or spend the night on the street. Other children are placed by their parent under the authority of a street entrepreneur, who employs them in return for some remuneration paid directly to the parent. Some children are sent out on their own by their parents, but more often by a stepparent, and are expected to return home with a minimum amount of money. Failure often entails punishments of varying types and severity. Some children work after school and during vacations; others work every day. Whereas a surprising number manage to go to school, many do not, and attendance by those who do is in most cases so sporadic that they never really become literate.

It should be mentioned that the boundaries between the two categories of children described above are not impermeable. Children from the second category can pass to the first one and vice versa at any time. Even though the alternation is not systematic, a great number of children we encountered were in either category at one time or another. Moreover, regular income-generating activities do not prevent many children from getting involved in recreationally and socially pleasurable activities.

Other factors that are directly concerned with the street include preliminary contacts that the kid may have had with individuals who know the street; conditions of access to the street; the initiation rites into the street culture; the insertion of the child into a street milieu; the representation that the kid makes of the street; survival opportunities in the street; police repression and internal group violence; the degree of identification with the street culture; the degree of resilience of the individual child and his ability to cope; the degree of insertion into the informal sector of the economy; forms of street sociability and socialization; and contacts with crime.

All of the above-mentioned factors are interdependent, and their possible combinations are numerous. These combinations and the nature of the factors that constitute them either enhance or inhibit the street child career. Appendix 1 provides profiles of some of the children we came to know in order to illustrate the diversity in the trajectories that led them to the street as well as the diversity in street life circumstances and styles.

In the foregoing, I argued for the necessity of recognizing the diversity in the children who are found on the street. I have described this diversity mostly in terms of individual differences with respect to the trajectories that lead them into the street as well as the lived experiences on the street. However, the kid in the street is not just an individual being, he is also a collective being, which is the focus of the next section.

Contextualizing the Phenomenon of Street Children within Street Societies

The difficulty regarding consensus building around a universal definition of what constitutes a street child is related to the fact that most efforts have focused on street children as if they existed in isolation from other street populations and arrangements. Early observation work indicated that for the most part, street children do not live on the street as isolated individuals. To be able to survive in the street, one has to establish some form of paternal/family relationship, which may be strong though informal, to improve one's chances of survival. Thus, most of the time street children associate with other children, adolescents, and adults of both sexes in 'groupings' that can be viewed as street milieus and communities, and which we coined 'street societies.'

Accordingly, any understanding of the street children phenomenon is inadequate to the extent that it fails to dissect the nature and dynamics of the relationships existing in street communities. Furthermore, contextualizing the phenomenon of street children within the broader phenomenon of street societies—in which the children are viewed as social actors able to cope and survive under circumstances that most of us would find unbearable—would pave the way to representing the street child as a cultural entity, which cannot be reduced only to a definition articulated around the prefix 'anti-'—anti-social, anti-productive, anti-moral, and so on.

It is within the context of street societies that the socialization of deviance in the street takes place and influences the identity construction of street children. Therefore, in order to capture the entirety of an individual's life in the street, we need to elucidate the organic daily ties the individual maintains with surrounding street milieus.

The Street as Habitat

Street societies refer to social groupings composed mostly of youngsters nested in the heart of a metropolis in an area that geographers call 'the central business district,' where there is a concentration of the most important economic and political activities, as well as the most intense real-estate speculation. Street children also occupy space in the principal markets, red light areas, commercial districts, and main transport terminals, that is, where there are large agglomerations of people and activities, and city life is at its peak. While it is quite common to describe these groupings as 'marginal,' the fact that they live and occupy central city districts requires an explanation of their marginal status. If marginality does not refer here to remote geographic boundaries, the question to be answered is: in what ways are these street groupings marginal?

The street, as we came to see it through participant observation and accompaniment of the children, is composed not only of physical space, but also of mental, personal, relational, and cultural space. Street populations are the world of those who have set themselves apart from conventional society and exist outside accepted social rules. The street is the space shared by the 'drop-outs,' the 'runaways,' the 'jobless,' the 'homeless,' the 'judicialized,' the 'addicts,' and many of those identified as 'marginal.' They constitute a population that is at the edge of the continuum of human existence. By sharing the street they make it their home, their school, their job, and their culture. It is in the street that they live their fears, their anguish, and their revolts, as well as their friendships, passions, and loves. In this sense, the street is certainly a place for different forms of significant socio-cultural expression.

When occupied by street people, the street, as a public space, becomes a space for a certain intimacy and visibility where a different form of social rapport is expressed and collective representations are forged. This more or less open consumption of the street, the ultimate public space, by children and other populations can be conceptualized as an open act of resisting exclusion. Let me explain.

The act of occupying the street and making it a habitat is one of transforming parts of a public place into 'territories' for multiple usage including sleeping, working, socializing, and recreational activities. As such, it is an act that defies public order. However, it is also, and mostly, a political act. By holding onto these territories and continually resisting eviction and relentlessly re-occupying spaces, street people are interpellating society. By making their exclusion visible in the public place, street people are *de facto* resisting their exclusion.

As such, contrary to widespread belief, the street is neither a vacuum nor a place of complete ruin and everlasting damnation. Instead, the street can be conceptualized as a space for socializing, a field of adventure, pleasure, difference and novelty, as well as a space for solidarity, and identification with peers. It is a place for passage and fleeing, in which one can exercise some power over oneself and the environment. It is also a place where survival requires endless rounds of negotiations with different sources of authority. Obviously, there are disadvantages to street life, especially for children. Unable to secure their basic needs, many of them often have to resort to different means to survive, such as prostitution, begging, theft, selling drugs, and other illicit activities. These activities obviously have repercussions, such as being at odds with the legal system, exploitation, malnutrition, deficient health, and social exclusion.

By occupying a public space (the street), which is officially regarded as devoid of any positive forms of socialization, street children come to be perceived as threatening, and as a consequence, repressive and violent measures are taken against them. The central issue here is that these young populations create a new use of space and time, and new rules of sociability and exchange, as well as new representations of their bodies and their relations to their environment. This new form of socialization is characterized by the absence of official control over these youngsters and the absence of positive interactions with the world of mainstream adults. Street socialization creates a lag between what the street youngsters live and believe on the one hand, and what mainstream society generally claims to offer the child on the other.

Lastly, I want to point out that the diversity in the different street territories created by street populations does not only reflect the different uses they make of the street. These territories also often reflect different subcultures and organizational modes. Appendix 2 provides some profiles of different street territories to illustrate this diversity.

Having captured some of the diversities in the realities of street children and street life, it became quite clear that the answer to the question "Who is a street child?" was bound to include as many variations as those observed in this population. It became necessary to identify a theoretical framework that provided an adequate lens for reading and pursuing the analysis of the various realities of street children. A return to theory proved worthwhile in identifying such a lens, as I elaborate below.

Theoretical Considerations

In his review of the literature on street children, de Moura observes that in most discourses they are depicted either as victims whose basic rights are violated or as deviants with deficient characteristics. He argues that this depiction fits well with a representation of street life "as the outcome of an organic and linear chain of adverse factors including migration, economic hard-ship, family dysfunction, and child abuse" (de Moura 2002, 353). Indeed, this dominant discourse in the literature is informed by causal theories to identify pre-existing factors that explain why children end up on the street. One can further argue that by naming poverty and family dysfunction as the main factors that produce victims and deviants—street children—this discourse fails to explain why the vast majority of children brought up in poor dysfunctional families do not end up on the street. Furthermore, this discourse blurs the question of the *agency* of these young actors since it only recognizes it in a negative sense when their representation as 'independent adventurers' is associated with deviancy.

The diversity in the street-child phenomenon includes the processes that lead and sustain the children in the streets, which are variable and complex. In other words, there are no necessary or sufficient conditions that create and/or maintain the street-child phenomenon. Instead, a number of alter-native, interacting conditions seem to contribute to the phenomenon, as a function of a number of contingent conditions. As such, the concept of linear causality that maintains that we need to know the causes in order to act seemed to have little operational value for us when we were grappling with the material collected through street ethnography.

We needed a conceptual tool that could help us to unravel the diversity of 'causal paths' in the lives of street children, and one which could accommo-date the view of the street kid as a cultural entity, a social actor who cannot be reduced to a mere 'deviant' or 'victim' of structural processes. The agency of the children through self-generated processes needed to be recognized, as it often helps to alleviate the weight of structural determinants. In short, we were looking for a lens to help understand not so much *why* but *how* these children ended up on the street, what they made out of it, and how they became socialized into deviancy. To this end, we turned to the concept of 'career' developed by the sociology of deviance.

Deviance as Career

Socialization processes that do not conform to mainstream values and take place within deviant and less institutional contexts, such as the street, have been relegated to a sociology of deviance, which has traditionally reduced the concept of deviance to a consequence of social disorganization, social pathology, and delinquency (Becker 1964; Lemert 1972; Spector and Kitsuse 1977). From this perspective, deviance is conceived as a mere detachment from orderly currents of social life, societal values, or social bonds, and as a phenomenon that needs to be controlled. Shaw and McKay's *Juvenile Delinquency* (1942) is a classic in this tradition. Within this school of thought (the Chicago School), street children are often represented as antisocial, foot-loose vagrants. Most discussions depict them as victims or delinquents and project deterministic notions of disaffiliation (Aptekar 1994).

The late 1950s and early 1960s witnessed the emergence and growth of a new sociology of deviance led by Howard S. Becker (1963, 1964), Erving Goffman (1959, 1961, 1963), John Kitsuse (1964), and Edwin Lemert (1951, 1972), whose work constitutes what has come to be known as the New Chicago School.

Whereas the members of the older school, who were focused on the deviants, concerned themselves with the structural causes of deviance and believed that deviance led to social control, the new school, built on symbolic interactionism, was focused primarily on the social construction of deviance.[21] Within the interactionist approach, it is assumed that human beings are actively engaged in the creation of their worlds of experience by acting according to the meanings that objects (including other people and themselves) have for them (Blumer 1969). They construct and shape these meanings through interaction with others as well as through self-reflectivity. Viewed as a community phenomenon, the study of deviance from an inter-actionist perspective puts the focus on the processes by which: some phenomena are defined as deviant; individuals and groups become identified as deviants; deviants become involved with, develop, and sustain subcultures;[22] formal and informal control agencies attempt to regulate deviance; and some deviants attempt to disengage from a deviant career (Prus 1996).

According to this theory, the socialization of deviance is understood in terms of 'career' or 'natural history,' a concept that includes the growth/trans-formation of 'identity,' based on a series of experiences of self and others (Goffman 1959, 1961). Essentially, the concept of career refers to the pro-gression of related experiences and identity changes through which the actors move in the course of their involvement in particular settings over time. It directs attention to the 'processual' nature of this involvement in terms of the ways in which the actors become initially involved in any situation, when they are more likely to continue, how they become disengaged from those settings, and when and how they might become re-involved in earlier pursuits (Prus 1996). Equal attention is paid to the contingencies the actors take into account as they work their way through these different stages.

'Stages' and 'contingencies,' the two main features of the concept of career, are useful analytical devices for investigating the processes of the socialization of deviance. Composed of objective status elements, social reactions, and conceptions of self, the concept of career sheds light on the interdependence between identity, socialization, and career. Its value lies in the fact that it provides a two-sided perspective that shifts back and forth between the self and significant others; it *dialectically* relates the actor's self-image to the social identity derived from interaction with surrounding social groups. A career study is thus an analysis of this dialectics in terms of the socialization processes through which an actor acquires the language, the values, and rules of conduct of a certain culture. The actor continually interprets the experiences lived within these processes by attending to the accounts of others. In Goffman's words: "The concept of career, then, allows one to move back and forth between the personal and the public, between the self and significant society, without having to rely overly for data upon what the person says he thinks he imagines himself to be" (Goffman 1961, 127).

The socialization of deviance in the street can be sorted out by following the children's socialization, based on the theory of social interactionism mentioned above (Lucchini 1996a, 1996b). The notions of career and contingencies provide a coherent way to focus on the processes of choice and the development and transformation of the actors' identities as they move through the stages of a street career (Visano 1993). Indeed, a child does not become a street child overnight but through stages of gradual detachment from the household, as well as the gradual forging of a street identity. Although an extended period of street life may be an important factor distinguishing the street child from other children, it is insufficient to designate street children as a particular social category. Therefore, research efforts need to be directed toward capturing the diversities within the phenomenon in order to avoid an approach that defines street children *ipso facto* as problems. These diversities can be dissected by charting the child's movement from home to street, as well as by identifying the contingencies related to the different stages of this movement.

The contemplation of departure from home, the preparation for it, experimenting with it over a period of alternation between home or institution and street, establishing some permanence in the street, building relationships, acquiring new skills, negotiating role and status with peers, developing and changing identities, going through periods of disconnection from the street, and the contemplation of giving up street life are some of the elements that constitute a street-child career. It can be argued that each of these elements corresponds to a certain stage in the street career and are associated with specific contingencies related to conditions and consequences of interactions with others. These conditions may include, for example, the strategies used to ensure recognition and acceptance of self, the reactions of others, the ways in which the actor manages and seeks out supportive relationships, and the ways in which identity is established and sustained.

Furthermore, the movement through career stages is contingent upon the interplay of a number of situational and subjective conditions, including the benefits and costs of street life, the nature of the relationship and ties with the family of origin, the actors' survival skills, and the availability of survival opportunities, the degree of resilience of the actors, their age and sex, the nature of attendance to the reactions of others, the degree of identification with street groups, the degree of integration/disintegration of the street group, and the ability to establish non-street contacts and relationships.

To summarize, in the face of a rather overwhelming diversity in street children, the concept of career developed by the sociology of deviance helps to capture the meaning of this diversity. It makes it possible to go beyond the dominant conception of a street child as victim or deviant to see these children as social actors able to survive under circumstances that most people would find unbearable. While the concept of career does not prescribe directives for intervention with street children, it does provide insights for practice.

Implications for Practice
Preclusion of Universal Rescuing Approaches

There is a prevalent assumption that the provision of various resources for street children will easily divert them from street life and cure them of their delinquency. This is the main assumption behind many intervention programs with street children, which are implemented with a view to 'rescuing' them from the misery of the street. However, this assumption fails to recognize the fact that the vast majority of street children are socially, economically, and culturally embedded in the intricate fabric of street societies.

There are at least two problems with the dominant rescuing approach. Firstly, because of their past experiences, many of these children are wary of adult authority in general. Not having the protection of a family, school, or village, their autonomy becomes the precious something that belongs to them. They should not be expected to give it up readily.

Secondly, to a great extent, the rescuing mentality requires that street children forget, if not repent, their deviance in the street. The general underlying assumption of the rescue approach is that street life cannot be anything except detrimental to the children's well-being. This assumption is reflected in the attitudes of the 'rescuers' and elicits the resentment of those for whom the street may have some positive meaning. Street children are apprehensive of attitudes that tend to trivialize their lived experience in the street. Asking them to be resilient in pursuing a non-street career—without appropriating their past street life—not only negates the meaningful relationships that they may have developed, but it also dismisses the value of the skills that they may have acquired, as well as their experiences and the lessons they may have learned.

What street children have in common is the *distinctive culture of street life*, which possesses its own logic and articulates its own normative value claims. While internally consistent, the latter are often antithetical to those adopted by mainstream society. In other words, the culture of the street is often difficult to reconcile with dominant values, and mainstream interests do not necessarily match those of street children. For a reconciliation to happen, it needs to be critical. By this I mean that the responsibility for reconciliation cannot simply be placed on the shoulders of street children. Indeed, the mere existence of street children interpellates the societal institutions concerned with childhood on the one hand, and questions the authoritarian guardian, the school, or the workshop from which they run away on the other. The failure of these institutions to keep an increasing number of children off the street ought to be a source of concern for policy makers and researchers.

It should be stressed that the nature of street life requires participants to engage in behavior that differs to such an extent from values and forms of 'acceptable' behavior that it often elicits coercive correctional and punitive approaches, even when undertaken under the guise of rehabilitation. Not surprisingly, successful rehabilitation is rarely achieved. Therefore, it is not a question of 'curing' the juvenile delinquent. Rather, social intervention should aim to offer the street kid the opportunity to explore voluntarily other venues of socialization and become involved in other forms of sociability.

The Challenges of Intervention

A major feature of 'good intentions' programs is their inflexible resolve to take the children off the streets by any means, at any cost, and as fast as possible. Those who do not cooperate with practitioners to facilitate family reunification or institutionalization are usually classified as 'hopeless cases,' 'hard-core,' and/or 'chronically delinquent,' and they are often deprived of services and care. Many of the children who do cooperate return home or join an institution and resume street life shortly afterwards. Practitioners remain perplexed and discouraged when faced with families who are not very keen to reunite with their runaway offspring. The sober and sometimes uncomfortable fact is that for many children, the street is often a better place than a home that may be nothing more than a tin roof covering a variety of forms of abuse. The successful cases of children reuniting with their families of origin often involve children who would have returned home anyway since they could not adapt to street life. Repeated failures in achieving family reunification or institutionalization for the great majority of 'seasoned' street children often make practitioners feel discouraged and burnt out.

While family reunification is certainly a noble objective, it is important to recognize that just as children do not become street children overnight but go through a process of joining the street, they abandon their street careers only through another such process. Temporary disconnection from street life is a common feature among many of the runaway children and adolescents we came to know and accompany. The length of these breaks can be a few days or weeks or sometimes as much as a month or two. Longer breaks usually reflect serious consideration and an effort to disengage from street life. Yet the children often return to the street, either because they were unable to negotiate an improvement in the pushing factors that led them to run away in the first place, or because they found it difficult to abandon the close and relatively stable friendships and relationships with their street peers. The stronger the sense of identification of peers with one another, the greater the bonds that unite them. Specifically, the smaller the street grouping, the less likely street children are to jeopardize their street life. These bonds do not disappear quickly, given the emotional dependency that characterizes group relations.

Accordingly, the challenge of intervention with street children lies in the ability to acknowledge the agency these children display in joining street life and the meanings the street has for them on the one hand, and simultaneously offering them supportive accompaniment and the opportunity to enlarge the scope of their socialization through non-formal education on the other hand.

Importance of Sustained Support, Accompaniment and Non-formal Education

By rejecting the uncritical use of correctional and/or rehabilitative approaches, as well as family unification as the primary objective of intervention, not only do I emphasize the importance of socio-educational actions, but I also contend that the most urgent need of street children is the promotion and protection of their basic physical, mental, and social developmental needs and rights rather than removal from the street per se. This can be achieved through genuine social support and accompaniment in their daily street existence.

The special relationships of trust that street workers build with street children—whose experiences with adults and mainstream societal institutions have for the major part been negative—not only demand the investment of a considerable amount of time, but also a *sustained, meaningful,* and *participatory* presence in the street milieus where these youngsters live. It is through such a presence that 'intimate familiarity' with ongoing community life is achieved, and that street children, both individually and in small groups, come to realize that there are adults who genuinely care for them.

Disengagement from a street career, as already mentioned, takes place through a process of identity transformation and reconstruction, which is more manageable when support from significant others is perceived as trustworthy. Street children need to appropriate their street career before plausible alternatives can be developed with their active and voluntary participation. To help with the emergence of a new self-concept, the role of the street worker is to accompany children through this process, without exerting excessive pressure to hasten the disengagement decision. Experience has shown that hasty and poorly planned decisions only result in repeated failures.

Sustained support and accompaniment work, coupled with constant dialogue, non-formal education, advocacy activities, and dealing with the problems of the children's everyday lives entails a process of education for life. By the same token, it provides the vehicle for a re-socialization process whereby the scope of the context in which street children develop mentally, socially, and culturally is widened. Only then can these children consider reconciling with a society that they perceive as hostile and rejecting. And only then can alternatives to institutionalization as well as means to support voluntary withdrawal from street life be envisaged and planned for in a participatory manner.

Capitalizing on the Strengths of Street Children

To proceed with PAR, it was not enough to join in the social situations of the street children and remain confined by the role of researcher—as in many participatory research projects—contending with a sympathetic accompaniment through the risks and hazards of the street. For accompaniment work to be meaningful and engaged—that is, to go beyond participatory research into PAR—it was necessary to try, with the active and voluntary participation of the actors involved, to change their situations for the better. For this to happen, the actors needed to be 'confirmed' in their capacity as agents of change in their own lives. Therefore, we had to discover and recognize in accompaniment work, not only the 'delinquency,' hazards and risks to which they had been exposed, but also the abilities, skills, talents, and strengths they had acquired through street socialization and that had been occluded by mainstream representations, depicting them as 'helpless victims' and/or 'hopeless delinquents.'

In mainstream society, institutions such as the family, school, mosque, or church are the agents of socialization. In street societies, socialization agents for street children and youth are mainly their peers and the surrounding adults. In the street, children and youth are rarely on their own; most of the time, they are affiliated with and in the company of others in what constitute milieus of living. Unlike mainstream children who grow up in a safe and protective family environment where basic needs are fulfilled, street children and youth grow up in situations that impose constant demands for coping and adjustment. Not only do they have to fend for themselves, they also have to adapt continuously to what are often unpredictable, uncertain, or threatening circumstances. The situational demands of street life necessitate the development of specific skills in order to increase chances of survival. The development of such skills culminates in the acquisition of both cognitive and instrumental competencies:

Cognitive Competence
- Observing and learning about others.
- Recognizing and interpreting risky and dangerous situations, making a pertinent judgement, and acting accordingly.
- Knowing which posture, attitude, and language to use in different situations (impression management).
- Learning and creating coded languages, gestures, and so on.
- Learning, respecting, and benefiting from street rules and culture.
- Possessing thorough knowledge of public space, including suitable refuge and/or sleeping spaces, different resources, and so on.

Instrumental Competence
- Creative use of public spaces by converting them into places for work, life, recreation, refuge, and so on.

- Capacity to give off, foster, and manage impressions with the aim of controlling the reactions of others, provoking favorable responses, and acting accordingly. For example, street children and youth know how to elicit compassion, guilt, fear, or terror, as well as to handle any contingencies that may arise.
- Elaborate management of gesture and wording to simulate a handicap.
- Capacity to negotiate identity and a repertoire of different life stories.
- Elaboration of different survival strategies and use of the most appropriate strategy, according to the situation.
- Ability to organize in small groups by developing sophisticated forms of cooperation and solidarity, as well as setting rules for the group to follow.

Apart from cognitive and instrumental competence, for many of the children, the act of leaving home (or an institution) and living in the street is in itself an empowering one since it often offers emancipation from oppressive institutional and parental structures. This factor is notoriously absent from the majority of discourses on street children, and whenever we mentioned it we were met with bemused looks. However, in seeking and finding relative freedom in the street, these children often become autonomous and are capable of actively defining their situations in their own terms, of challenging the roles assigned to children, of making judgements, and of developing a network of niches in the heart of the metropolis in order to resist exclusion and chronic repression. In short, many street children and youth are already actors actively engaged as agents of change in their own lives. As self-reflecting beings, they can and do direct, monitor, assess, and adjust their own behavior over time (that is, they exhibit human agency). Accordingly, the role of street workers is "to recognize them as agents in the transformation of reality, through a constant dialogue which gives priority to their participation in the whole process" (UNICEF 1987).

Capitalizing on the strengths of street children and youth was part of our discourse, further situating us in opposition to the dominant rescue and behavioral modification approaches, in both their correctional and rehabilitative versions. It also meant that the PAR process sought not so much to empower street children and youth as to discover and valorize their strengths and build on them to engender enhanced empowerment and emancipation. With this aim in mind, we designed a rather broad strategy of non-formal education, coupled with soft and collective advocacy.

In this chapter, I paused to reconstruct the PAR process that I began to describe in the previous chapter, with a view to presenting the conceptual framework that was developed according to the data obtained from street ethnography. In this framework, the dominant representation of street children as victims and deviants is rejected in favor of one that recognizes their capacity for intentional and meaningful activity, that is, their capacity for human agency, as well as their awareness of self as an object, that is, self-reflectivity. Furthermore, I highlighted the observed diversity in the phenomenon and argued that this diversity precludes the dominant single-model approach to practice based on rescuing the children.

Let us now resume the reconstruction of the PAR process.

5

Continuation of the Story

In this chapter I resume the reconstruction of the PAR process that I began in Chapter 3, in which I described the technical and political goals that needed to be accomplished during the first phase of 'getting in.' Ethnographic street work constituted the essence of fieldwork undertaken during this phase. The socio-political act of going onto the street, infiltrating street milieus, and developing relationships of mutual trust and acceptance with street children and their surroundings involved, as we saw, bridging a formidable gap between a mainstream society and a 'deviant' society. The construction of the necessary bridges for this operation was facilitated by the implementation of a non-obtrusive and carefully designed street work methodology. This allowed us to access marginalized and dissident street children in the very context of the street organizations and milieus in which they were active actors. The building of non-threatening identities and relations of solidarity was the first task that had to be undertaken in order to develop reciprocal trust and respect.

In establishing a meaningful, participatory, and sustained presence in the street milieus frequented by the children, the street workers were able to develop accompaniment relationships that were not exclusively, or necessarily, 'help-oriented.' Instead, the objective was to develop rapport and relationships that were basically ones of acceptance, trust, complicity, and solidarity, created by the repeated sharing of the ordinary, warm, and tender gestures of everyday life: laughing together, seeing each other in different situations that might even be ridiculous, allowing the other to live and express different emotions, playing and having fun, contemplating, creating, going for walks, joking, and allowing the other the right to live a crisis, to express disappointment, fear, suffering, and a desire to die. As such, the primary role of street workers was to offer their 'being' through the use of self in a sustained participatory presence in the everyday life of the children they came to know.

It was through this kind of participation that the street workers were covertly observing behaviors, informally interviewing and collecting accounts, which gradually added to our understanding of the realities of the street children and the milieus in which they live. In Chapter 4, I presented this understanding within a conceptual framework that highlighted the agency the street children displayed in managing the matters of their lives in order to go beyond the view of them as victims and deviants.

Equipped with this understanding, we pursued our fieldwork with the primary objective of increasing the children's participation by inviting them to join with us in a PAR enterprise, which I describe below, beginning with the opening of the drop-in center.

Opening the Drop-in Center

Preparing for the Drop-in Center

In our plan, the setting up of a drop-in center was intended not as a substitute for street work, but as a physical structure to serve as a landmark or point of reference for a concrete community mobilization, with the aim of advocating improved well-being for street children. Accordingly, the focus in the drop-in center was to be placed on capitalizing upon the strength and skills of the children and widening the scope of their socialization, not on removing them from the streets. The plan did not include the design of a well-defined program. We wanted the center to develop step-by-step with the active participation of the children. Therefore, it was necessary to adopt a flexible approach, open to constant reevaluation, and accommodation of changes.

I had explained to the street workers that the introduction of a drop-in center in the context of a street work program usually took place after establishing relationships of mutual trust with children, youth, and key members in the targeted street milieus. They had registered the information, but when the time came for action, they wanted to know the objectives of the center and the specifics of its operation. My non-specific answers and insistence on a step-by-step approach and the impossibility of foreseeing its exact development—to take place with experimentation and increasing participation of the children—left them worried. One of their main concerns was how they could present such a vague idea to the children. I suggested that we ask the core group of children, those we had come to know best, whether the idea of having a place where we could meet was appealing to them. A spontaneous answer from one of the children was, "Do you mean a club?" From then the drop-in center was always referred to by the children as "the club."

We had expected that floating the idea of a drop-in center would incite the children to ask questions regarding the sources of its funding. It was therefore time for us to come out to the children and divulge the hidden agenda behind our hitherto covert practice. The anticipated questions did come up, and our identities as action research practitioners were disclosed— our practice became overt. What facilitated the disclosure was the fact that many of the children were familiar with the only other NGO in Egypt that targeted street boys. These children were aware of the existence of donors that fund NGOs to help disadvantaged populations, and they communicated their understanding to peers and surrounding adults.

In order to establish the drop-in center, we needed to identify a suitable location and prepare the neighborhood for the arrival of the 'young devils.' Given the overwhelming housing crisis in the city of Cairo and our meager financial resources, we could only afford to rent an apartment. We wanted it to be situated in the vicinity of the Giza railway station, a key street locality where we had established good rapport with street children and surrounding adults. This was also the area where both Samir and Ranya had grown up and continued to live. They were thus well acquainted with a small neighborhood in the vicinity of the station, where, through their personal contacts, a small apartment (about thirty square meters), consisting of two rooms, a kitchen, and bathroom, was identified and rented. The apartment was situated at the street level of a six-story building inhabited by about fifteen middle-class families. The owner, the father of one of Samir's childhood friends, promised to let us use the building's courtyard (about forty-five square meters), which was accessed through the kitchen and had been used as a garbage dump.

Many of the children participated in the cleaning and renovation work, which lasted for almost three months. After removing three-meter-high piles of garbage from the courtyard, we found that two walls, at each end of the courtyard, were constructed adjacent to the courtyard fence. Roofing the area between each of these two walls and the fence would provide two additional rooms which would be dearly appreciated. We thought that one of these rooms could serve as a clinic to dispense medical and health care, which would be particularly welcomed given the difficulties that the children had experienced in trying to gain access to public dispensaries and/or hospitals. Being a visible minority, the stigma that they carried usually elicited maltreatment, if not refusal of access altogether. The harsh living conditions in the street made street children particularly vulnerable to many health hazards: skin diseases, respiratory infections, sexually transmitted diseases, and various types of injury were quite common. Accordingly, we recruited a nurse and two medical doctors, one male and one female, just before opening the drop-in center in April 1997.

After signing the lease and starting the renovation work, it became imperative to explain to the neighborhood what we were preparing, since many neighbors who saw the children coming to help were quite bewildered and upset by their presence. Ranya and Samir approached key, influential figures in the neighborhood to explain the 'project' that was about to be implemented. These included the barber, the carpenter, the mechanic, the ironer, and owners of other small businesses. The wealthy and charitable businessman, a couple of schoolteachers, police officers, and other professional neighbors were also among the individuals approached. Samir gave special importance to sensitizing the young men in the neighborhood, knowing that traditionally they were among the most hostile toward street populations and that they were keen to keep the neighborhood streets 'clean.'

We were aware that most people in the neighborhood would not easily welcome the street children. We expected them, like the majority of the public, to have an averse attitude toward the children, generally viewing them as a nuisance to be avoided. Therefore, in introducing the project, we had to present it in terms that would forestall possible rejection. To the people of the neighborhood, the project was presented as a welfare initiative to give a helping hand to these 'poor' children and to try to reunite them with their families. In so doing, the strategy was to capitalize on a deeply cherished value in Egyptian society, charitable assistance, which is also an obligation in Islam. Although this strategy may seem contradictory to PAR ideals, it was not possible at that stage to present the project as a PAR undertaking. Any reference to the objectives of community organizing with the street children, let alone their empowerment, would have sounded too revolutionary, if not 'crazy,' in this conservative middle-class neighborhood where activism, except for the forceful fundamentalists, was not welcomed. Our strategy was first to facilitate the infiltration of the children into the neighbourhood and the drop-in center, then gradually work toward changing the negative image of the public.

Start Up

At the beginning, the center was open two days a week for girls and another two days for boys. We were aware that this separation was artificial in light of the fact that in the streets, boys and girls did not lead separate lives but were intermingled in the social fabric of the street milieus. However, we were reluctant to have boys and girls together at the center since we knew that this would attract severe criticism in the Egyptian traditional context. Nevertheless, we opted to assume the responsibility of, once more, threatening the status quo and a few weeks after the opening, we started implementing an open-door policy for both sexes and all ages.

During the first three months of operation, the center's main activities consisted of preparing meals, using shower and laundry facilities, chatting with the children, playing some social games and light sports, and watching television. The drop-in center offered a suitable space for street workers to meet with the children who wished to talk privately about different concerns and/or problems. It appeared to us that many of the children who came to the center felt free to act like spoiled children, making us realize how much they missed and needed care and love. Obviously, the harsh circumstances of survival in the street do not permit this pampering, yet the moment the children were released from caring for themselves, the child in them surfaced and demanded care and unconditional love. This was characteristic of all age brackets that came to the center from children in their early years to youths in their late teens and early twenties.

We were surprised by the reluctance of the majority of the children to go to the clinic and consult the doctors, even when they were in need and in pain. Their few previous experiences with medical personnel had been enough to make them dread seeing a doctor. However, when a street worker with whom they had formed a special attachment offered to accompany them, they accepted and their fear gradually dissipated. The two medical doctors and the nurse we had recruited also managed to establish trust with the children by engaging with them in social activities outside the clinic.

During informal exchanges with the children at the center, we started to discuss with a core group some of the logistics regarding the operation of the drop-in center. These included the center's days and hours of opening, as well as some rules of conduct. We expressed our concern that consuming drugs on the center's premises jeopardized its very existence, and we also said that we did not think that it was the appropriate place for this activity. The children overzealously suggested forbidding drug consumption, and some of them even proposed quite strict measures to ensure respect for this rule, as well as punitive actions to be applied to the offenders. It was agreed, however, that through the cooperation of all, the no-drug consumption rule would be observed. Indeed, no one consumed drugs at the center. However, many of the children used to arrive already 'high,' after having their regular dose. And although fighting was also prohibited in the center, fights erupted as often as they erupted in the street, except that in the center there were adults from the mainstream watching, and they were called upon to judge and referee. Competition to get the special attention and care of the workers rapidly became a major dynamic.

The Participation Challenge

The observations described above made us realize the immense challenge that participation, as a problematic process, represented. When people with different power, status, culture, influence, and facility with language, as well as different personal, intellectual, political, and interpersonal abilities, come together in a PAR undertaking, the notion of participation becomes very problematic. We could not install democratic participation just by wishing it, permitting it, or ordering it. We realized that it needed to be incorporated into the PAR process as an objective to be pursued and reflected upon continuously. In other words, democratic participation, like other PAR promises, is an ideal toward which we could strive only through a process of dialogical exchanges, experimentation, and reflection. This meant that the ultimate responsibility for managing the center and the overall PAR process needed to remain ours while we were working toward its gradual diffusion.

Accordingly, participation at the drop-in center was initially to take place largely in the form of information sharing and consultation. However, we were keen to initiate, simultaneously and selectively, a process of closer participation with a core group of natural leaders and older children who were coming to the center. We shared with them some of our puzzlement and questioning, discussed more extensively what we were trying to do together, drew visions and dreams for the future, and identified potential challenges and obstacles. In short, we were trying gradually to involve them in a process of individual and collective reflection.

We started delegating some responsibilities and tasks to this core group of children. These included buying food, preparing and serving meals and tea, taking care of the younger children, cleaning the premises, delivering messages, answering the phone, assisting in recreational and drawing activities, and coordinating the children's access to the clinic. Not surprisingly, there were repeated failures on their part in meeting their commitments. We were determined not to let these failures, often heavily taxing and discouraging, make us give up and consequently fuel their negative self-image. As we learned to expect setbacks, we strove to manifest our unflinching commitment to these young leaders, just as a parent does not give up on a child who makes mistakes, exhibits poor judgement, or lies. Sustained support was paramount in the development of reflective and critical capacities.

In thinking about the repeated setbacks, we became aware of the challenges posed to individuals when they assume a different role. In assuming responsibility for some task at the center, individuals not only needed to learn new technical skills, to be present on time, and to be alert and cooperative, they also needed to deal with an emerging new identity, not an easy undertaking. These situations were further complicated by the reactions of peers, who often made it difficult for the leaders to perform their tasks adequately and often did not cooperate with them. Competition, jealousy, rivalry, provocation, and setting malicious traps between peers and within the group of leaders assuming responsibilities in the center were all forms of behavior that contributed to repeated fall-outs and setbacks. As we reflected on these dynamics, we realized that these repeated failures in assuming tasks and responsibilities were as much the outcome of a sort of collective sabotage as an outcome of the individual's deficiencies. The emerging new identity associated with the assumption of leadership roles outside the street context posed a threat both to the individual and to the individuals surrounding him or her. Therefore, we needed to deal with these repeated failures both at the individual and group level.

At the individual level, it was very important, as already mentioned, to continue supporting the children who 'failed' in the chores they had taken on at the center in order to avoid the trap of a self-fulfilling prophecy of marginality and uselessness. As Lemert (1972, 64) aptly remarked:

Awareness of unenviable features of the self is a complex rather than a simple reciprocal of societal insult to identity, and, further, adaptations can turn into maladaptations on the person's own terms. This comes to light when efforts at validating the self are complicated by distinct feelings of hopelessness, entrapment, or loss of control over actions presumed to be volitional. These can be observed in certain forms of deviance best described as self-defeating; their peculiar, illogical manifestations speak of underlying difficulty or dilapidation in the communication process by which self and other are constituted.

Therefore, we never gave in to statements such as: "You have done your best with me. Thank you, but I am sort of hopeless." It was important not only to tell them that trial and error was a basic right, but also to attend to the identity problems associated with the re-socialization process.

At the group level, interrelationships between groups were · oriented toward a mode of mutual accountability in order to promote a strong collective sense among the participants. The ensuing group-to-group discussions went beyond the organization and division of labor to grapple with issues related to values, beliefs, attitudes, and lifestyles. Under the general theme of 'how we are going to organize ourselves for a better being,' we were actively encouraging and promoting the development of dialogical relationships. This allowed for the consolidation of a group reflection practice and the sharpening of critical thinking and analysis, which, it must be emphasized, were already prevalent among many of the children. It was thus relatively easy to have participants engage in a reflective process of reviewing their realities, discussing alternatives for change, and suggesting advocacy actions to improve their situation and achieve further empowerment.

In ending this section, I want to mention that six months after the opening of the drop-in center, the municipal authorities, accompanied by a force of about eighty armed policemen, arrived one morning to enforce a court order to demolish the two rooms that we had built in the courtyard, on the grounds that their construction contravened municipal regulations.[23] Watching the demolition operation, we were all in a state of shock. Then the authorities left, leaving behind the rubble and ruins. As the feelings of sorrow and discouragement were becoming overwhelming, a couple of children started to clean up. We all followed and the spirit generated was so high that we worked all night removing the rubble through the tiny apartment out onto the street. If I mention this incident, it is to highlight the wonderful survival capacity of the children. We learned a lesson from watching the 'coolness' and pragmatism displayed by the children when faced with a situation of this kind. As well, we were quite happy to observe that the children were tidying up the center with the zealousness and enthusiasm that people display toward a place that is dear to them.

Progression of Non-formal Education

As already mentioned, during the first three months of operation, only a limited number of activities took place at the center as we were waiting for the children to express their desire for other activities. The opportunity to introduce some educational activities came about one evening when some children were playing *Monopoly*, which they enjoyed since it involved the use of simulated banknotes in large denominations. In this game there are instructions and orders to be read at each move. One of the children was fed up with calling on one of us to read the instruction cards. He said that he wanted to learn how to read. We took his wish seriously and offered to teach him. A couple of other children said that they too wanted to learn to read and write.

I was somewhat reluctant to start a literacy class immediately since none of us had any relevant experience. However, the children and one of the street workers were very impatient to start. Upon their insistence I briefed the street worker on the basics of the Freirian literacy methodology (Freire 1970, 1973). This method is based on teaching letters and composing words in a way that is particularly meaningful to participants (in this case, the word 'glue,' for example). At the same time, the participants engage in a 'liberatory dialogue' around the composed words, their meaning and the values they project. We bought pencils, notebooks, and a tiny blackboard, and the first literacy class started with four children.

As I watched the worker and the children in the improvised classroom, I noticed that the created learning environment was very much colored by the sincerity in the personal relationships between the 'educator' and the 'students.' The educator was not a teacher they only saw at school. He was also the street worker who went onto the streets and joined them, that is, someone with whom trust and complicity had been established prior to embarking together on a learning adventure. I was quite struck by the splendid creativity displayed by both the street worker and the children. They were enthusiastically engaged in identifying the means to facilitate the mental retention of the different letters by associating them, for example, with shapes of familiar objects. The master-servant relationship inherent in traditional education seemed to be replaced by a subject-subject relationship. Further, in the dialogues around existential issues evoked by the words that they composed, the children felt free to break through the limits of meaning construction, thereby moving from limitation to infinite possibilities. In other words, the learning relationship was a creative space in and by which a multiplicity of truths were constructed, enabling individuals to recreate themselves, while at the same time redefining their relations to others. It dawned on me that both teacher and students were collectively dismantling the rigid distinction between learning and creativity that characterizes the mainstream definition of education. The basics of non-formal education were all there in a non-intimidating, supportive, inspiring, and collaborative environment.[24]

At the children's request a painting activity was introduced in a similar fashion. Some children who were fond of drawing with colored pencils and crayons wanted to experiment with painting. A board member who was a painter brought brushes and paints to the center and showed the children how to prepare the colors and use the brushes. She sat with them doing her own painting and looked encouragingly at their first attempts, giving some advice every now and then, but avoiding a didactic fashion. We wanted them to express freely whatever they wanted, and they did. It was surprising to see some of the children spending hours silently painting, and seeming to enjoy it tremendously. Some other children would paint only sporadically, and many others gave it a try for a couple of times but never got really into it.

Gradually, a wide array of cultural, educational, sportive, and recreational activities was introduced within the framework of a non-formal educational approach that acknowledged the realities of street life in a safe and useful way. All the activities were introduced step by step with the active participation of the children, who suggested, planned, and managed them. The activities that developed through experimentation and flexible adjustments included painting, gymnastics, karate, table tennis, storytelling, collage, theater, sewing, percussion, stick dancing, social games, literacy classes, computer, beadwork, woodwork, carpentry, and watching educational videos.[25] The street workers were acting more as 'facilitators' than as 'instructors,' always involving the children in developing ideas and in decision making. The relatively large number of participants led us increasingly to rely on reciprocal teaching between the children. This method was an integral feature of their relational modes in the street, and we certainly capitalized on it rewardingly.

At another level, participation in activities that were more vocationally oriented, like sewing and carpentry, allowed the identification of those who were particularly talented and wished to develop their skills. They were accompanied to other programs and workshops that had more sophisticated facilities and training programs. In other words, the objective of the activities at the center was not to set up a comprehensive vocational training program, but to offer the children the opportunity to experiment with elementary vocational skills, which helped to identify talents and dispositions that could be further developed at the individual's request. We simultaneously identified a number of workshops where some of the children could be hired as apprentices. We selected these workshops according to criteria that would guarantee that the children would be treated humanely, be housed conveniently, not work endless hours, learn a vocation, and be allowed enough time off to pursue cultural and educational activities at the drop-in center. Many of these workshops were located in the vicinity of the drop-in center, and the street workers knew their owners. To motivate these owners, we offered them a modest grant to be paid in installments to help them in renewing their premises or acquiring a new tool. More importantly, we signed a contract with them stipulating all the above-mentioned conditions and, obviously, there was close follow-up by the street worker. The children who were referred to these workshops had to be fourteen years old, the legal age for employment.

Another function of the center emerged a few months after its opening when an increasing number of parents and/or relatives started coming to ask about children. It is common in Egypt to see parents whose children have run away or got lost, going down the streets where there are large numbers of street children and looking for their own. As the center and the street workers became known to many people in street milieus, they started directing many of these parents to the center. Sometimes, the parents or relatives arrived at the center and their children were actually there. On other occasions, we knew the children they were looking for or could find out where they were by asking their peers. Whenever this happened we seized the opportunity to mediate between the runaway and his family, while making sure to safeguard the best interests of the children by paying friendly visits to the household. It was during these visits that we came to realize why many children kept running away from home to the street—it was often safer and less exploitative than the home.

Collective Soft Advocacy

Under the title of 'The First Painting Exhibition by Children and Young People of the Egyptian Association to Support Street Children—The Front Line Street Intervention Program,' the Minister of Social Affairs, Dr.

Mervat El Tellawy, opened the exhibition on the thirtieth of November, 1998, at the British Council in Cairo, where it was open until the fourteenth of December. It was then shown at the British Council's branch in Heliopolis from the sixteenth to the twenty-third of December. The presence of the young artists at the opening of the exhibition and their welcoming the Minister of Social Affairs and the other guests definitely had a very positive impact. The minister and the guests took time to exchange and discuss with the children about their paintings, personal lives, and circumstances.

The exhibition has so far attracted an audience of more than three hundred people, including painters, movie directors, NGO representatives, businessmen, international donors, ambassadors, journalists, TV and radio presenters (including the BBC who reported the event on its Arabic and English stations), and social workers, who were impressed by the artistic value, originality, and bold colors of the paintings. Mr. David Marler, the Director of the British Council, wrote in the Council's newsletter, "The Link" (January, 1999), that the exhibition was 'one of the best-attended exhibitions we have had and an inspiring occasion.'

As a touring exhibition, it has been shown at a recently opened downtown art gallery, Townhouse, from the fourteenth to the twenty-first of January. It will be also shown soon at the British Council in Alexandria, and it is planned to keep it touring during 1999.

(The Egyptian Association to Support Street Children,
EASSC, Progress Report 2000, 8)

The above quotation from a progress report intended for EASSC's funders and friends describes one of the events that was held as part of our soft advocacy strategy. Indeed, the painting exhibition[26] referred to above was also the first time that the children more or less 'came out' and engaged with the public in a non-street setting.

Prior to that date, most of the advocacy was done 'on behalf' of the street children. As the program became increasingly known, we were continually receiving invitations to participate in different meetings, workshops, working groups, forums, and conferences on 'children at risk.' We were keen to be present and participate actively at such events, knowing that they constituted arenas for the construction of the social problem(s) regarding the street-child phenomenon. The prevailing tendency then was, as already mentioned, to define street children, in and of themselves, as the problem and to prescribe rescue approaches for the 'eradication' of this shameful phenomenon. Obviously, our 'empowerment' discourse encountered strong resistance, if not outright hostility, on the part of policy makers and social affairs bureaucrats. The very few who were secretly in agreement with us were those who had adopted a participatory rhetoric to please the funders. The latter had increasingly pressed for adopting participatory approaches in local community development strategies, making it, as well as the objective of empowering the poor, a condition for allocation of grants. However, most participants in public forums concerned with street children were very keen not to run counter to mainstream ideologies, especially since the state bureaucrats, including social affairs officials, were represented at these forums. Even the support of UNICEF and the international community could add little credibility to our discourse, which was persistently dismissed by the bureaucrats as being culturally alien to Egyptian society.

The strong opposition to our approach was somewhat dampened when individuals came to visit the drop-in center and interacted with the children. Gradually, we were able to attract the attention and support of several professionals and policy makers, as well as some media people. However, for the most part, alliances were formed on the individual level, and not on the institutional level. As for the resistance and the attacks that we often encountered at public meetings, they were softened whenever we were allowed to bring some of the children along with us.

The idea of involving the children in the arenas where their realities were being constructed was not so much motivated by the desire to dampen resistance and gain supporters, as by the desire to give the children an opportunity to talk for themselves, whether directly or through their works of art and handicrafts. 'Advocacy on their behalf' was gradually substituted by 'advocacy with them.'

The participation of the children in public events was not restricted to these arenas. They took part in several cultural activities, summer camps, and other socio-educational and sporting activities where they interacted with mainstream children.

Many of the children were very eager to take part in public events, and preparation for such events usually took place with a great deal of excitement and joy. Indeed, their participation, especially in events that lasted for more than one day, required a great deal of organization and self-discipline. Most of the children refused to go to public meetings in their shabby street clothes, and many of the meetings would start at nine o'clock in the morning. This meant that they had to come to the center quite early to wash and to try on some of the donated clothes, and after a rapid breakfast, quickly rush to the meeting. Afterwards, they would go back to the street to resume their lives and come back to the center the following morning—if they had not been arrested—dusting off their clothes, which they had tried to keep clean throughout their night on the street. Those who had dirtied their clothes, would, though they felt quite embarrassed, nonetheless start bargaining for a new set.

After participating in a couple of these events, it was interesting to observe one of the children suggesting to the organizers a three-day workshop to start at ten in the morning instead of nine, in order to accommodate the special circumstances of those who spend the night in the street. His suggestion was adopted and from then on it became a consistent request that we would make to the organizers of the events to which we were invited.

The children's enthusiasm, zealousness, eloquent spontaneous responses, assertiveness, and critical capacities were often quite thrilling to observe at public events. On many occasions, the children's input incited other participants to adopt a more realistic and reflective position. Their outstanding performance made some participants think that we had achieved a 'miracle' with these children, and they would come to congratulate us. This probably reflected the very poor prognosis usually made regarding street children. Actually, the 'miracle,' if any, was created by the convergence of the children's persevering will for empowerment with the benefits of sustained accompaniment, non-formal education, and collective advocacy organizing.

Reflective Commentary
Sensitive Issues: Drug Consumption and Sexuality

The intensification of accompaniment work described above allowed us access to an array of morally sensitive information, especially with regard to drug consumption and sexual matters. We had to deal with uncertain, complex, ambiguous, and value-laden situations that raised ethical and moral dilemmas. Supplementing our own observations, many children increasingly confided to us details of behavior regarded, in the context of traditional societies like Egypt, as highly immoral. Adults who witness or come to know about such behavior are expected to severely reprimand the deviant and take necessary action to correct him or her.

We adhered to a strong belief, according to which accompaniment of deviant populations demands an increased 'tolerance' with respect to use of drugs, violence, sexual activities, and all those values and lifestyles usually condemned by mainstream norms and considered detrimental to the well-being of children and youth. Yet we remained confused as to whether this tolerance required us to accept any kind of behavior. Recognition and acceptance of difference was indeed a major issue with which we grappled throughout the program. Below are some examples, taken from situations in which we were confronted with issues related to drug consumption and sexuality.

In the meager literature on street children, drug consumption and sexual matters are usually referred to as sensitive issues, and represented in terms of abuse, addiction, promiscuity, exploitation, and high risk behavior such as prostitution, homosexual activity, and anal intercourse (de Moura 2002). This representation, guided by the negative aspects attributed to street life, often reduces the debate regarding the ethical questions raised by these sensitive issues to the moral obligation of 'protecting' the children (Young and Barrett 2001). Researchers are advised to assess carefully the possible negative impacts on street children before divulging information regarding abusers and the children's spatial survival strategies to avoid retaliation from the police or other abusers. This 'protectionist' discourse is employed at the expense of dismissing and excluding other aspects of the lived experience, such as exploration, pleasure and adventure, which are not exploitative and can even be empowering at times. These aspects are not addressed in the literature.

In exploring closely the issue of glue sniffing and drug consumption, we came to understand that in the context of street life, there are very good reasons to engage in the use of inhalants: peer pressure, the need to belong to a group and the fear of isolation, to name a few. Moreover, the anaesthetic effect of glue helps to block out not only 'bad thoughts,' but also hunger pangs and the effects of harsh weather. In this sense, glue sniffing is vital for street survival. However, we were also concerned with the possibility of cognitive deterioration and detrimental repercussions on the nervous system, which are widely believed to result from the use of inhalants. As such, we were at a loss as to how best to react when children informed us about their drug consumption and sniffed glue—sometimes provocatively—in our presence. On the one hand, we felt that criticizing, discouraging, or condemning this kind of behavior was obviously negating the unique context and circumstances associated with it. On the other hand, we felt an urge to 'protect' the children from the detrimental health effects of drug consumption. It was not without pain that we came to realize that for any prospect of behavioral change regarding drug consumption to emerge, the living circumstances of the young 'addicts' themselves needed to change.

This early concern with how best to 'react' to drug consumption and the concern to 'protect' the youngsters may have concealed some of our own value judgements, prejudices, and ignorance. We did not differentiate between different usage of inhalants (moderate, occasional, or chronic), and we assumed that every kid who sniffed glue must be an addict. It was only later that we came to observe and understand that many children used drugs socially and were not drug dependent. We also learned that the alleged negative effects of inhalants in the form of cognitive and personality disorders were far from being conclusive (Jansen et al. 1992). Therefore, it became important not only to be aware of the unique street circumstances that led to glue sniffing, but also to start identifying and discerning differences in usage.

The concealment of our own cultural specifications was even more apparent when reflecting on sexual matters. The street workers felt ill at ease discussing the children's sexual promiscuity, even though they did not seem to elicit much shame or guilt on the part of the children. It must have elicited great discomfort among the workers as our discussions—as in the literature—tended to focus on issues of prostitution, paedophilia, sexual abuse, and exploitation. This tendency among the street workers resulted, once more, in an overemphasis on the protection dimension, blocking deeper reflection. However, unlike researchers who were in contact with street children for only a limited period of time, we could not continue with a protectionist discourse and attitude since our relationships with the children would have remained patronizing. Let me explain.

Notwithstanding the fact that drug abuse and sexual exploitation take place in street culture, representing the children's sexual relationships and use of drugs solely in terms of exploitation and abuse not only, as already mentioned, excludes other pleasurable aspects, but also confirms the victim label. To accompany the children in a meaningful way, we needed to identify, recognize, and relate to both the victim and the actor in them. Furthermore, the street culture context in which the sensitive realities of abuse and exploitation are lived and experienced needed to be specified and discerned in order to avoid the trap of adopting a universal perspective, informed by mainstream values. But to go beyond the protectionist obstacle, we first needed to deconstruct.

As a trainer and ethnographer, I was aware of the fact that, publicly at least, the street workers in their own life worlds adhered to mainstream values. Regarding sexual behavior in particular, I was also aware that, privately and secretly, this adherence was often less strictly observed. While open and public discussion of sexual matters is generally frowned upon, and the mention of deviant behavior is whispered about and severely condemned, in both practice and beliefs, a rather surprising 'tolerance' is observed among both the affluent and less privileged classes.[27] The two cardinal rules for indulging in socially unacceptable sexual behavior, such as premarital, extramarital, homosexual, or anal sex, are silence and secrecy. Thus, the challenge for me was to establish enough trust with the street workers for the whispers to become louder and for them to acknowledge painfully the inevitable phoniness/paradoxes that often color mainstream values. That was the prerequisite for embarking on a process of critical analysis not only of the realities and lived experiences of street children, but also of our own.

Through the dialogical relationship with the street workers, we came to recognize that by referring to the children's sexual behavior only in the negative terms of exploitation, abuse, and risky behavior, we were negating any possible pleasure or exploration/experimentation that might be there as well. This orientation was in flagrant contradiction with our own observations: the majority of the children had reached an age at which their sexual maturity and their bodily changes aroused curiosity and the desire to discover and experiment. We also observed that both boys and girls were often involved in sexual relationships that were not necessarily exploitative but had more to do with exploration, intimacy, and even love. From our privileged position in the daily lives of the children, we witnessed the genuine, sincere, and intense emotions associated with many of these relationships. This made us think that the absence of parental restraint might have been of positive benefit to the street children by enabling them to experiment more freely in comparison with children growing up with the security of parental love and protection.

We also came to understand that the sexual and physical abuse of street children was not committed by their peers or adults in their milieu as often or as brutally as we had imagined. Instead, the abusers were too often the very same individuals whom society had appointed as their protectors: the various policing agents and their informants (Human Rights Watch 2003). Exploiting the exclusion and voicelessness of the street children, these abusers committed their acts of abuse quite freely, confident that the children's voices would be easily muted and never reach a sympathetic ear. We knew that reporting such abuse would not result in any significant change, except for our removal from the scene. Both governmental and non-governmental organizations know about the abuses and exploitation of street children, yet a law of silence prevails; the threat of the counter-accusation of defaming Egypt is too intimidating.

It was perhaps paedophilic and homosexual relationships that were the most difficult to 'accept.' Struggling with the issues that these relationships raised helped us realize that acceptance of the other in the work of accompaniment did not require accepting or sanctioning just any kind of behavior. Instead, it meant not suppressing the other's words and experience and being non-judgmental, realistic, and capable of facing facts, rather than ignoring them. It also entailed recognizing the right to trial and error. Accepting the other required us to reject the desire to control the other, and to engage instead in a liberatory dialogue that invites the questioning of certain assumptions without feeling threatened or pressured, but empowered by an evolving critical consciousness.

Silent Practices

This attitude of recognition and acceptance of the other enabled the gradual incorporation of silent practices, especially in relation to reproductive health issues. The children's sexual promiscuity required us both to convey general information and advice about reproductive health and especially about the means to prevent the transmission of STDs and HIV/AIDS.

Another 'tricky' silent practice was the accompaniment of teens and young adults during their pregnancies in a cultural context where pregnancy outside marriage is so severely condemned that the very life of the female is threatened. The shame that she incurs justifies killing her to wipe it out. Therefore, we were quite alarmed when young women and teenagers became pregnant, even more so when they decided to keep the baby. In addition to our concern that they were putting their lives at risk, we were worried about the difficulties of giving birth and nurturing an infant on the street. With time we were able to identify and develop several rudimentary emergency resources for such situations, including shelter and medical care. However, the burden of nurturing the infant when the mother's own survival was so precarious inevitably led to entrusting the baby to an acquaintance, often with an informal agreement that the mother could not see her newborn again.

On some occasions, a young man from the street who was not the father—and in love with the young mother—offered to marry the mother and register the baby under his name. Incidents of this kind are examples of how an individual act of solidarity in a context of exclusion can freely occur in a collective space.

We went through other dramatic situations when newborns had handicaps or were in precarious health. I still recall the sad incident involving Samar. A few weeks after giving birth, Samar came to us one morning at the drop-in center, holding her newborn tight in her arms. She was looking very worried and told us that she did not know what the matter was—the baby was dead. Being a single mother with no birth certificate for the infant meant that the legal procedure for burial would be complicated. If the mother had gone to a hospital or a police station, she would have been considered a criminal offender, been humiliated, and been locked up. A couple of leaders hastily decided to take the baby to the hospital. On their way, as they told us later, they realized that they could not come up with a convincing story with respect to the identity of the baby and how they found him. Burying the baby remained quite a difficult issue to resolve.

This incident, like many others, occurred within what might be called the gray zone of practice. Such incidents often took place suddenly and created some shock as well as panic given the uncertainties they evoked and the immediacy of action they required. The burial incident related here reflects a situation of extreme marginality in which the baby had no civic name, that is, he did not officially exist, and as such no burial permit could be issued. Further compounding the situation was the non-recognition of Samar's status as a single mother.

Some of the children's silent practices also raised difficult dilemmas. One example involved Mervat, whom we came to know shortly after she had run away from her village in the governorate of Minia, about three hundred kilometers south of Cairo. She was about twelve years old, with white skin and blond hair (such features are less common in Egypt and highly valued). She was quite witty, as well as good-looking, and was successful in gaining our love, care, and attention. Despite her age, origin, and physical features, all of which made her particularly vulnerable in the street, Mervat managed to extract herself from precarious situations with the least possible damage by investing dramatically in her boldness, her capacity for seduction, and her unusual survival instincts. In fact, her family situation, as we came to observe later, was quite stable, and her father had complied several times with her wish, expressed to him in a heartbreaking letter, to return home and he had come to Cairo to take her back. However, Mervat always ran away again, and even helped her younger brother to do the same.

Mervat wanted to continue with street lifestyles, and it was clear that she had adapted exceptionally well in terms of taking the greatest advantage of the free and adventurous aspects of street life, as well as experimenting with a variety of petty jobs usually reserved for boys, such as shoe-shining and fire-eating. Mervat was also a convincing liar, displaying the proper emotions and gestures for whatever dramatic situation she was relating, and naturally, she wanted to become an actress.

At the age of sixteen, four years after running away, Mervat was developing into a mature and charming young woman, and in her street career she had managed to become a leader. Acquiring this status was contingent upon her ability to establish that she was not an easy sexual prey for speculating males, and this was no easy task. Unlike some other females, who become leaders by acting tough and hard, inflicting on themselves additional razor cuts, and dressing and behaving like men, Mervat, although she smoked, sniffed, took pills, did karate, and worked like the boys, was feminine and quite proud of it. Acting tough in order to survive and establish status was not her strategy. To avoid sexual harassment from males, Mervat managed to establish a tacit pact with two key figures in the street locality where she spent most of her time. These two men, a police informant and a tea maker, were her friends and, using the clout of the first, they always tried to be the first exploiters of female newcomers to their street locality. The two males had a pact with Mervat whereby she quickly linked up with female newcomers and led them to the den of these two exploiters. In return, Mervat was not only spared the viciousness of these two monsters, they also provided her with protection from other preying males, as well as protection from police harassment and abuse. This protection, as well as Mervat's attributes, including her ability to read and write, definitely placed her in a privileged status among the leaders.

Mervat's example was one of many that made us realize that in street culture, values are often paradoxical. For each value, one inevitably finds its very opposite. Group solidarity and intense individualism appear to go hand in hand. Selfless sharing and selfishness are equally widespread. And although tolerance is valued, there are no compunctions about turning a friend in, in order to avoid problems. Our bewilderment and feeling of unease with these paradoxes were attenuated when one day one of us said, after some reflection, that she would, in all likelihood, deceive her buddies if her own survival was seriously threatened. This made us realize that these paradoxes do not reflect behavior and characteristics specific to street children. Indeed, they are aspects of human nature.

Drop-in Center and Street Work: Two Complementary Strategies

It is important to emphasize that the opening of the drop-in center did not mean the cessation of street work. On the contrary, accompaniment work in the street localities where we had established our presence had to be sustained and intensified in the less infiltrated localities. This was partly because the children were always on the move in the street. They constantly needed to identify temporary, often precarious refuges and niches until the regular raids to clean up their preferred areas calmed down. It was during these round-ups that many children were arrested. Those few who managed to escape were afraid and had to be awake and alert all night. Solidarity and a supportive presence during these rough times were greatly appreciated and enhanced the rapport.

Yet this was not the only important reason for sustaining street work after the opening of the drop-in center. The children who came to the center returned at the end of the day to the street localities which were their living milieus and habitat. Ensuring a presence here gives accompaniment work its full meaning. Our street work philosophy held that the relationships developed in the street with the children should not be conditional on their coming to the center. In fact, not all the children came to the center on a regular basis, nor were they expected to do so. Some never or only rarely came to the center, others came only occasionally, while others came regularly but with intervals of absence. It is true that regular attendance was often, but not necessarily, associated with positive prospects for change, and it definitely motivated the workers. Yet making regular attendance a condition would have resulted in instituting a selection mechanism whereby the more 'difficult' children would, all too easily, be dismissed, thus focusing the approach on the individual. Therefore, we needed to remind ourselves constantly that accompaniment work targeted both the individual and the milieus and the communities—the collectives—in which he or she lived and interacted.

Sustaining active street work was important for settling problems and difficulties at the center itself. On many occasions when some of the children were displaying extremely disturbing and provocative behavior for no apparent reason, the answer to our bewilderment was to be found in the street. We came to realize that the children and the people surrounding them in the street were conducting a form of continuous assessment and evaluation of the center. The provocative behavior of the children at the center was a message from the milieu that there was something about which they were not happy; they wanted to negotiate, and we always welcomed such requests. This dynamic occurred on more than one occasion when a street leader was assigned tasks and responsibilities at the drop-in center, failed to measure up to them, and was asked by us to step aside until he was more ready for them. The leader would then use his influence on the children to stir up trouble, using the pretext of our 'unfairness.' In situations like this, we made sure not only to go and seek this leader to clarify issues, but we made sure that this happened with the participation of other children and leaders.

Street children programs that operate drop-in centers in isolation from the street milieus of the children who frequent the centers often end up in a conflictual relationship with these milieus. Programs of this kind usually do not have an open-door policy. Access to their school-like centers is usually reserved for a certain age bracket and is conditional upon appropriate behavior and adherence to a rigid program consisting of classes and some recreation. These programs usually apply what has come to be known as a 'tough love' policy. Children who are admitted to the center are expected to be resilient and determined to break with the bad habits that they displayed on the street. In replicating the same authoritarian family and school structures from which many of the children run away, it is not surprising that such programs appeal only to the children who are 'nice' and 'easy' and on their way back to a family or an institution. Furthermore, this selective approach usually requires that the more 'seasoned' and 'turbulent' children be warned a couple of times, excluded temporarily, and then expelled permanently. These seasoned children often retaliate so that many of the managers of these programs feel the need to protect themselves from the street milieus. The story does not end here though. For these programs to survive, some street children must come to the centers. To find them, the staff needs to go into the street—as they did when they first opened their center—and attract some children. But this time the staff is likely to face a rather hostile milieu. Hard negotiations take place, and it is not uncommon for the staff to resort to dubious maneuvers such as threatening to report street people to the police. Attitudes such as these hasten an escalation of animosity, and the requested police interventions, far from settling the dispute, result at best in temporarily silencing the vocal street leaders, and at worst in widening the gap and the mutual feeling of resentment and hostility between mainstream and street milieus.

Undoubtedly, many of these programs and their staff have good intentions. The point I am making here is that intervention efforts conducted in isolation from the context of the street milieus in which the children are embedded, not only suffer from serious limitations, but also run the risk of being counterproductive. Furthermore, for drop-in centers to be effective tools of intervention and re-socialization, they need to offer alternatives to traditional, authoritarian school settings by making education a pleasant, exciting, and voluntary experience that can pave the way to better reintegration.

Implications of the Open-door Policy

The open-door policy adopted at the drop-in center entailed the intermingling of children who were of different age brackets (from newborns to early twenties), of both sexes, and from different street locations. The space provided by the center was used to tackle many community organizing issues: disputes were settled; news about absent peers was shared; difficulties and problems encountered in the streets were discussed; and trips and other events were planned. However, this open-door policy resulted in relatively large numbers of children and adults coming to the center, and this presented an immense challenge. There was an average daily presence of about sixty youngsters in a rather small space under the supervision of six street workers and a couple of volunteers. Therefore, the management of space, resources and people was dependent upon prompt improvisation and creativity, given that every day was different in terms of the numbers, the individuals and the groups present, and in terms of the ensuing dynamics. Flexibility and continual reorganization of the space were necessary in order to accommodate the different activities that changed on a daily basis, as a function of who was there, their numbers, and what they wished to do. Serving two meals and drinks required elaborate organization and accurate estimation, as did lining up for the shower, using the laundry facilities, and visiting the clinic. With different activities often taking place in very close spatial proximity, clashes and fights were bound to erupt. These situations were further complicated by our keenness to avoid disturbing the neighbors and abusing their tolerance.

The management of what often seemed like a situation on the verge of chaos raised dilemmas with which we continuously grappled at our meetings, in which we had started including some of the leaders. The question of when and how to use authority to keep functioning adequately and to avoid jeopardizing the existence of the center was not an easy matter and needed to be discussed. We sometimes resorted to actions that from the perspective of our early appraisal did not fit with the 'ideals' of the open-door policy that we wished to implement. Several times on very busy days, the only measure we could take in response to extremely disturbing behavior by some children was to ask them to leave the premises for the day. While it was true that the relationships of trust that had been developed allowed for this measure to take place without eliciting violent reactions, we still made sure to go out at night after the center closed to find these children and settle the issue with them.

Grappling with the authority issue, we became aware of the family dynamics that were at work at the drop-in center. There was no escape from assuming parental roles in this substitute family. For example, Samir, the most experienced of the street workers and their leader, acted like the father of the children, while Ranya played the mother role. With older individuals, these parental relationships alternated with adult-to-adult ones. In a similar fashion, while Samir and Ranya were, professionally speaking, senior to the other workers and assumed supervisory and training tasks, they were also like their older siblings. As for myself, in addition to my professional role as the person in charge of the PAR program, I was also father/big brother to the workers and grandfather to the children, who on many occasions did not hesitate to solicit my intervention when their wishes were denied by the workers.

The identification of these different roles helped us to address the associated problematic issues of power and authority, and in exposing these issues to group discussions with the core group of leaders, a form of collective monitoring of these issues emerged. As for the punitive measures to which we sometimes resorted, they came to be integrated as part of culturally acceptable family rules.

While we consciously attempted to implement a democratic family—constantly reminding ourselves that the culture of the street possessed its own logic and articulated its own normative value claims—there were times when value clashes caused what seemed like strong and insurmountable emotions. For example, one morning a group of children arrived at the center holding Hassan, a young boy around ten or eleven years old, by the arms.[28] Hassan was obviously in great pain and could hardly walk. They told us that Hassan had been forcibly "taken" by Tarek, an older kid of about fifteen, who also visited the center. While trying to comfort Hassan and reach the doctor over the phone to ask him to come earlier than usual, the street worker with whom Hassan had a special rapport looked quite disturbed by the situation. A few minutes later, when Tarek walked recklessly into the center, this street worker grabbed him and proceeded to beat him up. As we watched with mixed emotions the physical punishment of 'the monster,' and before any of us would intervene, the street worker stopped as suddenly as he had started and walked away.

Later, the street worker told us that he could tolerate deviant behavior like homosexuality and paedophilia, but he could not tolerate sexual assaults. Our grappling with the issue inevitably led us to wonder about the psychological repercussions of sexual violence on the victims. Over the eight-year duration of the program, we came to face several other situations similar to the one experienced by Hassan. The children told us many other stories about their experiences with being sexually assaulted. It was definitely surprising to us that these children did not seem to have been particularly 'damaged' by the event. Although they would only tell us about such incidents when enough confidence had been established, observing the ease with which, among themselves, they humiliated each other jokingly for being forcibly taken, helped us to contextualize the incidents of sexual assault. We came to understand that one of the very early pieces of advice that newcomers to the street obtain from their peers is a repeated warning to protect themselves against such assaults. However, newcomers also learn that most peers have experienced being taken by force, which is usually marked by a razor cut on the face inflicted by the offender. Despite the obvious cruelty involved in these assaults, we wondered whether the expectation of the trauma could result in better survival. We also wondered whether the fact that there was no shame attached to these public incidents alleviated the emotional and psychological repercussions of the assault. What seemed certain to us was if children brought up in a safe and secure family were to be exposed to this kind of brutality, the lack of awareness of the coming threat and the subsequent 'privatization' that usually follows would make the situation more complicated for them than for street children. The apparent absence of psychological damage to many street children who are exposed to sexual assault may, after all, be explained in the words of Hamada, a seasoned kid, who in reply to our bewilderment regarding the frequency of these assaults told us: "It's only natural; when you are young you get taken, and when you grow up you take."

The drop-in center's open-door policy also allowed children to come to the center without necessarily participating in any of the activities described above. Indeed, many of the children came just for a meal, a shower, the laundry facilities, to consult the doctor, to have a word with a street worker, or simply to sleep in a safe atmosphere. Furthermore, participation in the activities was not conditional on regular attendance. This would not have been a realistic expectation on our part. Many of the children kept trying to return home while others enjoyed traveling to Mediterranean cities in the summer and to Upper Egypt in the winter. Some of those who wanted to maintain continuity in their activities at the center were picked up by the police regularly and detained for days, if not weeks, before they were released, humiliated, angry, and in pain. Recovering from this maltreatment required a degree of determination and strength that many could not sustain. They thus understandably succumbed to depression, heavy drug consumption, or self-mutilation, and for those who were engaged in exploring avenues of withdrawal from their street careers, it often meant another setback. This made us feel very angry and frustrated with our own powerlessness and incapacity to denounce more loudly police brutality. It also made us realize how such repressive actions and attitudes tend to confirm the children's mistrust of adults and mainstream society. They made us realize and witness how for many seasoned children, police brutality and the general hostility of the public over the years had resulted in so many physical as well as psychological scars that the prospect of disengaging from a street career often looks unattainable to them. They knew that they were unwanted and that the only place offered by society was behind secure fences in isolation. Many end up internalizing social degradation and spend the greater part of their lives behind bars.

In accompanying the children through their many arrests and maltreatment, the challenge was not so much in lending empathy and support: their formidable insistence on survival and the solidarity generously displayed by their peers handled that quite well. The challenge lay in the difficult task of capitalizing on their experiences of repression in order to increase their empowerment and emancipation. As we expressed our own anger and frustration to the children with regard to our inability to protest their maltreatment, it made us realize that in a sense we were in the same boat, despite the obvious fact that we were much more privileged and enjoyed many more comparative advantages. Nevertheless, the knowledge that we were together trying to do something different from the mainstream kept emerging throughout our experience, further strengthening our complicity, and providing a solid base for planning and strategizing the action component of PAR, articulated through street work and non-formal education, as well as through collective soft advocacy.

In this chapter, I resumed the reconstruction of the PAR process undertaken in Cairo with street children, which was begun in Chapter 3. In this second phase, our identity as street workers-researchers was revealed to the children with whom we had established trust relationships during the first phase of ethnographic street work. This 'coming out' was needed so we could shift from doing research *on* street children to doing research *with* them within a PAR framework. The opening of the drop-in center and the intensification of accompaniment work, along with the non-formal educational activities and collective soft advocacy, were the major features of this second phase. I narrated and reflectively commented on the major ethical issues and dilemmas that surfaced during this phase of the PAR process. This second phase, which began in 1997, came to an abrupt end in 2001 with the dismantling, by MISA, of the EASSC, the association that was sponsoring the PAR programme. However, the beneficial effects of this program had already begun to appear, as I discuss in the following chapter.

6

Impacts and Concluding Commentary

I n this last chapter, I will discuss some of the changes brought about by
eight years of action and research on and with the street children of Cairo.
I will highlight and discuss changes that we observed at the individual and
the group level, as well as changes with respect to street children policy in
Egypt. I will then summarize and discuss the methodological features that
characterized the PAR process presented in this book before ending with a
discussion of some of the unresolved issues.

Impacts

> Another consequence for seeing deviance as an interactive process is that
> we are able to correct false impressions fostered by earlier theoretical
> assumptions. For instance, if we assume, as has been often done, that
> deviance is somehow a quality of the person committing the deviant act,
> we are likely to suppose without looking any further that the person who
> commits the deviant act is somehow compelled to do so and will continue
> to do so. On the other hand, if we view deviance as something that arises
> in interaction with others, we realize that changes in interaction may pro-
> duce significant changes in behavior. (Becker 1964, 3)

Individual Level

As a non-institutional social intervention practice that subscribes to the
humanist tradition, street work with the street children of Cairo aimed at
establishing a sustained accompaniment of otherwise inaccessible marginal
and excluded populations of youngsters, who are often repressed, deprived
of their fundamental rights, and who, understandably, adopt behaviors

considered to be deviant according to mainstream views. This sustained accompaniment—in the street, in non-formal education activities, and in collective advocacy—led to the development of authentic relationships between the street workers and the children, at the heart of which was the 'recognition' of difference, as well as the basic and fundamental acceptance of the 'other.' This facilitated the construction of rapport based on reciprocity through a dialectic movement between self and other. In turn, the reciprocal consideration for each other was the basis for the development of a subject-to-subject dialogical relationship rather than a relationship of expert to client. Dialogue and interaction became the basic tools for the co-construction of meaning, which is the prerequisite for the development of a critical consciousness able to question certain assumptions, to specify underpinnings, to elucidate choices, and to evaluate them. Gradually, the children, individually and collectively, began to assume an active role in making decisions about the issues central to their lives and about the means of enhancing their lives.

Indeed, the interactive and relational approach adopted throughout the duration of the PAR undertaking has, like Becker (1964) believed, produced significant changes in the behavior of individuals and groups. The situation of Hind can be quite illuminating as an example of change at the individual level.

With the nickname *al-sal'awwa* (a type of coyote that frightens many villagers in remote rural areas and sometimes attacks children), Hind, a fifteen year old female, only about one meter tall, sturdy and fully developed, was indeed quite 'wild.' She mumbled her words and never exchanged more than a couple of sentences. Failure to understand her was met either with her giving up on you or having a fit of bad temper. Calling her by her nickname would make her so furious that she would bite the person responsible and, paradoxically, confirm the appropriateness of her sobriquet. Biting was also her method of fighting, and she fought a great deal. On the days when she came to the center, we would look at each other in anticipation of the difficult hours ahead of us. She was so demanding, particularly because of her tantrums, that we often had to dedicate the full attention of a street worker to her. More about her background is found in Appendix 1, Vignette 5.

One day Hind took a colored pencil and began to draw. Her drawing drew our attention, and we were quite encouraging. She would draw only occasionally until she started to form some attachment to the volunteer female painter, the board member who introduced the painting activity. A series of wonderful paintings followed fairly rapidly and she acquired a new nickname, 'the artist.' Calling her by her old nickname did not seem to bother her as much, her heavy consumption of drugs became more discerning, and she stopped biting. When an exhibition of the children's paintings was organized a few months later, Hind was the missing star on the opening evening. She made her appearance only on the second day. After closing time, as I was looking alone at the paintings, Hind came up to me, took me gently by the hand, and said: "Why are you standing alone; come and sit with us," pointing to where the other young artists and a couple of street workers were sitting.

The story of Hind, like that of many other children, lends credit to the claim made by Becker (1964) regarding the importance of positive interactions for eliciting behavioral changes. It also adds credit to the value of non-formal education: changes in behavior need not be, and seldom are, the outcome of strict correctional measures. Instead, enhanced self-esteem and self-confidence, and a wider scope of awareness and creativity change the way individuals feel about themselves, and their behavior is modified accordingly, almost naturally, I venture to add.

Collective Level

At the collective level, we had set as an indicator of meaningful change the children's capacity to take responsibility for their own affairs and to develop a collective voice. This was partly achieved by virtue of the fact that a small group of children were able to assume supervised street work tasks just before the abrupt end of the process. Furthermore, the group-to-group negotiations and participation in organizing and strategizing collective advocacy activities seem to have equipped many of the children with the necessary tools and capacities to address politicians and policy makers publicly and within the arenas concerned with their realities. We were pleasantly surprised and indeed moved when, in the midst of the confrontations with the state bureaucrats in the period preceding the dismantling of EASSC, a group of six children came to show us a copy of a letter they had written themselves and had presented, without our knowledge, to the MP of the jurisdiction where the association was registered, and with whom they had managed to obtain an appointment. In the letter, which took them days to write, they eloquently described their undertaking with EASSC, and asked the MP to do whatever in his power to ensure the sustainability of the association. This initiative confirmed the validity and value of the PAR endeavor, and it gave me the bittersweet feeling that the imminent abrupt ending would not nullify the emancipation at both the individual and collective levels.

With regard to changes at the policy level, the National Council for Childhood and Motherhood (NCCM), closely associated with Egypt's First Lady, Mrs. Mubarak, who chairs its Advisory Technical Committee, announced in March 2003, in a spectacular ceremony that received lots of media coverage, a national strategy to 'eradicate' the phenomenon of street children (NCCM 2003). In this strategy, the core of the discourse and recommendations we had developed over the years of PAR with the street children was adopted: the diversity of the phenomenon and its organic link with street societies, the importance of viewing the children as active social actors capable of participating in the search for the means to improve their situation, the necessity of establishing drop-in centers and shelters that the children can voluntarily join, developing training courses to sensitize public servants concerned with the phenomenon, and so on.

It is interesting to note here that despite the fact that EASSC had a good working relationship with NCCM (with whom we shared our views and analysis of the phenomenon), the council, notwithstanding its influence, did not do much to prevent the dismantling of the association. The question that can be asked here is whether the act of adopting our discourse and recommendations—almost word for word—was one of co-optation. While it is true that the adopted policy appears sophisticated and constitutes a powerful tool for the Egyptian State to respond to accusations of maltreating street children (Human Rights Watch 2003), it remains to be seen whether it will result in meaningful changes at the practical level.

Regardless of the outcome of the NCCM initiative, its value resides in the fact that the street children phenomenon has been mainstreamed. Gone are the days when state officials denied the very existence of the phenomenon and accused those who addressed it of defaming Egypt. International donors have allotted generous funds to address the phenomenon and the number of NGOs working with street children is increasing. The scaling up of the drop-in strategy will take place in 2007, funded by the EC and implemented by the NCCM.

Methodological Considerations

The production of replicable methodological formulae has never been an objective in PAR. Indeed, it would even be considered contradictory to its tenets. As an open-ended process, each PAR needs to progress along the emerging, sequencing, and unfolding realities of a group's life, which are continuously shaped, forged, formed, and constructed by the interactions among the different members. While the PAR process described in this book could not be replicated as such, I nevertheless propose to identify the main methodological traits and concerns that characterized it and which in my view could inform future PAR undertakings.

The Processual Nature of PAR

As an open-ended process, the PAR described in this book has all the characteristics of generic social processes noted by Blumer (1969). It encompassed the interpreting, planning, anticipating, doing, experiencing, assessing, and readjusting features of action. It incorporated the perspectives of participants, as well as people's capacities for reflectivity, their ability to influence one another and their tendencies to develop and act upon particularistic relations with others. In addition, the PAR process actively assumed the problematic and uncertain features of group life, the dilemmas the actors experience, and their *savoir-faire* in coming to terms with them. However, the PAR process presented in this book went beyond the parameters of Blumer's interactionist ethnography. The practitioners-researchers became involved in educational as well as therapeutic relationships with participants, were politically positioned in favor of the participants' fight against exclusion, and organized advocacy activities both *for* and *with* them.

PAR processes of this kind are understandably very time-consuming, labor intensive, field based, longitudinal, and engaged undertakings that require extensive patience, perseverance, and a capacity to handle a great deal of ambiguity. They also require a certain experiential knowledge that allows practitioners to venture into the life-worlds of the other while being careful not to provoke fusion and confusion problems by over-identifying with the other. Moreover, by taking the side of the excluded, PAR practitioners put their own identities on the line and subjugate their viewpoints to those of the many "moral entrepreneurs" (Becker 1963) who may have a variety of vested interests regarding either the non-respectability of some people or practices being studied or the ethics of aspects of methodology.[29] Furthermore, the promotion of values and notions such as empowerment, equity, self-reliance, and commitment to the interests of local participants often entails challenging oppressive political and social arrangements, such that the research group is often positioned in opposition to dominant and mainstream forces.

For an undertaking with such a wide scope of multiple and diverse issues, the PAR process must necessarily be conceived along a multi-component approach—rather than a single-model approach—in order to allow for different issues to be addressed in a parallel fashion. The case presented in this book is one that has conformed to this requirement. Let us examine this claim more closely.

Multiplicity and Diversity in Methodology

As we saw, the eclectic methodology that was used for the implementation of the present PAR process combined street ethnography, street work, and action science. The beginning of fieldwork consisted of street ethnography (observation and participant observation) that allowed access to the street milieus frequented by street children. After establishing an 'intimate familiarity' with these milieus and building relationships of mutual trust and respect with individuals and groups, fieldwork gradually incorporated accompaniment and non-formal education components. In so doing, fieldwork marked a shift from an ethnographic inquiry (that is, studying and understanding deviance) into street work that meant becoming involved and taking sides. The reflective approach that was adopted from the outset ensured the training and education of both street workers and participants, focusing on enabling them to use their intuitive *savoir-faire* to continually add to the construction of their experiential knowledge.

The 'multiplicity' feature in the present PAR was by no means restricted to its eclectic methodological framework; indeed, this feature characterized all three dimensions of PAR—participation, action, and research.

Participation

The multiple stages and facets of participation observed in the PAR described in this book were carried out in conjunction with the processual nature of the undertaking. Contrary to the promises by some PAR rhetoric, democratic participation, like other PAR ideals, cannot constitute a fixed feature and mode of operation from the outset. As I have argued, it may be more realistic to view PAR ideals as goals that serve to guide and inform the process. Accordingly, democratic participation as a major PAR ideal cannot from the outset of a PAR process be the actual state of affairs. This kind of democratic participation requires a wide range of abilities, including personal, intellectual, political, interpersonal, group management, and data management skills, in addition to a capacity for self-awareness and reflexivity. It is very unlikely at the initial stage of a PAR enterprise with marginal and excluded populations that practitioners would be able to constitute a group that is more or less homogeneously equipped with these abilities. Therefore, the promotion of democratic participation requires educating participants to acquire such abilities so that they can eventually participate more actively.

In the PAR case narrated in this book, the increasing participation of two groups of actors was of vital importance for the PAR process to progress democratically. For their participation to be meaningful and to become fully operative, both the street workers and the targeted children needed to be equipped with practical and theoretical tools and concepts to sharpen their self-reflectivity and to increase their capacity to work in a collegial fashion.

With regard to Ranya and Samir, the street workers' group leaders, who started as volunteers conducting street ethnography under my supervision, they needed to be coached to acquire both street work and research capabilities, that is, to become practitioner-researchers. During the initial ethnographic street work, the hands-on experience in the street, which was continuously subjected to reflective analysis facilitated the gradual acquisition of skills and the construction of their experiential knowledge. Gradually, Ranya and Samir progressed from mere data collectors to full participants in the management of the overall PAR process, including the recruitment and coaching of additional street workers.

Likewise, the participation of street children also followed a coached progression. As the scope of their socialization kept widening, new dimensions of their participation were gradually incorporated into the process. Many of the youngsters who started by being mere providers of data and recipients of care and accompaniment were able to acquire enough knowledge to participate in the interpretation of data, that is, to critically examine themselves both individually and collectively. Some were also able to participate in the planning of change and its implementation. And just before the abrupt ending of the process, a couple of the children had assumed street work tasks and responsibilities under the supervision of Samir and Ranya.

Lastly, it is important to note that at different moments in the overall process of the construction of democratic participation, different actors are found at different stages, and this requires vigilant monitoring on the part of practitioners, as we have seen in Chapter 4, to attend to the many issues related to these variations in the degree and forms of participation.

Action

The action dimension in the present PAR incorporated several features, and its content was determined in conjunction with the unfolding process. Initially, the action took the form of going up and down the streets of Cairo to locate the targeted youngsters in living environments. This was followed by socially infiltrating some of the identified street milieus and building relationships of trust with key informants. These relationships gradually developed to accommodate actions of support and accompaniment of the children through the sustained, meaningful and interactive presence of practitioners in the accessed milieus. With the opening of the drop-in center, the non-formal education activities coupled with on-going individual and group negotiations for increasing participation paved the way for the political action of organizing advocacy activities.

Research

The research dimension was equally multifaceted. The combination of symbolic interactionism and ethnographic methodology, the plurality of fieldwork areas (different street localities and the drop-in center), the triangulation of methods used (observation, participant observation, informal discussions/interviews, open-ended, semi-structured and in-depth interviews, focus-groups, and collection of biographical accounts), the techniques employed (field notes, personal notes, drawings, street workers' reports, observation of participants in different settings and by different observers), the active involvement of participants in the analysis and interpretation of data, and the longitudinal nature of the research undertaking all contributed rich data for critical reflection, analysis, and the gradual construction of knowledge.

Savoir-faire, Ethics, and Reflectivity

The 'intimate familiarity' developed with the groups of street children that we worked with often involved unpredictable situations in which uncertainties and ambiguities gave rise to a large number of ethical issues. From the outset, reflectivity became for us a sort of survival mechanism to feel our way, to manage the dilemmas raised by ethical issues, to acquire and develop conceptual understanding, and to contain our own affective states.

When reflectivity is instituted as a group activity, the varied knowledge and competencies of the participants come face to face with one another and produce a dialectic tension that allow them to engage in definition, interpretation, intentionality, and assessment. Increasingly, participants develop the capacity to attend to the lived experience of the other, to take the viewpoint of the other with respect to oneself, and thereby become objects of their own critical awareness. This capacity to see themselves from the standpoint of the other and to talk about themselves fosters the participants' sense of awareness of self as an object, that is, their self-reflectivity, and enhances their capacity for intentional and meaningful activity, that is, human agency. The momentum for growth and empowerment generated in this way can then be exploited to its full potential.

Furthermore, reflectivity in groups often gives rise to an array of issues that are often described in dualistic terms or dichotomies such as subject and object of research, theory and practice, research and practice, participatory and top-down research, academia and fieldwork, individual and collective, oppressor and oppressed, advocacy *for* and advocacy *with*, democratic and authoritarian action, ethical and unethical, professional and unprofessional, empowerment and alienation, education and social control, expert and popular knowledge, private and public, to name some of those that were addressed within the PAR process described here. In exploring these dyads, we followed the Southern tradition of PAR in terms of developing a dialectic sensitivity that was concerned less with solving contradictions than with developing the capacity to identify and dissect them, to recognize them in the self and in others and to struggle with them actively, both individually and collectively.

This vigilance in maintaining a reflective approach and dialectic sensitivity is paramount in PAR undertakings. In a process that requires political involvement and taking sides with the excluded, a critically reflective stance can act as a safeguard against the pitfalls of reproducing dyads, of accusations of treachery, and of longing for innocence and purity.

Unresolved Issues

In this final section, I would like to present some of the issues and concerns that the present PAR would have needed to address had it continued to operate. These are issues that we had been reflecting on around the time of the forced dismantling.

Street Workers and Street Educators

With regard to the complementarity of street work and the drop-in center, I argued that while street work was articulated along a strategy of building bridges to access the excluded in the margin, the strategy at the drop-in center aimed, through non-formal education and collective advocacy,[30] at more emancipation and empowerment for participants. While most contemporary street work activists adopt this dual strategy, we had internal debates with people who questioned the appropriateness of practitioners who implemented street work activities being involved at the drop-in setting. In their view, the street worker is a practitioner who basically works in the street and develops a *savoir-faire* and knowledge articulated through being and working in the children's territories. The space created within a drop-in location is viewed as a shared territory in which the street worker may have to resort to the use of authority, if only at times, to keep a minimum of order within the locale. For example, practitioners in the street would never ask the youngsters to stop sniffing glue. They may talk and exchange with them about glue sniffing as a habit, its effects, and the like, but they would not feel the need to take any meaningful measure should one or more of the youngsters start sniffing in their presence. However, within a drop-in center, practitioners would feel more compelled to try to stop such behavior, especially when agreed upon rules do not permit it. In this view, then, the street workers who do not assume responsibility within a drop-in center stand a better chance of developing an egalitarian relationship with the youngsters.

The debate is far from being conclusive. As discussed earlier, the issue of the use of authority was on the reflective agenda at the drop-in center, and the practitioners grappled a great deal with the question of when to assume a parental (authoritarian) role. My view is that those who favor the separation of tasks may want to avoid 'confrontation' situations with the youngsters, and do not seem to realize that issues of power and authority are bound to surface in the relationship between street workers and the youngsters. This avoidance is bound to be challenged by the youngsters sooner or later. More importantly, such 'difficult' situations can be very emancipating when handled collectively, that is, when individual deviance is contextualized within the larger group and the latter is challenged to take responsibility for its own actions.

Furthermore, the separation of the street worker and the street educator tasks artificially creates unnecessary areas of expertise. By both accompanying the youngsters in the street and becoming involved with them in informal educational activities at the drop-in center, street workers can really claim that their work of accompaniment is full and meaningful.

Gender

A second concern I would like to discuss here was whether it would be more beneficial for girls if they had time and space reserved only for them at the drop-in center. Initially, boys and girls came to the center at different times. As mentioned before, we had days for boys and others for girls in order to be congruent with policies adopted in public schools. However, in the street milieus, children and adults of both sexes intermingle, so we decided to let everybody come at the same time. While this policy reflected the living realities of participants, it may have overlooked some particular needs of female participants. This concern was triggered by repeated observation of many of the girls' behavior in the presence of male peers. Some of us had actually started to be irritated by the display of stereotypical female attitude and seductive behavior on the part of many girls competing to seduce male peers. We also noticed that this kind of behavior was much less prominent when the girls were engaged together in some kind of activity apart from the boys.

We came to realize that we might be able to deal with the issues associated with this behavior if some space and time were reserved for girls and female workers to undertake activities together, apart from the males. While there were always occasions when the girls preferred to be alone or with female workers to privately discuss different matters, including their relationships with the boys, many times they had to specifically request to be left alone. Furthermore, we felt that the elucidation of the meaning of their stereotypical behavior could not occur only through dialogue with the girls. Our view was that if the girls become involved in some activities together, as in sports where the focus is on notions like team building and personal skills rather than just their femininity, there might be more opportunities for exploring group emancipation and the development of identities other than stereotypes.

Shelter

A third concern that became urgent before the PAR described here came to end was that of shelter. As an increasing number of youngsters decided to try to disengage from their street careers and as they were exploring other venues, it became quite clear that to continue sleeping and living in the street was hindering them from fully exploring alternatives to street life. We rapidly realized that offering some shelter in the form of institutional settings (reception centers) was not the answer. Many street children develop an autonomy that is suppressed by the authoritarian and paternal treatment they receive in such settings, and not surprisingly most run away the moment they get the chance. Therefore, we started to experiment with forms of supervised apartments in which the participants collectively assumed the supervisory task themselves. As was expected, many problems arose and needed to be attended to. Conflicts with landlords and other tenants often reflected the prejudices most people held with regard to street children. Whenever there was theft or other infractions in the neighborhood, the children were suspected and accused. However, these initial experiments were encouraging, and they demonstrated the organizing skills that many of the youngsters had acquired by virtue of surviving under the harsh circumstances of the street.

The 'In-between' Position

We were quite aware of the fact that in accompanying street children we were situating ourselves in an in-between position: dissident youngsters on the one side and a scornful and hostile mainstream society on the other. While mediation between the children and family, school, police, social and probation workers, reception centers, and other instances was certainly an important aspect of fieldwork, it did not mean that we remained neutral. On the contrary, we sided with the children as a means of validating their experiences, not so much as victims or deviants but more as active actors who were trying to cope with being excluded. Obviously, this was a politically sensitive position. However, it enabled us to witness their day-to-day reality and to advocate not only for an increased mutual tolerance between mainstream and deviant street societies, but also, and more importantly, to advocate for a genuine, humane representation of a young excluded population living precariously on the fringes of society.

Despite the fact that we had opted for a soft collective advocacy approach, it did not save the NGO under whose auspices the PAR project was undertaken from being dismantled by Egyptian state officials in April 2001. The NGO went to court to contest the decree and the case is still being reviewed. This raises a question regarding the appropriateness of soft advocacy in light of escalating conservatism in the North and repressive regimes in the South. Behind this question is the issue of 'resistance,' an issue which fortunately seems to be making its way again onto the agenda of social activists, albeit slowly and tentatively.

In both the North and the South we are witnessing the rise of a wave of political discourses that heavily invest in the revival of one of the most pernicious, yet stable, dichotomies constructed by human thought, namely, 'good versus evil.' This can only add fuel to a mounting fundamentalism, which may have well started in the South but is today equally manifest in the North. Resisting this global and exclusive binary of 'good and evil' as advanced by the fundamentalists is no easy task for today's activists in light of the intensification of surveillance mechanisms[31] and the blatant exercise of power (under the guise of preemptive security measures). Activists in the North are now experiencing some of what has been until recently considered to be the 'fate' of their Southern counterparts, namely, the shrinking of the democratic margin of maneuver permitting the existence of nuances and a dialectical sensitivity to go beyond the simplistic/fundamentalist discourses of good versus evil.

In the face of such a regressive state of affairs many activists understandably feel pessimistic regarding the prospect for any meaningful emancipation in terms of social justice, at least for the immediate and medium terms. However, even if the prospects for emancipation at the structural level seem dim, if not nil, this does not preclude the prospect of pursuing emancipation through social processes at the local level. This becomes even more important when we realize that the present situation is further aggravated by the resonance the fundamentalist discourses have among the masses. This resonance carries the risk of waking the dormant totalitarian in us and we are likely to witness the insurgence of moral entrepreneurs with different vested self-interests ranging from fear and desire to protect oneself to power trips and even psychotic disorder. These moral entrepreneurs are familiar faces in the South and include those who give themselves the right to impose on others what they consider to be the right and good way to live. They are not found solely in the ruling hierarchy, but are also comfortably niched in the social fabric of the day-to-day reality of ordinary people. In the North, some moral entrepreneurs seem to be coming to the surface in the context of such groups as the moral majority as well as in the context of rising patriotism and the war against terrorism.

It would thus seem that today's activists increasingly need action strategies at the local level that aim at resisting the trickle down of oppressive tendencies with a view to saving some of the essential values of the humanist project. Such action strategies can be articulated using the practice of 'emancipatory resistance.' Emancipation here gets its (new) meaning in the collective process of resisting fatalism, of elucidating the dynamics and the underpinnings of the global situation and its ramifications at the local level, and of identifying means to resist. While these acts of resistance may not have a significant impact at the macro level, their values reside in the very process through which local communities and groups come together to resist the hegemony of fundamentalist discourses, of individualistic and market values, of capitalist rationality and the often ensuing fatalism.

In April 2001, after the forced closure of the NGO, participants including myself felt overwhelmingly discouraged, if not depressed. It took more than a year to recover and to start reorganizing. In December 2002, Ranya and Samir, along with two other street workers and the children who had started to assume street work tasks just prior to the dismantling of the NGO, decided that they would not wait an extended time period for the court to settle the dispute between the NGO and state officials. Instead, they began to study the feasibility of establishing a new NGO. In November 2003, the new organization was officially set up and resumed operation in September 2004 upon reception of grants from the very same donors who were supporting the dismantled NGO. The emancipatory process with Cairene street children was thus re-launched.

Salwa, 15 years old

Paintings by some of the children who frequented the drop-in center. Painting workshops were held weekly by artist Huda Lutfi, who would spend the whole day with the children painting, discussing, and reflecting on their works. The paintings often reflected the everyday experiences of the children and their vision of a happy or a traumatic childhood.

Dalia, 16 years old

Hind, 16 years old

Hussein, 15 years old

Ali, 14 years old

Appendix 1
Profiles of Street Children

In this Appendix, I sketch the profiles of some of the street children we came to know in order to illustrate the diversity in the trajectories that led them to the street, as well as the diversity in street life circumstances and styles.

Vignette 1: Ashraf, male, thirteen years old

Ashraf was born to a father who worked in a 'beans and falafel' restaurant and a housewife mother who took care of him and his younger sister. The family lived with the maternal grandmother. When Ashraf was about ten, the father decided to move to a piece of land he owned on the outskirts of Cairo, where he set up a tent for the family in which they lived until completion of a one-story house. Ashraf had difficulties adapting to the new shanty neighborhood and complained that at the school the teachers treated him with violence. He started missing school and roaming the streets, and in so doing came to meet and befriend some street children who introduced him to street life.

Ashraf's performance at the school deteriorated and he quit. His father placed him as an apprentice in a mechanic workshop, from which he ran away a few weeks later because of violent treatment by the owner. This scenario was repeated several times, and each time ended with his father becoming increasingly violent toward him.

Around that time, fights were endlessly erupting between the mother and the father, and the latter was often absent from home. The mother started to bring a man home during the father's absence, and Ashraf complained that "this man started acting as if he was our real father, and he used to beat up my sister." This is when Ashraf ran away from home and linked up with the street children he had befriended. He spent most of his time in Zone 1 (see Appendix 2). In the vicinity of this zone, he met a man working as a driver for a microbus network of communal transportation, who took him to work with him, calling passengers and collecting fees. Ashraf slept at the man's house; the man was kind to him.

Ashraf's uncle happened to see him one day in the street. He took him to his place, and a few days later returned him to his mother. To avoid living with her, Ashraf told his uncle and grandmother about the relationship the mother secretly had with "that man." This resulted in the mother running away with her daughter and friend to a distant neighborhood where she later, after divorcing Ashraf's father, married her friend. Ashraf succeeded in identifying the mother's new address and, curiously enough, went to live with her and the friend "because I loved my sister very much and I was attached to her." However, the mother and the friend constantly fought with Ashraf who 'even' tried to convince his sister to run away with him. But the sister told the mother about the plan, and Ashraf was severely punished. He went back to the father, who again placed him as apprentice in a workshop. He only ran away again with LE20 he stole from the owner.

Ashraf spent a few months on the street with his friends in Zone 1, and they introduced him to the entertainment street locality in Zone 2 (see Appendix 2), where they spent the money they made from begging and wiping car windows on watching karate movies, sniffing glue and gambling. When asked about how he spent his days on the street, Ashraf replied:

> On Fridays I wake up in the morning and got to El . . . mosque at the time people are coming out of prayer and I beg for money and food. There are lots of people there who distribute food and vows after Friday prayer. After that, I go to a café to watch one or two video movies and then I start looking for a place to sleep. As for the other days, we go for breakfast near the mosque, and then each one of us goes off to make some money. Sometimes we go wiping car windows and begging, and with the money we make we buy cigarettes and glue. Sometimes, we go to the sea [the Nile Corniche] under the bridge where we bathe and do good business. Because every one standing there has a woman with him, we keep sweet talking them by begging and sometimes we bring some flowers and sell them to them by force.

Ashraf was found once more by a relative of his (this time, his aunt's husband), who took him to live with them and got him a job at the wood factory where he worked. Once more, despite his love for his aunt, he went back to the street, this time because he was upset to find out that the boss at the factory knew that his aunt's husband had "picked him up from the street." He found that out on one of the occasions when he was reprimanded violently by the boss, the boss said to him "you street beggar, who wants to sleep in the street and sniff glue." But this was not the only reason he went back to the street. He said that he made more money there than at the factory.

Ashraf kept in contact with his aunt, and would periodically try to go back to the living arrangement with her and her husband, but always ended up going back to the street. After the opening of the drop-in center, the aunt regularly came to see him or ask about him. One of the street workers became increasingly involved in trying to negotiate one of Ashraf's many returns. One arrangement was made whereby the aunt and her husband agreed not to use violence with Ashraf, who promised not to run away again. Additionally, Ashraf asked that he be able to bring along one of his friends to work and live with him at his aunt's house. The request was granted, and the new arrangement worked fine for a while. During this time, Ashraf's relationship with his aunt and her husband became more peaceful and loving, until the day his friend ran away after stealing some money from the household. Ashraf was punished by the aunt and the husband on the grounds that he was responsible for his friend's deed.

Back on the street, Ashraf told the street worker:

The street is better. My father doesn't care and my mother, it's finished, she doesn't exist, and my aunt beats me. Finished. What can I do? From the time my mother ran away with the man who used to come up to our place, and one feels that really there is no use for anything. Finished. If it wasn't for my mother's story, may Allah forgive her, we could be living well now.

Vignette 2: Sahar, female, twenty years old

Asked to tell her story, Sahar starts by saying:

I have gone through a lot of difficult things in my life. My father divorced my mother when I was still in diapers. And I knew nothing about my mother until I grew up and discovered that she was quite the opposite of what my father said about her. She remarried and gave birth to three children. My father remarried, and I lived with him and my stepmother, and she is kind and I love her and call her mama. I was twelve when I first left home.

Sahar left home because they were living in a small place with her uncle, his wife, and their five daughters. The uncle's wife hated Sahar and managed to turn her father against her by accusing Sahar of misbehaving. Her father started to beat her often and violently for even small mistakes. However, Sahar still loves her father, who she says once wept after beating her feet with a strap.

The death of her uncle's wife had a strong impact on Sahar. She died after catching fire and going around screaming, and when Sahar tried to help, she tried to grab onto her so she would die by fire as well. This is what Sahar believed, and she still believes that her uncle's wife set fire to herself because she was continually sneered at and shamed by her husband and neighbors for giving birth to five girls and failing to give her husband a son.

After that incident, Sahar says she felt psychologically disturbed and started to "see imaginary things." She "saw" her uncle's wife around the place and was afraid to go to the bathroom by herself. These hallucinations and visions continued to curse Sahar's life. She asked her father to move to another place, but he refused, claiming he didn't have enough money. Instead, he brought one of the Qur'an readers to Sahar to pray over her head for her salvation.

When she was ten, she began to run away from home and spend time in the street, mostly in Zone 1 "because the atmosphere at home and the whole neighborhood made me feel suffocated." In this area she made friends with a girl who ushered her into a downtown district where she introduced her to a woman (Auntie N . . .) who let her live with her, took good care of her, and bought her fancy clothes. When Auntie N . . . was arrested for running a prostitution ring, Sahar was placed in a reception center where she managed not to be returned home by lying about her identity and origin.

The reception center in which Sahar lived for about a year was half-closed. She could go out and she met a young man with whom she fell in love. She gave him her father's address in order to bring him to get her out of the center on the understanding that they would marry. The young man convinced the father, paid him a sum of money as a dowry and married Sahar the *'urfi* way.[32] They lived together for two years (from about the ages of sixteen to eighteen), and Sahar resumed her relationships with the street friends she had met prior to being placed in the reception center. The couple began to fight, and the marriage ended in divorce.

Once back to the street, Sahar spent most of her time with her friend Salwa in Zone 3 near the mosque, surviving on begging and prostitution in the milieu of taxi and microbus drivers. Explaining how she ended up in prison, Sahar relates:

> I used to sit with Salwa near the mosque and we were regularly arrested for possessing drugs. I was once arrested for vagrancy and sentenced to one month at the reception center, and then I got out. Salwa and I were always fighting. Every time she wants to pick a fight, Salwa takes all her clothes off except her underwear. One day she did that while we were fighting, a policeman saw us. He arrested us and we were charged with indecent exposure on a public road. We were sentenced to six months in prison.

Sahar was six month's pregnant when she was sent to jail. Two months later, she gave birth to a premature baby who needed an incubator, but because of lack of money the baby died. Sahar vehemently denies that she let the baby die as many of her female friends claim. When they fight with Sahar, these friends shame her for her father's knowledge of her work as a prostitute, and they claim that both he and her ex-husband are Sahar's pimps and make money out of it.

Once out of prison, Sahar went back to hanging around the mosque in Zone 3 and re-established contact with her biological mother. She resumed her street life, oscillating between periods where she was high on drugs, unclean, wearing shabby clothes, roaming around, and periods where she took excessive care of her appearance, wearing fancy clothes that she kept at her mother's place. This was the period during which she became involved in different prostitution deals either with taxi drivers or with Arab tourists.

In 2000, Sahar became pregnant for a second time. She insisted on keeping the baby, gave birth, and took care of him for three months before confining him to the care of a woman friend who worked as a taxi driver, which is rare in Egypt. The arrangement seemed to be working all right, as every now and then Sahar would meet the woman to spend some time with her child.

Vignette 3: Nihal, female, twelve years old

This vignette illustrates the situation of a kid who spends most of the day-time in the street working to contribute to the family's income and returns home by sunset.

Nihal's family consists of her biological mother and two sisters, a step-father and three stepsisters. They live in a village near the Pyramids that is part of an agglomeration of small and poor shanty villages where poor immigrants from upper Egypt squat.

> We live in one room, and in this room we sleep with my mother and my stepfather. In the room next door Dalliah and her sisters live, and on the other side Hoda and her children live. All these people make their living through begging and mendacity.

Indeed, Nihal's entire family are engaged in menial work. Her sisters, who are sixteen years old or above, are not permitted to work; they stay home waiting to be married. Nihal is allowed to work without her parents' supervision and in the company of one the neighborhood girls. They sometimes wipe car windows and sell paper tissues in front of a famous supermarket. At other times, they receive some money by lighting incense and going around street stores or simply begging from pedestrians.

Nihal is very keen to present herself in a manner that differentiates her from street children, although she does have some relationships with them. She believes she is on the street to work, and is proud of contributing to her family's income. She is also proud of the fact that her mother warns her about going to the "dangerous" Pyramids Boulevard, and that she consistently turns down offers from young men to get involved with them in "impolite behavior." She also turns down offers from other girls to work with them in prostitution. Nihal considers begging and petty jobs better than indulging in such behavior. She feels angry when some store owners or passers-by treat her like a street kid:

> People look at us as if we were dogs, not human beings. Once, a lady took me and my friend Laila and asked us to help her carry things from her car to her flat. As we were coming back down the stairs, she called us again and as we entered the flat, she started beating us with a stick she was hiding behind her back, and she also touched Laila's hand with a live electric wire and kept saying 'this is so that you stop begging.'

Nihal says that she loves her family very much, including her stepfather. However, she complains that her mother and stepfather beat her if she comes back home without money or with less than what she usually makes. When her parents found her a job as a servant in a wealthy household, she refused to take it, saying "I am freer working on the street."

Vignette 4: Sherif, male, seventeen years old

Sherif was born to a father who had no fixed job, working most of the time on construction sites as a day laborer. His mother is the family's main bread winner; she begs and sells tissues at traffic lights in a wealthy neighborhood. Sherif has an older brother who alternates between the street and juvenile institutions. A younger brother died after a car accident when he was with his mother working at a traffic light and was hit by a car. Sherif was six when his brother died; he continued accompanying his mother on the street. He had infrequently attended school, which he finally quit when he was eight.

Sherif gained much of his knowledge of the street world from his older brother, with whom he would spend a few days at a time on the street before returning home. They wanted to be away from home because of the increasingly common fights between their parents and because their father pressured them "to work with their mother while he would spend most of his time at home consuming drugs."

When Sherif was about ten, his father asked him to prepare some tea, but Sherif said there was none left. When the father later found some tea in the kitchen he grabbed a knife and threw it at Sherif, causing an injury to his thigh. His mother complained to the police, but Sherif denied what had happened, claiming that he had fallen on a piece of iron that was sticking out of the stairs.

Sherif continued alternating between the street and home, sometimes accompanying his mother in her work, until he was about thirteen at which time his father was arrested and jailed after his mother informed police about his drug consumption. She then sent Sherif to her parents in a rural village, where he helped doing farm work. Sherif did not enjoy living in a rural village and did not appreciate the fact that he was not paid for his work. He returned to his mother in Cairo only to discover that she had married a one-armed man who worked with her at traffic lights. His father had divorced his mother, and after getting out of jail went back to his hometown in Upper Egypt. Sherif describes the situation that followed his return to Cairo:

Every time I go to stay at my mother's, my mother's husband wants me to work with him selling tissues and the like. My mother tells me to go to my father. She tells me, "Ali [the stepfather] is no good for you; he's a bum." So I ask her, "Why did you marry him? You're not my mother, you're more like a stepmother."

Once back on the street, Sherif learned from peers about 'Hope Village,' a reception center that seemed to treat children rather nicely. He made up his mind to join it. To be accepted, his mother had to go and sign a declaration that she did not want Sherif to live with her. Sherif managed to get her to do this, and was accepted in the permanent boarding department at Hope Village. For about a year, Sherif stopped sniffing glue and worked as a calligrapher's apprentice in a workshop. He was then accused of sexually assaulting a boy in the neighborhood where Hope Village was situated, and was severely punished both by the monitors at Hope Village and by the boy's family, who almost killed him. Sherif maintains that he was innocent, and that it was another child who committed the assault and pretended his name was Sherif.

After this incident, Sherif's relationship with Hope Village started to deteriorate and he eventually ran away. He took with him a bicycle that Hope Village loaned him to run errands for the center and left behind his identity card. He headed to his grandparents in the countryside where he sold the bicycle and from there travelled to where his father lived in Upper Egypt. There, he lived with his father, who found him a job in a laundromat. He constantly fought with his father, who wanted to take his earnings and who prevented Sherif from buying himself new clothes. Sherif left his father and returned to Cairo, where he met up with the street children he had known previously. He resumed living in the street.

At that time Sherif met one of the street workers and started coming to the drop-in center, where he gradually became active in assuming different responsibilities. A few months later, after saving enough money, he paid for the bicycle he stole from Hope Village, and was given back his identity card.

Vignette 5: Hind, female, fifteen years old

Hind is petite, very short, and looks like an eleven or twelve year-old girl, though she is fully developed. She thinks that she is ugly with her thin hair and crooked teeth. She spent most of the time by herself in Zone 1, high on dope, and was very aggressive with her peers.

Hind lived with her mother and a younger sister in a room they rented in a *sha'bi*[33] neighborhood, where her mother sells arugula salad on the sidewalk. Six of her older brothers and sisters are married and live independently.

> My mother goes out with my sister to work and leaves me alone. I clean the room and wash until they come back. A guy who lives in a room

next door used to eye me, especially when he had his friends with him. I ignored them until one day he came with three of his friends and he called me as I was cleaning our room. When I went to see what he wanted, he pushed me back into the room, lifted me and put me on the bed, took out a knife and told me to take off my clothes, and he started to do bad things with me from the front, but his friends were from behind. I was screaming as I became very tired, but no one cared to check what the matter was.

When the mother came back and learned about what had happened to Hind, she complained to the assailant's parents, who denied their son's deed and argued with her. All this made Hind feel that she hated their room, especially since most of the time she was there on her own. This is when she started going out on her own, roaming around the nearby Central Station, but returning home at night. One day Hind met a woman who had a tea stand on the sidewalk, and who asked her to work with her. Working there, she met a lot of people who hung around the station, and she befriended Amani, a black girl who often successfully managed to look like a boy with her short hair and masculine attire. Together, Hind and Amani had fun in an area that was not very popular among street girls.

As Hind began to spend more and more nights on the street, her mother complained to one of Hind's older brothers about her behavior, who punished her by inflicting burns on her arm. She and Amani decided to run away, and they went to hang around and live in Zone 1, which was familiar to Amani. She stayed there for five years, surviving on begging and prostitution. Despite her aloofness and bad temperament, Hind managed to forge a place for herself in Zone 1, but not without being vulnerable to rape and exploitation. She is often picked up by security agents who try to get information from her about prostitution activities in the area. While some of her friends claim that she gives information to the police, Hind says that she only did that once, when she was taken to the police station, where, because she refused to answer their questions, "they undressed me in front of the soldiers, and gave me electrical shocks, so I told them about Nancy sleeping with Moustafa and doing bad things under the blanket."

Over the years, Hind kept in contact with her mother, whom she visited every two or three months: "I spend some time with her and come back here. I don't like to stay there because the young men keep insulting me and shaming me for looking ugly and say that I belong to the street."

Vignette 6: Yasser, male, twenty-two years old

Yasser lived with his mother, two brothers, and two sisters in a tiny place in one of the semi-urban shanty agglomerations on the outskirts of Cairo. His father had divorced his mother, remarried, and lived with his wife in the port city of Damietta, one hundred and thirty kilometers north of Cairo. His father visited and contributed money to the household occasionally. His mother worked as a nurse's aid until her health deteriorated and she had to stop working. Yasser and his brothers had to help support the family.

Yasser was placed as apprentice in a mechanic workshop at the age of seven. He ran away from his apprenticeship to join his younger brother in Zone 1, where he begged and wiped car windows, which was more profitable than his job in the workshop. Yasser decided to go back to the workshop after he was arrested by the police. There, he endured the owner's abuse for a couple of weeks before returning to work with his brother. Together, they tried many petty jobs, discovered several street localities, and continued moving from one place to another. When they managed to save some money, they would go back home to give it to their mother.

When Yasser was thirteen, his father came to Cairo and took the whole family to live in Damietta. However, Yasser, his siblings, and their mother were set up in a dilapidated house next to the fancy one in which the father, his new wife, and their children lived. Yasser and his siblings were not happy with this arrangement and felt jealous of their half-siblings and stepmother. His father worked in Saudi Arabia and sent money mostly to his wife and her children, while Ahmad and his brothers had to work at the port to support their family.

Around that time, his younger brother hurt his eyes badly while playing soccer. A considerable amount of money was needed for surgery to save his sight. His father refused to help, so his mother went around asking the neighbors for assistance. His father accused her of begging and ruining his reputation, and assaulted her in a very demeaning manner in front of his wife. Yasser was so infuriated that he hit his father and ran away with his brother, leaving his younger handicapped brother and mother behind.

Once back in Cairo and Zone 1, Yasser, now fifteen, re-established contact with some of the street children he had met before moving to Damietta, and he and his brother resumed street life, surviving mostly by begging and wiping car windows. They often wore rags and acted as if they were mentally disabled. As he grew older, begging became more difficult:

Here I am. I stand with children wiping car windows at the traffic light even though I said 'That's it, I am old now and I'm not wiping cars anymore.' Only yesterday someone gave me a dirty look that made me hate myself, but here I am wearing a shirt and pants, begging and wiping cars. I even thought that I should start wearing rags again.

At times, Yasser becomes obsessed with the idea of making as much money as possible. For example, when he was nineteen, he worked at a welding workshop during the day and begged at night in an effort to afford a normal life with a family. At other times, Yasser is completely nonchalant, and roams around, sleeping in different places and working as little as possible, providing for himself primarily through begging.

Despite the considerable time Yasser has spent on the street, he thinks often about his family. He constantly mentions them, speaking bitterly about his cruel father and stepmother, but referring lovingly to his mother, sisters, and younger brother. On more than one occasion, his father has come to Cairo to ask about Yasser and his brother and incite them to return to Damietta to help their mother. They would occasionally return, but only long enough to provide their mother with some money. Thereafter, they would return to their street life in Cairo.

Appendix 2
Profiles of Street Localities

I n this appendix, I sketch the profiles of some of the street localities in which the street workers established a meaningful presence. My purpose is to highlight the diversity in the use of public space by street people as well as the diversity in the milieus that they create.

Zone 1

In Zone 1 (see map of Cairo on page xiv), situated south of Cairo, the street workers were actively engaged in ten street localities. Two of these localities are described below.

Locality A

It is in this locality that Ranya started street work. The main area is a very busy, noisy, and polluted public square situated directly in front of the railway station serving Upper Egypt. This is the south gate of Cairo for people coming from the poor rural governorates in the south, including runaway children and landless farmers, who are looking for work in the capital. In the square and the surrounding area, a great diversity of commercial activities take place, including street food vending, *sha'bi* restaurants and cafés, shoeshining, tea stands, a large number of stores reputed to be heavily frequented and cheap, and sidewalk vendors of various commodities.

For street people who hang around this locality, an area they call the 'garden' constitutes the main territory where they create their living milieu. The garden is about 3,500 square meters of fading green space with benches, a few trees, and a small water fountain. During the day, street leaders who occupy the garden manage a large number of tea stands and small shoe-shine operations that employ street children. The proximity to the railway station is advantageous as it provides street people with access to public toilets and water. At night, the garden becomes the dormitory for many of the street children as well as adults who mostly inhabit the street.

It is also a space for socializing and socialization. The social interactions that take place here are numerous and diverse by virtue of the variety of the actors engaged in this milieu. The street children who are found in this Locality are often newcomers from Upper Egypt who disembark at the station and after a few exploratory missions manage to overcome their fear and establish contact with street people. They spend some time here under the protection (and sometimes exploitation) of one of the area's leaders before they discover other zones and start to navigate the city. In the experience of some leaders, many children come once or twice and never show up again.

Besides newcomers, the garden is the place to which many children return for respite from other localities, at times they are driven out of their new locales by police raids, other times they are avoiding troubles with peers, or for a simple change of scenery. The fact that the garden is heavily infiltrated by police informants, who are omnipresent, has the advantage minimizing acts of violence in the area, which has made the garden more attractive to street girls especially. In the opinion of several street girls the substantial police presence makes this milieu relatively safer for them. However, the garden is not spared from periodic police cleanups, which usually leave it deserted for a couple of days, after which street people return and resume using the space as they had prior to the raid.

Indeed, police informants and police officers are an integral part of the street milieu in the garden. They often use their discretion to overlook many of the infractions committed by street people, including glue sniffing, gambling, sexual activities, and all the commercial activities of selling tea, shoe-shining, and others that are officially prohibited. In return for this, they obtain free tea, some money, or the sexual services of one of the girls. Many of these police officers and informants become involved in the daily interactions in this dynamic milieu, sharing the news of newcomers, the follow-up on many individual stories, the different gossip, and the love stories between boys and girls that continually erupt and often end as suddenly as they started. Some even invest small amounts of money in one of the micro-businesses and become involved in settling some disputes and fights. In short, these police officers and informants often become part of the social fabric of the garden milieu. Whereas some of them use their discretion for the purposes of exploitation, others seem to genuinely care for the children, and others appear apathetic.

The leaders in the garden are adult males whose ages vary between early twenties and late forties. Most of them adopted the street as a main habitat from the time they were in their teens or even earlier. While some of them live permanently in the street, others manage to periodically rent a room in one of the neighboring shanty towns on the outskirts of Cairo. Most of these leaders are arrested regularly and serve sentences varying from a few months to a few years, depending on the crime they are charged with (mostly theft and fights).

An example of a street leader in the garden is Zaki, a thirty-seven-year-old male. Although he is reputed to be a paedophile, Zaki does not feel in the least bit shameful or guilty. On the contrary, he presents himself proudly as a 'do-gooder' for street children, who helps them by giving them work and protecting them from the bums. Zaki, who has no fixed address, has been living mostly on the street and in the area around the garden for as long as he remembers, interspersed with numerous periods of incarceration. Whenever he makes enough money, he sometimes rents a hut or a room not far from the garden. At such times, he works as a manufacturer of gates for stores, a trade he claims to possess. However, most of the time, Zaki makes shoe-shine boxes, which he sells, but keeping some for the children under his protection. These children obtain what amounts to a fair daily wage of about LE5, in addition to food, a 'safe' sleeping arrangement, and a generous provision of glue and cigarettes, which the children pay for out of their wages.

"I love the garden because I found a father there, Zaki. He is very tender, and I wish he was my real father; I would have never left home," said one thirteen-year-old girl, whose words are quite indicative of Zaki's genuine popularity among the children. They refer to him as "uncle," and they love him not only because he is "tender" and "compassionate," but also because he makes them laugh when he imitates Ismail Yasin, a famous Egyptian comedian who, though he died some thirty years ago, is still very popular among many Egyptians, including these street children who see him on television. Zaki's talents as an entertainer are not limited to imitating Ismail Yasin. He is also a master in the art of telling jokes, and has created some funny skits that he acts out with the children during the evening entertainment time at the garden. These evenings often end with a euphoric group dance, for which the children and Zaki improvise musical instruments, and they somehow always manage to have a *tabla*. The joyful ambience that Zaki creates in the garden is indeed very well appreciated by the children. During the month of Ramadan, when we organized *iftars* at the drop-in center, which was followed by an evening of entertainment, the children insisted on inviting 'uncle' Zaki; whenever he came he was also the star of the evening. No wonder, then, that Zaki's popularity among the children is envied by the other leaders in the garden, who often try to set malicious traps for him.

Locality B

About five hundred meters from street Locality A, Samir started infiltrating another locality, situated right after the exit to an underpass over which the trains cross a major commercial thoroughfare leading to the Giza Pyramids. This area also harbors one of Cairo's most active red light districts. This street locality is situated stategically close to a mosque, with access to toilets and water. Also, the heavy traffic there facilitates begging and wiping car windows. Many of the car drivers stop there to buy water, cigarettes, ice cream, chips, or other items from the area's many, small variety stores. Many of these people are often on the way to some leisure time, and as such are good targets for soliciting activities. Furthermore, the children who hang around this locality have developed a rapport with many of the shop owners, who pay them small amounts of money in return for cleaning the sidewalk in front of their shops, bringing tea from a nearby café, going to change a large bill, and other menial tasks.

This locality has been occupied since the early 1990s by a group of street children who had started their street career in Locality A described above. Most of them were then in their mid-teens and had come from Upper Egypt. Three influential figures among them came from the same town. From the beginning of their work in transforming this locality into a territory, this group of children was very keen to establish a 'quiet' living space in order to minimize hassle with the police (detention, investigation, and so on). To a large extent, they succeeded and benefited well from the lucrative opportunities available in the area in addition to the excitement associated with its active nightlife. Work and pleasure for this group of children were pleasantly merged with a sort of diffused leadership. Quite a cohesive group, they seldom fought over the sharing of the money they made, and displayed great solidarity at times of arrests, car and other accidents, and had fun together gambling, sniffing glue, going to the cinema, and other recreational activities. From the beginning they agreed not to admit girls into their group because they were 'trouble makers.' Very few exceptions to this rule were observed. When one of the children fell in love with a girl, the 'fiancé' was sometimes cautiously admitted, but not for a long time.

Throughout the years, these children had to defend their territories from other children by controlling access. The territory was not open to just anyone who wanted to make a living. If force was needed to prevent this, it was used without much hesitation. This, however, did not prevent the group from establishing strategic alliances, ties of solidarity, and even friendships with some street food vendors, tea makers, police informants, and security agents. This small community managed to establish a rather 'quiet' milieu that was less of a target for police harassment and brutality.

When this group of children became a few years older, they started having difficulties making their living from begging and wiping car windows. They became too old to elicit pity. Besides, the fun side of the business lost its appeal. The joy and fun associated with wearing rags and making-up with mud, simulating different handicaps, and the like ceased to be attractive to these young men who started to wonder about their future. Some managed to disengage from their street careers, others tried but failed, and others still preferred to continue in their careers. In order to be able to continue, these young men started to employ younger children with whom they shared the winnings in return for protection. This was a major transformation in their career that resulted, among other things, in antagonizing the relationship with the milieu of the garden in which many of them had started their street careers, as I already mentioned, and with whom they had managed to maintain cordial ties. However, when the young men from Locality B started recruiting children from the garden, they fueled the competition over the children among the leaders there, and an abundance of conflicts arose.

Zone 2

This zone is situated in a traditional, *sha'bi* neighborhood in old Cairo, which may account for the fact that the street children's use of the street there is less marked by identification to a territory. This zone attracts younger children since they can go around without being harassed by people. Since most of the workshops in this neighborhood employ children, it is a common sight to see children going about the street. Here, younger street children can also benefit from the 'kindness' usually attributed to inhabitants of such traditional neighborhoods. For example, the children can ask for food from *sha'bi* restaurants without being scorned; indeed, their request is often granted.

This neighborhood is named after a female relative of the Prophet Muhammad, and a mosque bearing her name is situated on a large square. In the mosque, her shrine and mausoleum attract huge numbers of people who come to pray, visitors, and pilgrims. Here people pray to the Lady to fulfil their wishes, and vow to give to the poor should their wishes be granted. Thus, it is quite common to see people distributing food, clothes, or money to crowds of poor people who hang around the mosque waiting for the visitors whose wish has been fulfilled. These crowds consist mostly of professional beggars—organized into networks—who limit access to these 'distributions of vows.' It is only the younger street children who can manage their way through such crowds, as they melt in with the other children in the company of the professional beggars.

Another attraction for street children in this neighborhood is the many narrow alleys and back streets that cannot be accessed by police cars, and in which they can easily hide if they are chased. The children can also find a relatively safe place to sleep in one of the vacant lots in the neighborhood. These lots, many of which are garbage dumps now, are the result of the damage caused by the 1992 earthquake to many buildings in this old neighborhood. Some of these buildings collapsed, others were demolished because they were severely damaged, and others have been crumbling since 1992 because of damage concealed in order to avoid demolition.

In another street locality not far from the mosque, the children come in large numbers to watch karate videos in one of the many cafés situated along both sides of one of the narrow back streets some three hundred meters long. In most of these cafés, the space is divided into two. In the back area, there are regular 'café sitters' playing backgammon or cards, smoking from water pipes, chatting, or just watching television. In the front area, people can sit and watch karate videos for a nominal fee. The vast majority of the clients here are street boys in their early teens and younger. Observing them glued to these videos, one realizes that the boys must have seen the videos many times before, as they delight in drawing each other's attention to an upcoming movement or scene. Listening to their comments, one can appreciate the extent of their imagination in making up stories from the scenes they watch, despite their inability to follow the subtitles.

In this alley, the cafés stay open long after the official closing hour, and they tolerate the children who hang around. They can even gamble and often sniff glue around a small fire they make before falling asleep, huddled up like cats. After the cafés close, older children often come to the alley to harass the children, steal their glue and money, and sometimes try to take them by force. However, the younger children are usually able to defend themselves, especially when they outnumber the older ones. These older children are intimidated from harassing the youngsters when the alley is still awake; the café owners do not allow fights in their alley and tend to feel protective of the younger children, whom they view as important clients for their karate videos.

Zone 3

This zone is located in one of the new, modern neighborhoods, with a great deal of commercial activities, including fancy restaurants, movie theatres, modern cafés, fruit juice shops, take-away restaurants, American-style restaurants, fashionable shops, and utility stores. This zone attracts a large number of Arab tourists from the Gulf, especially during summer holidays, and many businesses have developed in the area around those tourists. Children and adults from neighboring shanty agglomerations come here hoping to make a living by begging or selling different items or services to wealthy tourists.

One street locality in this Zone is situated right in front a mosque named after a famous medical doctor who built it next to a hospital, which he owns and which also carries his name. This famous doctor is a public figure reputed to be a 'moderate Muslim,' who advocates the compatibility of Islam and science. He writes weekly articles that are published in prominent newspapers; he also hosts a weekly television show that promotes the same view. His hospital is reputed for charging moderate fees, and thus attracts large crowds who spend many hours and sometimes days waiting to be seen. Tea stands, street-food vending, taxi drivers, and other micro-businesses have flourished in this vicinity.

The street children who frequent this locality occupy the sidewalk along a small green space right in front of the mosque. For the most part, these children are in their late teens or early twenties and are of both sexes. They survive by selling tea and washing taxicabs. They also support themselves through female prostitution, which is protected, facilitated, and often exploited by the male members of the group. Nonetheless, these boys and girls often get involved in passionate love affairs, and often marry the 'urfi way in order to legitimize their relationships and be able to rent rooms in one of the surrounding shanty areas. They are heavy drug users and always aspire to make their way through the prostitution rings serving the tourists. These rings are highly lucrative and organized, and rarely admit street children. Some children occasionally manage, however, to 'hunt' a client through elaborate maneuvers and tactics that keep them very busy, but which seldom result in the lavish material gains they dream of acquiring. Most often they have to contend with a rather poor clientele consisting of taxi and microbus drivers.

Not surprisingly, this street locality is the scene of regular police raids despite the fact that the children spend much of their earnings bribing the officers and informants who are stationed there. During these raids, many of the children, especially the girls, seek refuge in Zone 1, Locality A, where most began their street careers.

In several other street localities in the vicinity of shopping malls and Western-style sidewalk cafés, other groups of younger street children beg and sell small items. Many of these children come from neighboring shanty agglomerations on their own or in the company of one or more family member, and usually go back home to sleep. Many of these children attend school, and work in the street in the evenings and during school breaks. While some seem to enjoy this lifestyle, alternating between the mainstream and an exciting marginality, feeling and acting 'adultish,' and being proud to contribute to their family's living, others complain about being forced to work and dread their guardian's punishment should they return home without the money they were expected to make.

Another group of children that compete with the preceding group of children come from a Gypsy community that has been living in the area since well before its urbanization in the 1960s. Surprisingly, this community succeeded in surviving the giant modernization of the area, and to date one can still see some of the women and children going around with a small herd of sheep and goats. Many Gypsy children beg under the supervision of an older person, and they seldom mix with the other children. As is the case with Bedouin communities, the tribal and ethnic ties in Gypsy communities are quite strong, possibly because of their dual marginalization by virtue of being poor and their nomadic lifestyle. As such, Gypsy children, like the older members of their community, do not trust the 'others,' whom they often refer to as the 'Egyptians.'

Notes

1 For reasons of confidentiality, all names, except for those of international organizations and state officials and institutions, have been changed.
2 The term 'Third World' was used before the collapse of the communist block to refer to what is known today as 'developing countries' and/or 'Southern countries.'
3 I discuss praxis in more detail on page 20.
4 According to Burrell and Morgan (1979, 283–84), critical theory represents "a sociological thought built explicitly upon the work of the young Marx . . . [and] seeks to operate simultaneously at a philosophical, a theoretical and a practical level." While critical theory usually refers to the work of the Frankfurt School of social theorists, the latter, Burrell and Morgan maintain, owe much to the work of Gramsci, and it is for this reason that they include him among the most influential critical theorists.
5 Actually, some writers consider PAR to be part of critical theory (Guba and Lincoln 1994; Healy 2001; Kincheloe and McLaren 1994).
6 See Foucault, M. 1980. *Power/Knowledge: Selected Interviews and other Writings.* New York: Pantheon Books.
7 A third mode of PAR operationalization consists of researchers themselves forming a group of individuals who are part of a disadvantaged population such as, for example, teenage mothers or physically handicapped children. In most cases, such groups dissipate with the end of the PAR activities. In some rare cases, the group continues and an organization is set up.
8 For those who still deplore the individualistic approach to the treatment of deviancy, it is interesting to note that almost a century ago Shaw and McKay were deploring it as well, and were complaining that it had been the dominant approach for a century.
9 "Life is an adventure of passion, risk, danger, laughter, beauty, love, a burning curiosity to go with the action to see what it is all about, to search for a pattern of meaning, to burn one's bridges because you're never going to go back anyway, and to live to the end. Terrified by this dramatic vista, most people just exist . . . for an illusionary security and something called status" (Alinsky 1969, viii).
10 Alinsky, S. 1971. *Manuel de l'animateur.* Paris: Seuil.

11 Popular education was a concept widely used after the Second World War. Its premises bear strong resemblance to today's call for non-formal education.

12 Note the similarity with Foucault's notion of power and knowledge.

13 The first clinic was called "Sainte Famille," and was affiliated with McGill University (l'ATTRueQ, 1997, 12)

14 See for example, Duval, M. and A. Fontaine. 2000. "Lorsque des pratiques différentes se Heurtent : les relations entre les travailleurs de rue et les autres intervenants." *Nouvelles Pratiques Sociales* 13 (1): 9–15.

15 Note the similarity with PAR.

16 This does not mean that street workers do not keep records of work progress and problems. However, these records remain their own.

17 In Latin America, Africa, Asia, and Eastern Europe, children and youth living on the streets are commonly referred to as 'street children.' In North America and Western Europe, the term 'homeless youth' is used interchangeably with that of street children to refer to this population.

18 It is interesting to note that at that time the term 'street children' was not used in Egypt in reference to the population in question. 'Vagrant children' was the most common term used by both the public and officials. Associating an individual or behavior with the street is pejorative, and it is a very serious insult to refer to someone as having been 'brought up in the streets' or as 'belonging to the streets.' The official adoption of the literal Arabic translation of the term 'street children' took place only in 1998 when Mrs. Suzanne Mubarak, wife of Egypt's President, used the term in Arabic in a public address. Following her utterance of the term, it was adopted by the National Council for Childhood and Motherhood (NCCM)—created by Presidential Decree no. 54 of 1988 and closely associated with Mrs. Mubarak, who chairs its Advisory Technical Committee. Since then the issue of street children has figured on the NCCM's agenda as one of the most pressing social problems (see the National Council for Childhood and Motherhood, http://www.nccm.org.eg).

19 'Sees' is the nickname for street children.

20 When in 1993 officials from the government and from the only NGO that was addressing the phenomenon of street boys were asked about street girls, they claimed that there were not any street girls, only prostitutes!

21 The term 'symbolic interaction' was coined in 1937 by Herbert Blumer (1900–1987), building on the 'interpretive/hermeneutic' tradition generated by Wilhelm Dilthey, George Simmel, and Herbert Mead, which set the basis for a social science grounded in lived human experience (Prus 1996).

22 The term 'subculture' signifies a way of life of a group of people; it denotes communities within communities, characterized by interaction, continuity, and outsider and insider definitions of distinctiveness (Prus 1996) The centrality of subcultures for understanding people's initial involvements and continued participation in deviance has been emphasized by many theorists of deviance as early as Shaw's (1930) discussion of delinquency and continues to be a prominent theme in contemporary studies of deviance.

23 A tenant in the next building had illegally opened a window overlooking the courtyard. The landlord of the building where the center was located had filed a complaint, obliging the tenant to close the window. In retaliation against our

landlord, this same tenant filed a complaint about the construction of two rooms in the courtyard, resulting in their demolition.

24   The street workers involved in literacy classes subsequently had the opportunity to attend a Freirean training session designed for literacy teachers. The workers' hands-on experience and experimentation helped them to be discerning and critical of the philosophy and the tools presented to them during the training. They were thus capable of adopting what they found useful, while feeling confident about adjusting and/or modifying other components.

25   The introduction of many of the activities had to wait until we were able to rent a second apartment next door. This added about fifty square meters to the overall available space, including a second shower room and laundry facility.

26   Some of the children's paintings are shown in the picture section.

27   This differentiation between professed values and the actuality of behaviors is analogous to the distinction in action science between 'espoused theories' and 'theories-in-use.' (Argyris and Schon 1974)

28   The approximation of the children's ages is due to the fact that many of the children did not know their real age and/or did not have birth certificates.

29   Becker's notion of 'moral entrepreneurs' includes both the roles of 'rule creators' and 'rule enforcers' that individuals and groups may play to regulate morality in a community context.

30   See Moreau 1990.

31   "The FBI is currently asking libraries to provide them with lists of the books and internet sites consulted by their members as a way of building 'intellectual profiles' of individual readers," *The Washington Post*, National Weekly Edition, 21–27 April 2003. Even more frightening is the creation by the Pentagon of a system of 'total surveillance' of all six billion individuals that constitute the inhabitants of the planet, as reported in *Le Monde Diplomatique*, August 2003.

32   The *'urfi* way of marriage in Islam requires just the signatures of two witnesses and is not registered in civic registries. Although frowned upon by the majority of Muslims, it is used by a variety of people, often to give legitimacy to relationships that are considered 'non-respectable.'

33   *Sha'bi*, literally 'popular' or 'of the people,' an Arabic word with strong socio-economic connotations, used in Egypt to refer to people of lower social status in Cairo and other Egyptian cities. When referring to a neighborhood, *sha'bi* usually denotes a district with significant poverty levels, often densely populated and deteriorating, its inhabitants sometimes, but not necessarily, living according to traditional mores and customs; when used to describe literature or art, *sha'bi* can mean 'folk literature' or 'folk art.' The word can also have slightly negative connotations as when used to mean 'common' or 'vulgar.'

Bibliography

Alinsky, S. D. 1969. *Reveille for Radicals*. New York: Vintage Books.

———. 1971. *Rules for Radicals*. New York: Random House.

Amegan, S. et al. 1981. "La Recherche-Action: Un processus Heuristique de Connaissance et de Changement." In *Actes du Colloque Recherche-Action*. Chicoutimi: UQAC.

Amin, S. 1974. *Accumulation on a World Scale: A Critique of the Theory of Underdevelopment*. New York: Monthly Review Press.

———. 1977. *Imperialism and Unequal Development*. New York: Monthly Review Press.

Aptekar, L. 1992. "Are Colombian Street Children Neglected? The Contribution of Ethnographic and Ethnohistorical Approaches to the Study of Children." *Anthropology and Education Quarterly* 22:326–49.

———. 1994. "Street Children in the Developing World: A Review of their Condition." *Cross Cultural Research* 28 (3): 195–224.

Argyris, C. 1980. *Inner Contradictions of Rigorous Research*. New York: Academic Press.

———. 1982. *Reasoning, Learning, and Action*. San Francisco: Jossey-Bass.

———. 1983. "Action Science and Intervention." *The Journal of Applied Behavioral Science* 19 (2): 115–40.

Argyris, C. and D. Schön. 1974. *Theory in Practice: Increasing Professional Effectiveness*. Berkeley: Jossey-Bass.

———. 1989. "Participatory Action Research and Action Science Compared." *American Behavioral Scientist* 32 (5): 612–23.

l'ATTRueQ, Collectif d'Écriture. 1997. *Le Travail de Rue: De l'Oral à l'Écrit*. Drummondville: Refuge La Piaule du Center de Québec.

Barbier, R. 1996. *La Recherche Action*. Paris: Anthropos.

Beazley, H. 2002. "'Vagrants Wearing Make-up': Negotiating Spaces on the Streets of Yogyakarta, Indonesia." *Urban Studies* 39 (9): 1665–83.

Becker, H.S. 1963. *Outsiders: Studies in the Sociology of Deviance.* New York: The Free Press of Glencoe.

————, ed. 1964. *The Other side: Perspectives on Deviance.* New York: The Free Press of Glencoe.

Bemak, F. 1996. "Street Researchers: A New Paradigm Redefining Future Research with Street Children." *Childhood* 3:147–56.

Bibars, I. 1998. "Street Children in Egypt: from the Home to the Street to Inappropriate Corrective Institutions." *Environment and Urbanization* 10 (1): 201–16.

Blumer, H. 1969. *Symbolic Interactionism: Perspective and Method.* New Jersey: Prentice Hall.

Bradbury, H. and P. Reason. 2003. "Action Research: An Opportunity for Revitalizing Research Purposes and Practices." *Qualitative Social Work* 2 (2): 155–75.

Brieland, D. 1990. "The Hull-House Tradition and the Contemporary Social Worker: Was Jane Addams Really a Social Worker?" *Social Work* 35 (2): 134–38.

Brown, L.D. 1985. "People-Centered Development and Participatory Research," *Harvard Educational Review* 55 (1): 69–75.

Brown, L.D. and R. Tandon. 1983. "Ideology and Political Economy in Inquiry: Action Research and Participatory Research." *The Journal of Applied Behavioral Science* 19 (3): 277–94.

Bureau de Consultation Jeunesse (BCJ). 1994. *Intervention et Action Communautaire, le BCJ en Évolution.* Montreal: BCJ.

Burrell, G. and G. Morgan. 1979. *Sociological Paradigms and Organisational Analysis.* London: Heinemann.

Burgess, E., C. Shaw, and J. Lohman. 1939. *The Chicago Area Project.* Chicago: S.N. (mimeographed edition)

Cancian, F.M. 1993. "Conflicts between Activist Research and Academic Success: Participatory Research and Alternative Strategies." *The American Sociologist* 24 (1): 92–106.

Child Law No. 12 of 1996. 1996. *Official Gazette,* no. 13, March 28 (in Arabic).

Cooke B. and U. Kothar, eds. 2001. *Participation: The New Tyranny?* London: Zed Books.

Coombs, P. 1968. *The World Educational Crisis.* New York: Oxford University Press.

————. 1985. *The World Crisis in Education.* New York: Oxford University Press.

Cree, V.E., H. Kay, and T. Key. 2002. "Research with Children: Sharing the Dilemmas," *Child and Family Social Work* 7 (1): 47–56.

De Boeve, E. 1997. "Travail Social de Rue entre Déni et Défi Européen," *EMPAN* no. 27:48–54.

DePoy, E., A. Hartman and D. Haslett. 1999. "Critical Action Research: A Model for Social Work Knowing," *Social Work* 44 (6): 560–69.

Dewey, J. 1916. *Democracy and Education.* New York: Macmillan.

——— 1938. *Experience and Education.* New York: Macmillan.

Doering, B., ed. 1994. *The Philosopher and the Provocateur: The Correspondence of Jacques Maritain and Saul Alinsky.* Notre Dame: University of Notre Dame Press.

Edgerton, R. and L.L. Langness. 1974. *Methods and Styles in the Study of Culture.* San Francisco: Chandler and Sharp.

Egyptian Association to Support Street Children (EASSC). 2000. *Third Progress Report.* Cairo: EASSC.

Fals-Borda, O. 1991. "Remaking Knowledge." In *Action and Knowledge: Breaking the Monopoly with Participatory Action Research,* eds. O. Fals-Borda and M.A. Rahman. London: Intermediate Technology/Apex.

Fals-Borda, O. and M.A. Rahman. 1991. "A Self Review of PAR." In *Action and Knowledge: Breaking the Monopoly with Participatory Action Research,* eds. O. Fals-Borda and M.A. Rahman. London: Intermediate Technology/Apex.

Fawcett, B. and B. Featherstone. 2000. "Setting the Scene: An Appraisal of Notions of Postmodernism, Postmodernity and Postmodern Feminism." In *Practice and Research in Social Work: Postmodern Feminist Perspectives,* eds. B. Fawcett, B. Featherstone, J. Fook, A. Rossiter. London: Routledge.

Finn, J.L. 1994. "The Promise of Participatory Research." *Journal of Progressive Human Services* 5 (2): 25–42.

Flax, J. 1993. *Disputed Subjects: Essays on Psychoanalysis, Politics, and Philosophy.* New York: Routledge.

Fook, J. 1999. "Critical Reflectivity in Education and Practice." In *Transforming Social Work Practice: Postmodern Critical Perspectives,* eds. B. Pease and J. Fook. London: Routledge.

———. 2004. "Critical Reflections and Transformative Possibilities." In *Social Work in a Corporate Era: Practices of Power and Resistance,* eds. L. Davies and P. Leonard. Burlington, VT: Ashgate.

Foucault, M. 1984a. *L'Usage des Plaisirs.* Paris: Gallimard.

———. 1984b. *Le Souci de Soi.* Paris: Gallimard.

Francis, P. 2001. "Participatory Development at the World Bank: The Primacy of Process." In *Participation: The New Tyranny?* eds. B. Cooke and U. Kothar. London: Zed Books.

Franklin, D.L. 1986. "Mary Richmond and Jane Addams: From Moral Certainty to Rational Inquiry in Social Work Practice." *Social Service Review* (December): 504–25.

Freire, P. 1970. *Pedagogy of the Oppressed.* New York: Herder & Herder.

———. 1973. *Education for Critical Consciousness.* New York: Seabury Press.

———. 1982. "Creating Alternative Research Methods: Learning to Do it by Doing it." *Creating Knowledge: A Monopoly. Participatory Research in Development*, eds. B. Hall, A. Gillette, R. Tandon. Toronto: International Council for Adult Education.

Gaventa, J. 1988. "Participatory Research in North America." *Convergence* 24:19–28.

———. 1991. "Toward a Knowledge Democracy." In *Action and Knowledge: Breaking the Monopoly with Participatory Action Research*, eds. O. Fals-Borda and M.A. Rahman. London: Intermediate Technology/Apex.

———. 1993. "The Powerful, the Powerless and the Experts: Knowledge Struggle, in an Information Age." In *Voices of Change: Participatory Research in the United States and Canada*, ed. P. Park. Connecticut: Bergin & Garvey.

Germain, C.B. and A. Hartman. 1980. "People and Ideas in the History of Social Work Practice." *The Journal of Contemporary Social Work* (June): 323–31.

Gigengack, R. and P. Van Gelder. 2000. "Contemporary Street Ethnography: Different Experiences, Perspectives, and Methods." *Focaal*, no. 36:7–14.

Glauser, B. 1990. "Street Children: Deconstructing a Construct." In *Constructing and Reconstructing Childhood: Contemporary Issues in the Sociological Study of Childhood*, eds. A. James and A. Prout. London: The Falmer Press.

Goffman, E. 1959. *The Presentation of Self in Everyday Life*. New York: Anchor.

———. 1961. *Asylums*. New York: Anchor.

———. 1963. *Stigma*. New Jersey: Prentice-Hall.

Gramsci, A. 1987. *The Modern Prince and other Writings*. New York: International Publishers.

———. 1992. *Prison Notebooks*. New York: Columbia University Press.

Graubard, A. 1972. *Free the Children: Radical Reform and the Free School Movement*. New York: Pantheon Books.

Groulx, L.H. 1997. Sens et Usage du Qualitatif en Travail Social au Québec, in J. Poupart, ed. *La Méthodologie Qualitative: Diversité des Champs et des Pratiques de Recherche au Québec*. Rapport Présenté au Conseil Québécois de la Recherche Sociale. Montréal: Centre International de Criminologie Comparée, Université de Montréal.

Guba, E.G. and Y.S. Lincoln. 1994. "Competing Paradigms in Qualitative Research." In *Handbook of Qualitative Research*, eds. N.K. Denzin and Y.S. Lincoln. Thousand Oaks, California: Sage Publications.

Hall, B.L. 1981. "Participatory Research, Popular Knowledge and Power: A Personal Reflection." *Convergence* 14 (3): 6–17.

———. 1992. "From Margins to Centers: The Development and Purpose of Participatory Research." *The American Sociologist* 23 (4): 15–28.

Healy, K. 2000. *Social Work Practices: Contemporary Perspectives on Change.* London: Sage Publications.

———. 2001. "Participatory Action Research and Social Work: A Critical Appraisal." *International Social Work* 44 (1): 93–105.

Hern, M., ed. 1996. *Deschooling our Lives.* Philadelphia: New Society Publishers.

Hesse, E. 1980. *Revolutions and Reconstructions in the Philosophy of Science.* Bloomington: Indiana University Press.

Human Rights Watch. 2003. "Charged with Being Children: Egyptian Police Abuse of Children in Need of Protection," *Human Rights Watch* 15, no. 1(E). <http://hrwo.org/reports/2003/Egypt2003/egypt0203.pdf.>

Ife, J. 1999. "Postmodernism, Critical Theory and Social Work." In *Transforming Social Work Practice: Postmodern Critical Perspectives*, eds. B. Pease and J. Fook. London: Routledge.

Illich, I. 1976. *Deschooling Society.* Harmondsworth: Penguin.

———. 1990. *Tools for Conviviality.* London: Marion Boyars.

Jansen, L., R. Richter and R. Griesel. 1992. "Glue Sniffing: A Comparison Study of Sniffers and Non-Sniffers." *Journal of Adolescence* 15:29–37.

Kefyalew, F. 1996. "The Reality of Child Participation in Research." *Childhood* 3:203–13.

Kemmis, S. 1993. "Action Research and Social Movement: A Challenge for Policy Research." *Education Policy Analysis Archives* 1 no. 1:<http://olam.ed.asu.edu/epaa>.

Kincheloe, J.L. and P.L. McLaren. 1994. "Rethinking Critical Theory and Qualitative Research." In *Handbook of Qualitative Researchi*, eds. N.K. Denzin and Y.S. Lincoln. Thousand Oaks, California: Sage Publications.

Kitsuse, J. 1964. "Societal Reaction to Deviant Behavior: Problems of Theory and Methods." In *The Other Side: Perspectives on Deviance*, ed. H.S. Becker. London: The Free Press of Glencoe.

Klein, M.W. 1995. *The American Street Gang.* New York: Oxford University Press.

Koller, S.H. and C.S. Hutz. 1996. "Resilience and Vulnerability in Children at Risk." *Coletaneas da ANPEPP* 1 (12): 36–47.

Lamoureux, G. 1994. "Histoire du Travail de Rue au Québec." In *Les Actes du Colloque du PIaMP: Une Génération sans nom ni oui*, ed. J. Pector. Montreal: PIaMP.

Lane, M. 1999. "Community Development and a Postmodernism of Resistance." In *Transforming Social Work Practice: Postmodern Critical Perspectives*, eds. B. Pease and J. Fook. London: Routledge.

Legault, D.S. et al. 1994. "Le Travail de Rue: l'Arrivée du Prêt-à-Porter." *Vie Ouvrière*, no. 248:24–37.

Lemert, E. 1951. *Social Pathology.* New York: McGraw-Hill.

————. 1972. *Human Deviance, Social Problems, and Social Control.* New Jersey: Prentice-Hall.

Leonard, P. 1997. *Postmodern Welfare: Reconstructing an Emancipatory Project.* London: Sage Publications.

Lewin, K. 1946. "Action Research and Minority Problems." In *Resolving Social Conflicts: Selected Papers in Group Dynamics,* ed. G.W. Lewin. London: Souvenir Press.

Lucchini, R. 1993. *Enfant de la rue, identité, sociabilité, drogue.* Paris: DROZ.

————. 1996a. *Sociologie de la survie: l'enfant dans la rue.* Paris: PUF.

————. 1996b. "Theory, Method and Triangulation in the Study of Street Children." *Childhood* 3:167–70.

Marx, K. and F. Engels. 1979. *Karl Marx, Frederick Engels: Collected Works.* New York: International Publishers.

Maurer, R. 1992. *Tout Va Bien : Travail de Rue En Suisse 1981–1991.* Berne: Gruppo Verlauto.

McTaggart, R. 1991. "Principles for Participatory Action Research." *Adult Education Quarterly* 41 (3): 168–87.

Moreau, M. 1990. "Empowerment through Advocacy and Consciousness-Raising: Implications of a Structural Approach to Social Work." *Journal of Sociology and Social Work* 17 (2): 53–67.

de Moura, S.L. 2002. "The Social Construction of Street Children: Configuration and Implications." *British Journal of Social Work* 32:353–67.

National Council for Childhood and Motherhood (NCCM). 2003. *Strategy for Protecting and Rehabilitating Homeless Children (Street Children) in the Arab Republic of Egypt.* Cairo: NCCM Project Document.

Park, P. 1992. "The Discovery of Participatory Research as a New Scientific Paradigm: Personal and Intellectual Accounts." *The American Sociologist* 23 (4): 29–43.

Pease, B. and J. Fook, eds. 1999. *Transforming Social Work Practice: Postmodern Critical Perspective.* London: Routledge.

Pector, J. 1999. *Le travail de Rue et l'Action-Recherche Réflexive.* Montreal: l'AT-TRueQ (Center de Documentation).

Petras, E.M. and D.V. Porpora. 1992. "Participatory Research: Three Models and an Analysis." *The American Sociologist* 24 (1): 107–25.

Prus, R. 1996. *Symbolic Interaction and Ethnographic Research.* New York: State University of New York Press.

Punch, M. 1986. *The Politics and Ethics of Fieldwork.* Beverly Hills, California: Sage Publications.

————. 1994. "Politics and Ethics in Qualitative Research." In *Handbook of Qualitative Research,* eds. N.K. Denzin and Y.S. Lincoln. Thousand Oaks, California: Sage Publications.

Rahman, M.A. 1991. "The Theoretical Standpoint of PAR." In *Action and Knowledge: Breaking the Monopoly with Participatory Action Research,* eds.

O. Fals-Borda and M.A. Rahman. London: Intermediate Technology/ Apex.

Reason, P. 1994a. "Three Approaches to Participative Inquiry." *Handbook of Qualitative Research*, eds. N.K. Denzin and Y.S. Lincoln. Thousand Oaks, California: Sage Publications.

————. 1994b. "Inquiry and Alienation." In *Human Inquiry: Research with People*, ed. P. Reason. London: Sage Publications.

————. 1994c. "Participation in the Evolution of Consciousness." In *Human Inquiry: Research with People*, ed. P. Reason. London: Sage Publications.

Rémy, J. 1990. "Les Courants Fondateurs de la Sociologie Américaine: Des Origines à 1970." *Espaces et Sociétés* 56:7–37.

Rizzini, I. 1996. "Street Children: An Excluded Generation in Latin America." *Childhood* 3:215–33.

Rosenau, P. 1992. *Post-modernism and the Social Sciences*. Princeton: Princeton University Press.

Said, E.W. 1994. *Orientalism*. New York: Vintage Books.

Sanders, M.K., ed. 1970. *The Professional Radical: Conversations with Saul Alinsky*. New York: Harper & Row.

Schapiro, R.M. 1995. "Liberatory Pedagogy and the Development Model." *Convergence* 28 (2): 28–47.

Schaut, C. and L. Van Campenhoudt. 1994. *Le travail de Rue: Nature et Enjeux : Rapport de Recherche pour la Fondation Roi Beaudouin*. Bruxelles: Center d'Études Sociologiques.

Schön, D. 1983. *The Reflective Practitioner: How Professionals Think in Actions*. New York: Basic Books.

————. 1987. *Educating the Reflective Practitioner*. San Francisco: Jossey Bass.

————. 1995. "The New Scholarship Requires a New Epistemology." *Change* 27 (6): 27–34.

Selener, D. 1997. *Participatory Action Research and Social Change*. New York: Cornell University Participatory Action Research Network.

Shaw, C. 1930. *The Jack-Roller: A Delinquent Boy's Own Story*. Chicago: University of Chicago Press.

Shaw, C. and H. McKay. 1942. *Juvenile Delinquency*. Chicago: University of Chicago Press.

Small, S.A. 1995. "Action-Oriented Research: Models and Methods." *Journal of Marriage and the Family* 57 (4): 941–55.

Smith, S. 1997. "Deepening Participatory Action-research." In *Nurtured by Knowledge: Learning to Do Participatory Action-Research*, eds. S.E. Smith, D.G. Wilms, and N.A. Johnson, 173–264. New York: Apex Press.

Sohng, S.S.L. 1996. "Participatory Research and Community Organizing." *Journal of Sociology and Social Welfare* 23 (4): 77–95.

Spector, M. and J. Kitsuse. 1977. *Constructing Social Problems*. California: Cummings.

Spergel, I.A. 1976. "Interaction between Community Structure, Delinquency, and Social Policy." In *The Juvenile Justice System,* ed. M.W. Klein. Beverly Hills, California: Sage Publications.

Stoecker, R. and E. Bonanich. 1992. "Why Participatory Research?" *The Americam Sociologist* 23 (4): 5–12.

Tandon, R. 1982. "A Critique of Monopolistic Research." In *Creating Knowledge: A Monopoly? Participatory Research in Development,* eds. B. Hall, A. Gillette, R. Tandon. Toronto: International Council for Adult Education.

———. 1989. "Participatory Research and Social Transformation." *Convergence* 21 (2): 5–15.

Touraine, A. 1992. *Critique de la Modernité.* Paris: Fayard.

UNESCO. 1972. *Learning to Be.* Paris: UNESCO.

UNICEF. 1986. *Exploitation of Working Children and Street Children.* New York: Executive Board.

———. 1987. *Paulo Freire and Street Educators: A Critical Approach.* Rio de Janeiro: Project for Alternative Treatment of Street Children.

———. 1989. *Protecting Working Children.* New York: Program Division, Staff Working Paper no. 4.

———. 2002. *The Situation of Egyptian Children and Women.* Cairo: UNICEF Egypt Country Office.

Vaillancourt, Y. 1981. "Quelques Difficultés Rencontrées dans la Recherche Militante." In *Actes du Colloque Recherche-Action,* Y. Vaillancourt, 62–72. Chicoutimi: UQAC.

Van Beers, H. 1996. "A Plea for a Child-Centered Approach in Research with Street Children." *Childhood* 3:195–201.

Visano, L. 1993. "The Socialization of Street Children." *Sociological Studies of Child Development* 3:139–61.

Weppner, R.S., ed. 1977. *Street Ethnography.* Beverly Hills, California: Sage Publications.

Whyte, W.F. 1943. *Street Corner Society.* Chicago: University of Chicago Press.

———. 1987. "From Human Relations to Organisational Behavior: Reflection on the Changing Scene." *Industrial and Labor Relation Review* (July): 487–99.

———. 1989. "Participatory Action Research: Through Practice to Science in Social Research." *American Behavioral Scientist* 3 (5): 513–51.

Young, L. and H. Barrett. 2001. "Ethics and Participation: Reflections on Research with Street Children." *Ethics, Place and Environment* 4 (2): 130–34.

———. 2001a. "Issues of Access and Identity: Adapting Research Methods with Kampala Street Children." *Childhood* 8 (3): 383–95.

Zuniga, R. 1981. "La Recherche-Action et le Contrôle du Savoir." *Revue Internationale d'Action Communautaire* 5 (45): 35–44.

Index

202   Index